Scottish Colonial Literature

Edinburgh Critical Studies in Atlantic Literatures and Cultures
Series Editors: Laura Doyle, Colleen Glenney Boggs and Maria
Cristina Fumagalli

Available titles
*Sensational Internationalism: The Paris Commune and the Remapping
of American Memory in the Long Nineteenth Century*
J. Michelle Coghlan

*American Travel Literature, Gendered Aesthetics, and the Italian Tour,
1824–1862*
Brigitte Bailey

*American Snobs: Transatlantic Novelists, Liberal Culture and the
Genteel Tradition*
Emily Coit

Scottish Colonial Literature: Writing the Atlantic, 1603–1707
Kirsten Sandrock

Forthcoming titles
*Emily Dickinson and Her British Contemporaries: Victorian Poetry
in Nineteenth-Century America*
Páraic Finnerty

Following the Middle Passage: Currents in Literature Since 1945
Carl Plasa

*Yankee Yarns: Storytelling and the Invention of the National Body in
Nineteenth-Century American Culture*
Stefanie Schäfer

Reverberations of Revolution: Transnational Perspectives, 1750–1850
Elizabeth Amann and Michael Boyden

*The Atlantic Dilemma: Reform or Revolution Across the Long Nine-
teenth Century*
Kelvin Black

www.edinburghuniversitypress.com/series/ECSALC

Scottish Colonial Literature

Writing the Atlantic, 1603–1707

Kirsten Sandrock

EDINBURGH
University Press

Edinburgh University Press is one of the leading university presses in the UK. We publish academic books and journals in our selected subject areas across the humanities and social sciences, combining cutting-edge scholarship with high editorial and production values to produce academic works of lasting importance. For more information visit our website: edinburghuniversitypress.com

Edinburgh University Press Ltd
The Tun – Holyrood Road,
12(2f) Jackson's Entry,
Edinburgh EH8 8PJ

First published in hardback by Edinburgh University Press 2021

Typeset in 11/13 Adobe Sabon by
IDSUK (DataConnection) Ltd,
printed and bound by CPI Group (UK) Ltd
Croydon, CR0 4YY

A CIP record for this book is available from the British Library

ISBN 978 1 4744 6400 0 (hardback)
ISBN 978 1 4744 6401 7 (paperback)
ISBN 978 1 4744 6402 4 (webready PDF)
ISBN 978 1 4744 6403 1 (epub)

Contents

List of Figures and Tables

Figures

Tables

Acknowledgements

One of the greatest pleasures I take away from researching and writing this book is how many people have contributed to it in intellectual, social and practical terms. The University of Goettingen has provided a rich and fruitful academic environment for my work, especially the English Department with its excellent staff and students. I particularly thank Barbara Schaff, who has been a constant source of advice, inspiration and encouragement over the years. My further thanks go to Anca Radu and Jan Thomas, who have been marvellous friends, colleagues and hosts ever since our Marburg years. For reading earlier versions of the manuscript and giving precious feedback, I would like to express my gratitude to Brigitte Glaser, Andrew Gross, Stephan Haas, Ralf Hertel, John Reid and Barbara Schaff. Likewise, I am grateful to Jens Elze, Marius Glowsky, Ralf Haekel, Karly Kehoe, Pat Mason, Anca Radu, Jessica Reid, Theo van Heijnsbergen and Heather Wells, as well as two anonymous readers for Edinburgh University Press for offering much-appreciated advice on earlier chapters. Thank you to all my delightful colleagues at Goettingen, especially Ellin Burnham, Anja Drautzburg, Claudia Georgi, Vanessa Kuenemann, Kathi Nambula, Frauke Reitemeier, Winfried Rudolf and Babette Tischleder. During a stay at the Gorsebrook Research Institute at Saint Mary's University in Halifax, I benefited from the hospitality and expertise of Karly Kehoe, Jackie Logan, Alexander MacLeod and John Reid. Colleagues and students at the University of Vienna were wonderfully welcoming and inspiring during a guest professorship there. I have also profited from the advice and support of many other colleagues. Among them are Bill Bell, Christoph Bode, David Creelman, Gwen Davies, Leith Davis, Thomas Devine, Ian Duncan, Stephen Greenblatt, Christoph Heyl, Martin Kuester, Lukas Lammers, Sylvia Mieszkowski, Monika Pietzrak-Franger, Carla Sassi, Felix Sprang, Christina Wald and many others. Thank you to all.

Michelle Houston and Ersev Ersoy at Edinburgh University Press have smoothed my way through the publication process and were brilliant to work with throughout. So were James Dale, Wendy Lee and Zoe Ross. The series editors, Laura Doyle, Colleen Glenney Boggs and Maria Cristina Fumagalli, offered valuable feedback at different stages of the book and enriched the discussion of the source material through generous conversations.

My family and friends have been most accommodating throughout the process of writing this book. Bob Skillen and Gisele LeBlanc have been family-away-from-home for many years now. Thank you also to David and Chantelle, as well as Anne-Marie and Tim and their families, for hosting me on various occasions. Numerous friends have motivated and helped me over the years. I particularly thank Stefan, Antje and David for their unfailing friendship and thoughtfulness. My immediate family has offered their time and support uncountable times. I thank my parents, as well as Arne, Heike, Siegmar, Sara-Kristin and Janna, for helping out whenever needed. I dedicate the book to Christian, Luise and Johannes. Your love, sense of adventure and humour sustain me every day.

Parts of *Scottish Colonial Literature: Writing the Atlantic, 1603–1707* have been published in earlier form elsewhere. Parts of Chapters 2 and 4 have appeared under the article 'The Legacy of Scotland's Colonial Schemes: From the 1620s Until Now', *Medievalia et Humanistica* 41 (2015): 231–46. Parts of Chapter 2 have been published in 'Ancient Empires and Early Modern Colonialism: William Alexander's *Monarchicke Tragedies*', *Renaissance Studies* 31.3 (2017): 346–64. I thank both publishers for allowing me to reproduce parts of my articles for this book. I also benefited from being able to present parts of my research at conferences in Bochum, Grainau, Port Hood and Wolfville. I would like to thank the audiences for their comments and feedback.

Series Editors' Preface

Modern global culture makes it clear that literary study can no longer operate on nation-based or exceptionalist models. In practice, American literatures have always been understood and defined in relation to the literatures of Europe and Asia. The books in this series work within a broad comparative framework to question place-based identities and monocular visions, in historical contexts from the earliest European settlements to contemporary affairs, and across all literary genres. They explore the multiple ways in which ideas, texts, objects and bodies travel across spatial and temporal borders, generating powerful forms of contrast and affinity. The Edinburgh Critical Studies in Atlantic Literatures and Cultures series fosters new paradigms of exchange, circulation and transformation for Atlantic literary studies, expanding the critical and theoretical work of this rapidly developing field.

For Christian, Luise and Johannes

Chapter 1

Introduction: Scottish Colonial Literature, 1603–1707

On 31 October 1700, the Parliament of Scotland ordered a book and pamphlet burning. After a passionate, nine-hour session, parliamentarians condemned 'two pamphlets by Walter Herries' and the anonymously published *Caledonia or the Pedlar Turn'd Merchant. A Tragi-Comedy, as It Was Acted by His Majesty's Subjects of Scotland in the King of Spain's Province of Darien* (1700) to be burned at the Edinburgh Cross.[1] All three works were concerned with the Darien scheme, Scotland's last colonial undertaking while still an independent kingdom in the 1690s. Like many oral and written narratives at the time, they dealt with the question of who was to blame for the premature ending of the Darien venture: Scotland or England? Not coincidentally, the English Parliament equally ordered a book burning related to Darien a little later. The work in question this time was *An Inquiry into the Causes of the Miscarriage of the Scots Colony at Darien* (1700).[2] It was published anonymously at the time but has since been attributed to the Scottish author George Ridpath. L. E. Elliott Joyce notes that the 'English Parliament ordered the book to be burnt by the common hangman in Palace Yard, Westminster, on 19 January 1701'.[3] Unlike the works burned in Edinburgh, the one burned in London held England responsible for not sufficiently supporting Scottish settlers at Darien.

As political and performative acts, the book burnings in Edinburgh and London mark the influential role that literary works played in the history of Scottish colonialism. This book explores how narratives of different genres and media formats shaped the Scottish Atlantic in the long seventeenth century. Its main focus is on three colonial undertakings: at Nova Scotia in the 1620s, East New Jersey in the 1680s and the Isthmus of Panama, then commonly known as

Darien, in the 1690s. In addition, it considers works written in the larger context of the Scottish Atlantic so as to illuminate how the Atlantic shaped Scottish literary production and vice versa. Textual narratives were powerful instruments of empire-building throughout the early modern period. In the Scottish context, they help to shed light on some of the tensions between internal and external forms of colonialism before 1707.

'A Sorry Poor Nation'[4]

One of the questions running through this book is the interaction between art and ideology. A place to start exploring the intertwinement of political and aesthetic practices of Scottish colonialism is *Caledonia or the Pedlar Turn'd Merchant. A Tragi-Comedy, as It Was Acted by His Majesty's Subjects of Scotland in the King of Spain's Province of Darien*. One of the works burned at the Edinburgh Cross, this satirical long poem is written in the style of a folk ballad, a genre that is common in seventeenth-century Scottish literature and which is often associated with the politicised nature of textual production.[5] In this case, the satire is aimed at the Scottish people themselves, who are portrayed as incapable of establishing an overseas colony. The tone of the ballad is cutting, which explains why it was burned at the Edinburgh Cross. *Caledonia, or the Pedlar Turn'd Merchant* consists of 127 stanzas. The title and subtitle set out the two main geographical reference points of the ballad – Caledonia/Scotland and Darien – which serve, both literally and metaphorically, as spatial structuring devices. The opening verses organise a complex set of ideas around the tropes of Scotland's poverty, the kingdom's lack of fertile land and its disadvantages vis-à-vis other nations. These tropes of dispossession serve as background against which the poem then presents an overseas colony at Darien as a solution to Scotland's domestic problems:

> A Sorry Poor Nation, which lies *as full North*,
> As a great many Lands which are *wiser*,
> Was resolv'd to set up for a People of Worth,
> That the *Loons* who laugh'd at Her might prize her. [. . .]
>
> Her claim was as fair, and as Just was her Plea
> To the goods of this Life as the best,
> And if *Sinners look green like a Fruitful Bay Tree*,
> That a *Scotch-man* should *Wither's* a Jest. [. . .]

And if their *Lean Acres* 'stead *Breadcorn* and *Wines*,
Bore 'em *Oats* to discover their *Natures*,
And they'd nothing but *Cole*-Pits in the Room of *Gold-Mines*
To shew what was *design'd* for such *Creatures*.

'Twas the very same thing since *Spain* and *Peru*
Had abundance of what they had none;
Could they steal it, no matter where the mineral grew,
Possession would make it their *own*.[6]

The satirical nature of the ballad partly accounts for its hyperbolic language. Beneath the surface of the satirical mode, though, the verses create a grander narrative about Scottish colonialism. They juxtapose the geosocial locations of Caledonia and the Atlantic to portray Scotland as particularly poor and Darien as particularly rich. Phrases such as the '*Fruitful Bay Tree*', the '*Gold-Mines*' and the fields of '*Breadcorn* and *Wines*' imagine the overseas colony as a space of plenty, where the 'goods of this Life' can be enjoyed. These images used for the Atlantic resonate highly, not only with other colonial narratives of the time but also with the genre of early modern utopian writing.

Like other utopianisms, the poem revolves around the aesthetics of abundance. *The Land of Cokaygne* is perhaps the most emblematic utopia of profusion, but numerous other narratives associated with the genre offer a similar vision of lavishness, or at least sufficiency.[7] *Caledonia or the Pedlar Turn'd Merchant* literally refers to the 'abundance' of Spain since it took possession of Peru. This formula, which associates overseas possessions with wealth, contrasts sharply with images of Scotland's domestic privation in the verses. The complaint about Scotland's '*Lean Acres*' that only breed '*Oats*' instead of '*Breadcorn* and *Wines*' signals the centrality of land as a motif of possession in Scottish colonial writing between 1603 and 1707. Rhetorically and ideologically, the ballad rationalises Scottish colonialism by pointing to the kingdom's material and political disadvantages, which are stressed in phrases such as 'Sorry Poor Nation', 'nothing but *Cole*-Pits' or 'they had none'. The ballad stanza, consisting of alternating four- and three-stress lines and a regular rhyme scheme, creates a catchy rhythm for a morally ambiguous message: that Scotland should 'steal' the land and possessions of indigenous populations in order to remedy the situation of Scottish citizens at home. This dichotomy between deficit and possession runs as a key binarism through Scottish colonial writing of the seventeenth century.

Herein lies one of the central conceptual difficulties this book deals with: how narratives of domestic dispossession aesthetically and ideologically intertwine with narratives of Atlantic possession.

Ania Loomba has written about the principal 'dichotomy' that underlies many postcolonial formations of nationalism, which are poised between '*both dispossession and privilege*'.[8] A similar narrative of possession and dispossession runs through Scotland's Atlantic literature of the seventeenth century. *Scottish Colonial Literature* raises complex questions about this dichotomy, which interacts, in the seventeenth century, with the utopian genre. To focus on the relationship between the colonial and utopian traditions means to interrogate the relationship between aesthetics and ideology.[9] This book assumes that all utopias are latent dystopias. *Caledonia, or the Pedlar Turn'd Merchant* gestures towards this ambivalent nature of utopian thought by suggesting that Scotland has the right, perhaps even the duty, to dispossess other people and the natural spaces of the Atlantic in order to improve its domestic situation. The satirical mode of the ballad does not lessen the ideological force of the verses. Rather, it adds to the persuasiveness of the colonial narrative by using humour as an emotionalising strategy. Readers today may find it uncomfortable, if not downright problematic, to think about colonialism and utopianism as working together in Scottish Atlantic literature. After all, there is a certain danger of linking the study of early modern colonialism to the literary tradition of utopianism. This danger is captured by Ruth Levitas's warning that '[t]here is a normative element in many definitions which excludes evil utopias and regards them as contradictions in terms.'[10] To avoid such normativity, the following chapters draw on Levitas's use of the term utopia as an analytic category.[11] It functions as a framework through which aesthetic devices can be conceptualised. Utopianism is not a normative category. On the contrary, the following chapters demonstrate that it is always based on the ideologies and biases of a given group. To make clearer the historical and discursive patterns upon which these arguments are based, it is useful to turn more fully to the utopian literary tradition and to illuminate its interaction with colonial thought in early modernity.

'The Room of *Gold-Mines*'[12]

Utopianism was a widespread framework of thinking about colonialism in early modern culture.[13] Bill Ashcroft points out that

Thomas More's *Of a Republic's Best State and of the New Island Utopia* (1516) was one of the *ur*-scenes of Tudor colonial ideology.[14] Although debates about the self-ironic nature of More's writing continue to spark controversy about *Utopia* and its relationship to early modern colonialism,[15] the conquest scene that narrates the creation of Utopia by King Utopus belongs to one of the less ironical passages of More's work:

> But King Utopus, whose name as conqueror the island beareth (for before his time it was called Abraxa), which also brought the rude and wild people to that excellent perfection in all good fashions, humanity, and civil gentleness, wherein they now go beyond all the people of the world, even at his first arriving and entering upon the land, forthwith obtaining the victory, caused fifteen miles space of uplandish ground, where the sea had no passage, to be cut and digged up.[16]

The scene is one of origins and destruction. Utopus conquers the land, renames it, changes the geography of the place from peninsula to island and henceforth dominates the inhabitants of Utopia as their ruler. It is also a scene of a self-proclaimed civilising mission. Utopus finds the inhabitants of Abraxa first 'rude and wild' but manages to turn them into epitomes of 'humanity, and civil gentleness'. Afterwards, he rules over them and turns Utopians into what he deems a cultivated, polite and peaceful people. Many tropes found in *Utopia*'s settlement scene have become standard tropes of colonial writing: nature as a resource, which can be shaped according to settler needs; indigenous populations as 'noble savages'; the spread of Western civilisation; sociospatial newness; control over the settled space and people; and the renaming of the colonised territory in order to mark it as a European possession. These intersections of colonial and utopian narratives also emerge in Scottish colonial writing of the seventeenth century, where they are often linked to narratives of domestic needs and desires.

Whereas *Utopia* uses a two-partite structure, first, to discuss England's problems (Book I) and, second, to offer the solution to these problems in the removed sphere of the island of Utopia (Book II), Scottish Atlantic writing fuses these two narrative strands. It offers a condensed version of utopianism by straightforwardly turning the overseas colony into a solution to Scotland's problems. Evidence suggests that Scotland developed a particularly powerful mode of utopian thought in the seventeenth century because of its domestic situation. In *Caledonia, or the Pedlar Turn'd Merchant*, the emphasis on Scotland's dearth contrasts powerfully with the emphasis on Atlantic abundance. Colonial and utopian thought overlap in the poem's aestheticised promise that Scotland can solve its problems by colonising other cultures. To focus on the generic links between utopianism and colonial literature means to deepen a perspective on the Atlantic as a space in which many Europeans, including a number of Scottish people, envisioned the solution to their own troubles and tribulations. Aesthetically speaking, they endowed it with idealising strategies that endorsed Eurocentric claims and helped to turn the Atlantic into one of the spaces in which narratives of the early British Empire were being developed.

One thing that *Scottish Colonial Literature* does not try to do is to argue for immediate intertextual references between utopian literature and Scottish Atlantic writing. Neither More's *Of a Republic's Best State and of the New Island Utopia* (1516) nor Tommaso Campanella's *City of the Sun* (1602) nor Francis Bacon's *New Atlantis* (1627) nor Margaret Cavendish's *The Description of a New World, Called the Blazing World* (1666) nor Henry Neville's *The Isle of Pines* (1668) is ever mentioned in Scottish Atlantic literature. Nor do the social reform texts by Gerrard Winstanley, Samuel Hartlib or the Fifth Monarchy Men play a direct role in the texts studied below, though an argument will be made regarding their structural interplay. Plato's *Republic* (c. 350 BC) and Aristotle's *Politics* (fourth century BC) are likewise never referred to in the texts studied below about Nova Scotia, New Jersey and Darien. Scottish Atlantic literature does not mention utopianism in the way Milton refers to it in *Areopagitica* (1644), which dismisses both 'Atlantick and Eutopian polities' as futile to 'mend our condition'.[17] The relationship between Scottish colonial writing and utopian literature is more subtle, and it rests on the very argumentative structures and aesthetic representations of Atlantic colonialism. The fact that Milton links the Atlantic with utopianism is a clear sign that connections between the Atlantic and the utopian imagination were already established in Great Britain by the mid-seventeenth century. Scottish writers drew on and advanced such links, even if the relationship is more one of 'confluence rather than influence', to adopt Rebecca Ruth Gould's argument for her exploration of settler colonial aesthetics in the twentieth century.[18] *Scottish Colonial Literature* shows that the connection between the Atlantic and utopian writing runs deeply throughout the seventeenth century and that it emerges, most strikingly, in generic links as well as ideological and aesthetic strategies.

There are prominent exclusions in the early modern utopian tradition that are central to my argument about the intergeneric conversations between utopianism and colonialism. In More's *Utopia*,
slaves are not part of the society of equals. Likewise, the islands that
are conquered when overpopulation sets in on Utopia are left to deal
with the power imbalances of King Utopus's society.[19] In Bacon's *New
Atlantis*, everyone not living in Bensalem is excluded from the possibility of improvement because only Bensalemites are in a position to
learn from the rest of the world.[20] Early modern utopias are frequently
based on such models of exclusion, which prioritise the needs of some
over the needs of others. The same is true for Scottish colonialism
in the long seventeenth century. The literature relating to Scotland's
colonial efforts between 1603 and 1707 makes strong claims upon the
Atlantic as a space in which Scottish people could prosper away from
home. Here, as elsewhere, the Atlantic becomes a space of opportunity
for some. For others, it is the opposite of freedom.

The cultural logic of dispossessing others to solve domestic problems was also at work in other British literature of the time, where
domestic pressures led to the idealisation of Atlantic settlement
sites.[21] The case of Scotland affords a powerful illustration of this
logic. The following chapters complicate discussions about power in
the colonial sphere by illustrating how some literary works exerted
new forms of mastery through emphasising privation. Throughout
the seventeenth century, people living in Scotland suffered from
socio-economic problems that were periodically more or less severe
between 1603 and 1707. There were also numerous other developments in seventeenth-century Scotland, and it would be wrong to
insist on a grand narrative of dearth or depravity for a century in
Scottish history that Jenny Wormald pertinently refers to with the
oxymoron 'Confidence and Perplexity'.[22] Yet, it would be equally
wrong to deny that repeated famines, rising grain prices, unemployment, land shortages and restrictions on international trade caused
many people to suffer, others to migrate and many more to die in seventeenth-century Scotland. The 'nightmare of uncertainty' pertained
to 'the landed classes' and the socio-political elite as much as to the
less privileged parts of society.[23]

Out-migration was one result of Scotland's predicaments during the long seventeenth century. Continental Europe and Ireland
remained the most common places for Scottish migrants and settlers
during the seventeenth century, with as many as '50,000 Scots' going
'to Ulster during the 1690s' alone.[24] Other early modern Scottish

migrants went to the Low Countries, to Scandinavia or to the Baltic.[25] The Atlantic was a far less established space for Scottish out-migration in the seventeenth century. And yet, increased interest in Atlantic colonialism constitutes one of the many co-existing literary and cultural identities of seventeenth-century Scotland.

'Just was her Plea'[26]

Despite the differences between early modern colonialism and early modern utopianism, there is plenty of wishful thinking in both traditions. Levitas's conception of utopia as an 'expression of the desire for a better way of being'[27] offers a way to think about utopias as generic formulas rather than content-based narratives. With regard to the early modern period, narratives of desire do not only relate to urban or island spaces or to societies without private possessions, as in More's *Utopia*. Narratives of desire also spur the thoughts and writings of colonial authors. This is especially true for settler colonists, whose initial aim is often, albeit not always, as Lorenzo Veracini states, the creation of 'an ideal social body' or 'an exemplary model of social organisation'.[28] The emphasis on 'desire' in Levitas's definition[29] and on the 'ideal social body' in Veracini's definition[30] asks important questions about the power constellations of utopian and colonial thought. What someone finds desirable or ideal may be the opposite of desirable or ideal for someone else. This is particularly true when desires concern the transformation of a status quo in which some groups seek to improve their situation while others are forced to lose their privileges, as is commonly the case in both utopian and colonial movements.

Karl Mannheim's *Ideology and Utopia* (1936) and Paul Ricœur's *Lectures on Ideology and Utopia* (1986) provide fruitful frameworks to reflect on the paradoxes involved in the Scottish Atlantic tradition. I would like to dwell on their writings for a moment in order to think about the relationship between power and utopianism more generally. Neither Mannheim nor Ricœur wrote about a colonial or Atlantic context. Yet, they conceive of utopias in relation to larger power struggles and ideological formations. They ask how utopianism is put into the service of social movements that try to shift the power from one group towards another. According to Mannheim's *Ideology and Utopia*, in utopian movements a given group tries to supplant the existing socio-cultural hierarchies with different kinds of hierarchy. More often than not, this power struggle results in the

liberation of some societal groups and in the simultaneous subjugation of others.

Although Mannheim does not directly address the history of
European colonisation, his points about the ideological nature of
utopian movements and the attempt to replace one hierarchy with
another speak to the power struggles many Scottish colonial writers
negotiate in the Atlantic context. A reading of *Caledonia, or the
Pedlar Turn'd Merchant* shows how the dispossession of foreign
countries and cultures was aestheticised as a natural process of
colonialism because it was seen as necessary in order to allevi-
ate Scotland's domestic situation. In one breath, the poem links
the lack of '*Breadcorn* and *Wines*' in Scotland to the desire for
'*Gold-Mines*' abroad. It rationalises the practices of 'steal[ing]'
from the populations of the Americas with the desire to make
indigenous '*Possession* [. . .] their *own*'. The phrase 'Just was her
Plea' euphemises the idea that Scotland's troubles at home justify
the subjugation of others abroad. It uses the word 'plea' to suggest
that colonialism is a gentle request rather than a forceful action,
which stands in awkward contrast to the confession of 'steal[ing]'
from others several verses below. According to Mannheim's general line of argument, such rhetorical naturalisation of colonial
dispossession can be understood as part of a power struggle in
which colonial authors and agents engaged by idealising both the
Atlantic and Scotland's role in it.

For Mannheim, utopian ideas and movements arise out of societal
conflicts in which different groups struggle for socio-political dominance. Those who wish to create a new society are frequently those
who are not in a leading position at home. And yet, they have sufficient
power – social, material, educational or political – to be able to voice
their desire for, and possibly accomplish the creation of, an alternative
society based on their ideals. They use this limited, though still sub-
stantial, power to imagine societies in which they are more powerful or
materially comfortable than before. Mannheim writes that

> the dominant group [. . .] is in full accord with the existing order
> [and] determines what is to be regarded as utopian, while the
> ascendant group which is in conflict with things as they are is the
> one that determines what is regarded as ideological.[31]

Interpreted in this way, Scotland's colonial ventures in the seventeenth
century can be read as outlets of a power struggle in which non-
dominant ideologies at home rise to become (more) dominant abroad.

Ricœur further theorises the power struggle outlined by Mannheim in his *Lectures on Ideology and Utopia*. Following Mannheim's argument, Ricœur asks whether it is possible for utopias ever to deinstitutionalise social hierarchies or whether they will always remain in a cycle of replacing one system of power with another. Ricœur does not simply mean a certain kind of social hierarchy, such as class relationships or political orders. Instead, he asks whether utopias could eliminate the very idea of social hierarchies and 'replace power by something else'.[32] Writing in a non-Atlantic context, Ricœur puts the question of power and utopianism as follows:

> The continual problem is how to end the relation of subordination, the hierarchy between rulers and ruled, by replacing it. The attempt is to find alternatives that work through cooperation and egalitarian relationships. This question extends to all kinds of our relations, from sexuality to money, property, the state, and even religion. Religion is revealed as such an issue when we consider that the only religions we know have institutions that rule religious experience through a structure and therefore a certain hierarchy. The deinstitutionalization of the main human relationships is finally, I think, the kernel of all utopias.[33]

Coming from an Atlantic context, the answer to Ricœur's question as to whether utopias can 'replace power by something else'[34] seems to be: no. Colonialism in its early, idealised form may attempt to transform existing social structures with different kinds of power relationship abroad, as the following chapters repeatedly illustrate. Feudal society gave way to capitalism in Atlantic colonies, dominant religious organisations were replaced with more open religious structures, and political rule changed, over time, from monarchy to democracy in North America. And yet, all these developments went hand in hand with the formation of other social and political hierarchies, which were designed to keep out of power those who were dispossessed in the process of colonisation. This pertains in an Atlantic context above all to the indigenous populations of the Americas and to enslaved Africans and African Americans. It also partly includes those who were involuntarily put into the service of colonialism, such as forced labourers or prisoners sent abroad, though in the long term these involuntary colonists frequently benefited from the racial hierarchies implemented by settler colonialism.[35] European colonialism, and the global order that arose out of it, are based on structural inequalities, which continue to organise global hierarchies until this day.[36]

'To the goods of this Life'[37]

It is common critical ground to read early modern utopias as a genre poised between intellectual jest and political reform. Chloë Houston argues that the seventeenth century saw a shift in the utopian genre from a dialogic toward a monologic mode of writing.[38] In the sixteenth and early seventeenth centuries, utopian texts were mostly written in dialogic form, where the emphasis on critical debate and intellectual wit is part of the structure. More's *Utopia* positions everything that is said in a conversation and frames the critique of the existing societal and political order as an interchange of experiences and thoughts. In so doing, it leaves deliberate room for interpretation. The puns and witticisms in *Utopia* further add to the fissures that have become characteristic of the genre. Nobody knows, or is supposed to know, whether what is said is meant straightforwardly or in jest. Towards the mid-seventeenth century, 'the concept of utopia became distinctly less imaginative in the hands of reformers who wanted to make use of it in order to promote social reformation'.[39] Houston situates the reformist mode of utopian writing in literary works associated with movements such as the Hartlib Circle (c. 1630–60), the Digger Movement (1640s–1650s) or the Fifth Monarchy Men (c. 1649–60). This shift from dialogic to monologic structure is crucial in aesthetic terms, and it raises questions about the assumptions commonly made about utopianism as a partially playful genre.

Scottish Atlantic writing of the seventeenth century calls attention to some of the more troubling aspects of utopian literature's shift from a dialogic towards a monologic genre. Colonial literature contributed to this shift. It turned the Atlantic into a reform space without, however, having to sacrifice the suaveness of the earlier tradition. There is much emphasis on the effortlessness and ease of overseas settlements in the sources studied below. Most authors promise the simplicity of acquiring land, the easy availability of natural resources, the smoothness of the voyage and the relaxed relationship with the indigenous populations. The utopian dimension of colonial writing emerges primarily in such idealisations of the Atlantic space and in the concomitant idealisation of the settlement process. In the wake of other reformist movements throughout the seventeenth century, the Atlantic was one of the spaces in which utopianism became a genre associated with practical reform. At the same time, colonial writing stabilised the links between utopianism and the struggle for power. Utopian elements in colonial texts are not mere playful devices. They turn the Atlantic into a space where narratives of political and societal reform are inextricably linked to hierarchical relations.

The utopian tradition, as coined in the British context by Thomas More, Francis Bacon, Gerrard Winstanley, Henry Neville or Margaret Cavendish, is known for its blend of factual and fictional universes. Travel writing in particular influenced the genre of utopian literature in its formation,[40] and so did the social reform writings that emerged in the mid-seventeenth century. Sarah Hogan identifies 'the strange tension between fantasy and hyper-rationality' in colonial literatures that 'might be best classified as utopia'.[41] This instability of the truth condition was part of an aesthetic system in which utopianism evolved in the early modern period and which closely interacted with the rise of colonialism. As the texts studied below illustrate, the relative unfamiliarity with the Americas is one reason why Scottish authors could praise the overseas territories in utopian terms and describe them as ideal settlement places. The utopian mode, with its fusion of fact and fiction and with its characteristic struggle for political, material and ideological power, was never a purely playful genre. It was one of the tools European authors used to establish power over the Atlantic, and its shift in aesthetic frameworks shows how serious this struggle over the Atlantic became in the seventeenth century. The colonies were turned into spaces of desire, on to which longings of different kinds could be projected: material possessions, spiritual riches, societal order, newness, social upward mobility, land acquisition, expansion and the conquest of other cultures and natures. These aesthetic frames are put into the service of diverse power struggles throughout the seventeenth century. Hogan uses the term 'Utopia of transition' to refer to texts that 'scheme a plan for radical sociospatial reform'.[42] In an Atlantic context, there is no denying the ideological resonances of such reform utopias. The narrative of change that characterises many seventeenth-century reform writings involves complicated networks of power, as a study of colonial utopian writing illustrates.[43] Stylistically and imaginatively, colonial authors turned the Americas into *eu topos*, a good place. But only for those who sought to profit from it.

'Spain and Peru Had abundance'

Scottish Colonial Literature situates Scotland's Atlantic activities in a framework of larger transnational power struggles. It specifically addresses the pan-British context but also notes how other European enterprises in the Atlantic served as interlocutors for Scottish colonial writing before 1707. Scotland's first official Atlantic undertaking began in 1621. In that year, James VI and I granted a large piece of land on the North American east coast to his Scottish courtier, Sir William Alexander. At that time, England was already well established in transatlantic trade and expansion,[44] as were other cultures such as France, Portugal, the Netherlands and Spain. The Virginia Company was founded in 1606, followed by the Newfoundland Company in 1610, the Dorchester Company in 1623 and the Massachusetts Bay Colony in 1629. French settlements in North America were emerging in the late sixteenth and early seventeenth centuries, with the founding of Port-Royal in 1605 and of Quebec City in 1608 serving as milestones for New France.[45] Similarly, the Spanish Empire spanned extensive parts of Central and South America by the early seventeenth century.[46] Many of the literary works studied below invoke the colonial efforts of other countries and make claims that Scotland, too, should become a global imperial player. Anglo-Scottish relations were central to the emergence of Scotland's colonial utopian tradition, as were larger intercultural trade networks and political relations in the sixteenth and seventeenth centuries. Here is where the question of power and utopianism enters the stage again.

Scotland was not a dominant player in the colonial sphere of the seventeenth century. More widespread schemes were developed by Dutch, English, French, Portuguese or Spanish colonial agents at the time.[47] The image of the 'Sorry Poor Nation, which lies *as full North*' in the opening line of *Caledonia, or the Pedlar Turn'd Merchant*, contrasts sharply with the idea that '*Spain* and *Peru* Had abundance.' In both cases, a generalisation takes place. The concept of the nation serves as both a symbol of and a projection screen for Scotland's colonial pursuits, which were certainly not national in the final decade of the seventeenth century or any time before. *Scottish Colonial Literature* recurrently addresses the role of the nation in discourses of Scottish colonialism in the seventeenth century and heightens the ambivalent interaction between nation-building and colonialism. It offers proof that the nation is frequently invoked as a symbol of unity in Scottish Atlantic writing, but that this unity was a discursive ideal rather than a real-life actuality. The chapters engage with discussions that consider nationhood a central, albeit problematic, concept in colonial and postcolonial studies.[48] In a Scottish context, the nation itself turns into a utopian rhetorical device. Several of the authors write about the nation as if it were a homogenous unity. In reality, seventeenth-century Scotland was profoundly heterogenous, some might say deeply divided and far from a homogenous nation. Dynamics of regional background, religion, language, gender, education, political association and race are only some of the factors that play a role in Scottish colonial writing, but which are frequently glossed over in invocations of colonial nationhood. Benedict Anderson's concept of the nation as an 'imagined community'[49] takes on additional meaning in the context of Scottish colonial writing in so far as the kind of nation that is imagined here is that of an elite.

Only a small circle of people living in seventeenth-century Scotland was involved in Atlantic colonialism. Whether as author, investor, settler, shipbuilder, political advisor, consumer or mercantile partner: the roles taken up in empire-building were highly divergent, and not all of them correspond to what we typically think of in relation to the word colonist. But even if we draw the circle as wide as possible, the group of Scottish individuals involved in Atlantic colonialism before 1707 forms a minority of the seventeenth-century Scottish population. From the 1620s onwards, Scottish colonial writing is mostly a product of the political, economic and social elite. Even though this elite at times intended large parts of the Scottish population to participate in overseas settlement schemes, most people in Scotland did not actively join in Atlantic colonialism. The chapters below demonstrate that public support for Scotland's overseas activities before the Union of Parliaments was low compared with other Atlantic colonial cultures of the time. Probably, the majority of the Scottish people not only were not involved in Atlantic schemes but may have never heard of Nova Scotia, East New Jersey or Darien, or any of the other Atlantic places where Scottish settlers were active before 1707. This also has effects on the archive of Scottish colonial writing on which this book can draw.

Scotland's Atlantic literature before 1707 includes a variety of genres and publication forms. Among them are poetry, song, drama, prose writing, political documents, travelogues, diaries, letters, colonial advertisement tracts, legal and administrative sources, manuscripts, print publications, closet dramas and royal charters, as well as, in later centuries, novels about Scotland's Atlantic schemes prior to 1707. The findings refute the idea that 'Traditionally, Scotland's seventeenth century has been viewed as a cultural wasteland.'[50] Many authors studied below did not consider colonialism their primary concern. Not every Scottish author or person discussed in the following chapters was necessarily a colonial activist, but many of the works helped to popularise thoughts about the Atlantic and its colonial dynamics. Some people also pursued financial interests in the Atlantic sphere and helped to push overseas colonisation through their speculative investments in a Scottish settlement at Darien. The scale of this tradition means that the following chapters do not strive for completeness. On the contrary, *Scottish Colonial Literature* attempts to break ground for further research on seventeenth-century Scottish Atlantic literature, much of which awaits to be rediscovered in archives, as well as printed form. Like other studies in the field that Kathleen Wilson calls 'A New Imperial History', the present book seeks to 'tell a story through competing fragments'.[51] It joins the efforts of scholars who question the existence of a unified Scottish or British Empire and emphasise instead the patchy nature of colonial pursuits in the larger history of the Atlantic.

As will be seen throughout the chapters, there is an inevitable bias in the source material towards Lowland, Protestant, male Scots. Gaelic-speaking authors, Highlanders and Islanders, women and children, as well as Catholics, are under-represented in the surviving sources. We know, however, that women were part of the colonial enterprises because mention is made of marriages on board colonial ships sailing to Nova Scotia,[52] and some Scottish women are listed as subscribers of the Darien scheme.[53] We also know that Highland Scots were among the settlers to the Darien expedition,[54] even if sources in Gaelic or by (openly recognisable) Catholics are absent from the corpus. Primary sources from indigenous populations and enslaved people are, unfortunately, also missing from the corpus. Hopefully, further research will unearth what protrudes as a regrettable gap in linguistic and cultural diversity in the present book. Language itself reflects this bias. English, or sometimes English mixed with Scots, is the prevailing language used in Scottish colonial writing of the seventeenth century. Gaelic texts or texts written in full-fledged Scots or in indigenous languages are virtually absent from the corpus. David Nicol's *The Fundamentals of New Caledonia* (2003) is the only work written in historical Scots, but it is a contemporary novel that makes a conscious choice to use the historical language. Only two Latin texts, King James's royal charters to Alexander and Gordon from 1621, are part of the corpus, which faintly hints at the range of languages used in early modern Scotland, even if Latin was surely part of the elite rather than the collective linguistic tradition. Scottish colonial writing is heavily weighted towards an elite that sought to carve out their political and material roles in the colonial dynamics of the long seventeenth century. The voices of the collective remain under-represented. This is a gap that *Scottish Colonial Literature* cannot close, but upon which it repeatedly dwells.

'The *Loons* who laugh'd at Her'

None of Scotland's colonial schemes prior to 1707 resulted in a long-term Scottish colony. This is not only historically striking but also, from a literary perspective, noteworthy because it hints at the idealistic quality that underlies some Scottish colonial writing of that period. Sometimes, the names survived, as in the case of Nova Scotia, Latin for New Scotland. Other times, Scottish settlers continued to live in the region of the original settlement site even after the colony was returned, as in the case of East New Jersey. In any official sense, though, Scotland did not acquire a long-term settlement in the course of the seventeenth century. Nova Scotia was returned to France as part of Charles I's peace negotiations with France at the end of the Anglo-French War, when the King ordered 'to remove all the people goods ordinance munition cattell and vther things belonging vnto that Colonie'.[55] The Scottish proprietors of East New Jersey returned the colony to the British crown in 1702, partially due to internal conflicts. Scotland's involvement with Darien ended with the premature departure of the settlers, many of whom died at the Isthmus of Panama while others left because of the climate, health issues and conflict with the Spanish settlers on site. In most cases, the dream of living a better life abroad turned out to be unrealisable for Scottish settlers.

Scotland's colonial imaginary is utopian in a twofold sense: it is *eu topos* and *ou topos*, a good place and no place. In many cases, this instability was a strategic device to promote overseas colonisation. While many narratives claim to represent reality, their depiction of the world outside could not always be verified by means of physical or material proof. To draw on texts about Virginia when writing about Nova Scotia, to promise that land would be willingly given to Scottish settlers by the indigenous populations of the Middle Colonies or to present Darien as a founding myth of a prosperous Scottish trading hub – all of these are rhetorical strategies that are meant to raise Scotland's stakes in the seventeenth-century Atlantic. For literary scholars, to engage with early modern Atlantic writing means to engage with the strategic instability of fact and fiction. It is a premise of this study, following Ignacio Gallup-Diaz, that colonial texts of whatever genre are 'more than literary artifacts that simply reflect the mental worlds of the Europeans who penned them for publication or to further political goals'.[56] Literature does not merely reflect reality. It actively shapes it. Many of the literary texts studied below frame the Atlantic as a space of desire and satisfaction. In this way, they produce an entire epistemology of thinking about the Americas that has influenced European thought from early modernity onwards.

Focusing on Atlantic colonialism means to leave out Ireland, England's and Scotland's earliest colony and, according to some, 'the last colony of the British Empire'.[57] While Ulster and Munster occupy a central place in the emergence of early British colonialism,[58] *Scottish Colonial Literature* excludes this part of Scotland's and Britain's colonial history for methodological reasons. First, it is difficult to argue for a 'Scottish' perspective on Ulster and Munster in a settlement scheme that was originally begun by English settlers and that is known for mixing English and Scottish settlers in the colonial plantations.[59] Although English and Scottish interests also intertwine in some of the schemes studied below, there is a pronounced emphasis on the Scottishness of the colonial schemes in literature relating to the Atlantic. The Americas became a space where some Scots wanted to establish an autonomous colonial tradition for Scotland and, in so doing, be on a par with England and other colonial cultures of the time. Second, colonial writing relating to Ireland developed a different kind of utopian rhetoric from that of Atlantic literature. Hogan's *Other Englands* includes Ireland as one of the places in which colonial and utopian thinking intermingled and which was a space of both desire and possession for settlers. Edmund Spenser's *A View of the Present State of Ireland* (c. 1598) serves as case in point. Spenser depicts the Irish who fought against the English in Munster as warriors who 'came creeping forth upon their hands, for their legs could not bear them', and they came '[o]ut of every corner of the woods and glens'.[60] According to Spenser's narrator, the Irish 'looked like anatomies of death, they spake like ghosts out of their graves, they did eat the dead carrions, happy where they could find them'.[61] In contrast to this connection between death and colonialism, Atlantic colonial literature frequently takes on a more idealistic tone by imagining the Americas as a space of new possibilities and societal improvement. This may partly be due to the larger distance to the Americas, which may have made the idealisation of the foreign place easier, especially at a time when the majority of readers would not have been able to disprove the authors. In Ireland, this was different. Robert Cecil (1563–1612), First Earl of Salisbury and advisor to Elizabeth I, was able to deprecate the call of the Irish Gaelic Lord Hugh O'Neill (c. 1550–1616) for an Ireland without English plantations as a 'Eutopia',[62] partly because he knew that Great Britain's power-grip on Ireland was too strong to be easily supplanted. Such a use of the term utopia in relation to Ireland suggests a different rhetorical and ideological approach to the neighbouring colony than to Atlantic settlements. Authors of Atlantic colonial texts could project their hopes, dreams and desires on to the foreign place much more freely because their readers' knowledge about the Americas was limited. In this way, utopianism became a powerful tool for shaping the Scottish Atlantic.

A growing body of literature engages with Scotland's role in the British Empire and the way literature and culture shaped this role.[63] The following chapters add to this work by investigating Scotland's Atlantic activities in the long seventeenth century from a literary and cultural perspective. Readers will recognise in the footnotes and citations that *Scottish Colonial Literature* greatly benefits from previous publications in the fields of Atlantic studies, Scottish studies, empire studies and, of course, literary and cultural studies. Many of the primary sources studied below were first mentioned, collected or sometimes reprinted in edited collections, scholarly articles or books. Where *Scottish Colonial Literature* sometimes departs from earlier scholarship on the period is in treating seventeenth-century Scottish colonial writing as a genre that actively shapes colonial activities through aesthetic practices.

Chapter 2 traces the emergence of a Scottish Atlantic tradition in the 1620s. At that time, a small group around the Scottish author and politician William Alexander, Earl of Stirling and a favourite of King James VI and I, promoted the creation of a Scottish colony at Nova Scotia. Later, Cape Breton was added as a colonial settlement site. Inner Scottish and inner British power dynamics are crucial to understanding why and how Scotland's cultural imagination turned towards the Atlantic at this particular time. So is the utopian literary tradition, which shapes the relationship between the spaces, temporalities and cultural agents of the Scottish Atlantic. The chapter closes with a consideration of how Scotland's colonial activities in Nova Scotia have been naturalised over the past four centuries. Naming devices and the ongoing use of the colonial flag and coat of arms for Nova Scotia, as well as the narrative of Canada's 'Scottish' province, show the extent to which Scotland's colonial history is still alive in the Atlantic sphere today. An examination of Scottish writing from the seventeenth century sheds new light on this enduring legacy of Scotland's colonial activities by showing how utopian framing devices were successful in establishing long-term power structures in the Atlantic.

Chapter 3 focuses on Scottish Atlantic literature from the 1660s to the early 1690s. It explores how the genre of colonial utopian writing broadened in the mid-seventeenth century to include, next to advertisement texts and propaganda, drama, life writing, legal sources and abolitionist texts. Colonial utopian thought entered not only literature directly linked to Atlantic expansion but also texts that are usually associated with domestic affairs. Starting with a discussion of Thomas Sydserf's *Tarugo's Wiles: Or, the Coffee-House. A Comedy* (1667) and Archibald Pitcairne's *The Assembly; Or, Scotch Reformation. A Comedy* (1691), the chapter situates Scottish literature from the second half of the seventeenth century in an intercultural context. Picking up on significant work that has been done lately on Scotland's relationship to slavery, the chapter reasons that Scottish literature must be looked at more fully in terms of the Black Atlantic. This is also true for Scottish literature from the second half of the seventeenth century written more directly in terms of colonisation. In addition to drama, the chapter looks at legal and governmental sources relating to New Jersey and East New Jersey from the 1680s onwards. These sources point towards one of the central paradoxes that characterise colonial utopian writing in general and Scottish colonial writing in particular, which is the paradox of freedom versus liberty. This paradox, which Laura Doyle conceptualised,[64] pertains above all to enslaved people and the indigenous populations of the Americas. The aesthetic devices authors employed to frame the relationship between European and non-European inhabitants of the Americas illustrate how utopianism was used to negotiate both internal and external forms of colonialism. It also served to create a narrative of Scottish benevolence in the Atlantic sphere. In some cases, it spurred the rise of abolitionist literature in settler colonial circles, most famously in Quaker communities.

Chapter 4 investigates the hitherto understudied literary tradition of the Darien scheme. It employs both quantitative and qualitative methods to establish Darien as a central *topos* in Scottish literature from the seventeenth century onwards. The first part of the chapter uses a mixed methodology of chronicling the Darien literary tradition and examining how this tradition interacted with larger political and ideological trajectories. Satire, nostalgia, romanticism, selective commemoration and historical revisionism are common narrative strategies in the Darien literary tradition over the past 300 years. As in previous chapters, utopian thought and aesthetic devices shape this tradition and continue the narrative of Scottish benevolence and moral superiority in the Atlantic. Sources from the seventeenth and early eighteenth centuries that portray Darien as excessively rich and Scottish settlers as especially benign support this reading. Images of gold and material possessions dialogue with narratives of the Scottish settlers' excellence and their alleged kindness towards indigenous inhabitants. By the late seventeenth century, the colonial utopian tradition has turned into a full-fledged myth of Scottish Atlantic writing. The mythologisation of the colonial sphere, together with the mythologisation of the Scottish settlers, functions as a powerful instrument that was meant to make Scotland a major player in the competition for power in the late seventeenth-century Atlantic.

Chapter 5 draws upon the earlier findings and sharpens the argumentative strands of *Scottish Colonial Literature* by turning to the concept of failure in discussions of Scotland's colonial schemes. Up until this day, there is a prevalent narrative tradition that marks Scottish colonial activities between 1603 and 1707 as failures. The main aim of the chapter is to address the ambiguous message inherent in this narrative, which is poised between discharging Scotland from an active colonising role prior to the Union of Parliaments and simultaneously naturalising the history of European expansion as an overall success story. A growing body of literature has investigated and questioned these links between normative conceptions of failure and colonialism. My aim is to use this body of literature to address why and how narratives of Scotland's alleged failure continue to frame both popular and academic accounts of seventeenth-century Scottish colonialism. *Scottish Colonial Literature* seeks to open up a debate about normative conceptions of colonialism in Scottish studies and to address how these interact with contemporary debates about Western modernity, conceptions of Scottishness, and Scotland's position in colonial and postcolonial studies.

Notes

1. Watt, *The Price of Scotland* 200–2.
2. Joyce, Introduction lxiii.
3. Joyce, Introduction lxiii.
4. Anon., *Caledonia, or the Pedlar Turn'd Merchant* 1.
5. Lindsay, *History of Scottish Literature* 143–52.
6. Anon., *Caledonia, or the Pedlar Turn'd Merchant* 1–4; italics in original.
7. Ferns, *Narrating Utopia* 41.
8. Loomba, *Colonialism/Postcolonialism* 187.
9. Ashcroft, 'Critical Utopias' 415.

10. Levitas, *The Concept of Utopia* 183.
11. Levitas, *The Concept of Utopia* 183.
12. Anon., *Caledonia, or the Pedlar Turn'd Merchant* 3; italics in original.
13. Hogan, *Other Englands*; Knapp, *An Empire Nowhere*.
14. Ashcroft, 'Critical Utopias' 415.
15. Knapp, *An Empire Nowhere* 21–5.
16. More, *Utopia* 50.
17. Milton, *Areopagitica* 23; italics in original.
18. Gould, 'The Aesthetic Terrain' 57.
19. More, *Utopia*.
20. Hogan, 'Of Islands' 40–5.
21. Linebaugh and Rediker, *The Many-Headed Hydra* 15.
22. Wormald, 'Confidence and Perplexity' 123–49.
23. Wormald, 'Confidence and Perplexity' 133.
24. Cullen, 'The Famine' 153.
25. MacKenzie and Devine, 'Introduction' 1. Also see Landsman, 'Introduction' 22.
26. Anon., *Caledonia, or the Pedlar Turn'd Merchant* 2.
27. Levitas, *The Concept of Utopia* 8.
28. Veracini, *Settler Colonialism* 4.
29. Levitas, *The Concept of Utopia* 8.
30. Veracini, *Settler Colonialism* 4.
31. Mannheim, *Ideology and Utopia* 203.
32. Ricœur, *Lectures* 288.
33. Ricœur, *Lectures* 299.
34. Ricœur, *Lectures* 288.
35. Linebaugh and Rediker, *The Many-Headed Hydra* 51–6.
36. Wolfe, *Settler Colonialism*.
37. Anon., *Caledonia, or the Pedlar Turn'd Merchant* 2.
38. Houston, *The Renaissance Utopia*.
39. Houston, *The Renaissance Utopia* 119.
40. Houston, *The Renaissance Utopia*.
41. Hogan, 'Utopia' 463.
42. Hogan, 'Utopia' 465.
43. The term 'colonial utopian' emerged in conversation with Laura Doyle.
44. Andrews, *Trade, Plunder and Settlement*.
45. Hart, *Empires and Colonies*; Roper and van Ruymbeke, *Constructing Early Modern Empires*.
46. Elliott, *Spain, Europe & the Wider World*.
47. Dandelet, *The Renaissance of Empire* 261; Elliott, *Spain, Europe & the Wider World*; Hart, *Empires and Colonies*; Roper and van Ruymbeke, *Constructing Early Modern Empires*.
48. For a summary of the debate, see Loomba, *Colonialism/Postcolonialism* 184–231.
49. Anderson, *Imagined Communities*.

50. Carruthers and McIlvanney, 'Introduction' 4.
51. Wilson, 'Introduction' 22.
52. Griffiths and Reid, 'New Evidence on New Scotland' 492–508.
53. Burton, *Darien Papers* 371–417.
54. Prebble, *The Darien Disaster* 100.
55. Laing, *Royal Letters* 68.
56. Gallup-Diaz, *The Door of the Seas* no page.
57. Kenny, 'Ireland and the British Empire' 1.
58. For example, Ó Ciardha and Ó Siochrú, 'Introduction' 1–17; Wormald, 'The "British" Crown' 18–32.
59. Wormald, 'The "British" Crown' 29.
60. Qtd in Hogan, 'Utopia' 462.
61. Qtd in Hogan, 'Utopia' 462.
62. Qtd in Hadfield, 'Afterword' 219.
63. For example, Devine, *Scotland's Empire, 1600–1815*; Gardiner et al., *Scottish Literature and Postcolonial Literature*; Mack, *Scottish Fiction and the British Empire*; MacKenzie and Devine, *Scotland and the British Empire*; Sassi and van Heijnsbergen (eds), *Within and Without Empire*; Stroh, *Gaelic Scotland*.
64. Doyle, *Freedom's Empire*.

Chapter 2

Shifting Paradigms: Nova Scotia and 'New' Scotland

In 1614, one of King James VI and I's courtiers published a long poem called *Doomes-day, or The Great Day of the Lords Ivdgement*. The author was the Scottish courtier, Sir William Alexander of Menstrie (c. 1577–1640), First Earl of Stirling, who became a key figure in the colonisation of Nova Scotia from 1621 onwards. *Doomes-day* gestures towards some of the core ideas of the Stuart colonial agenda. The poem crystallises certain underlying patterns that have shaped European approaches to the Atlantic from the seventeenth century onwards, including the religious, economic, philosophical and political interests in the Americas. *Doomes-day* is an ambitious poem consisting of twelve parts, each labelled as one 'hour' in a day leading up to final Judgement Day. One of the most forceful, though previously overlooked, motifs is the colonial thrust lurking in the religious rhetoric of *Doomes-day*. In the section titled 'The Second Hour', Jacobean Britain is portrayed as being destined, even obliged, to establish colonies in the Americas in order to fulfil its godly providence of bringing peace, Protestantism and civility to the world. The mission is particularly urgent because, as the subtitle states, Christian Judgement Day is near, and the discovery of the Americas is thought to be a sure sign of its proximity:

> From offring grace no storme the Word can stay,
> Ere judgement come to those who will receive,
> In this last age Time doth new worlds display:
> That Christ a Church over all the earth may have,
> His righteousnesse shall barbarous Realmes array,
> If their first love more civill Lands will leave,
>   *America* to *Europe* may succeed,
>   God may of stones raise up to *Abram* seed.[1]

There is an apocalyptic tone to this stanza, which also shapes the later ideological grammar of writings about Nova Scotia. The 'new worlds' are seen as missionary places, which Europeans must evangelise in order to prepare the planet for Christ's return to earth. In miniature, the stanza encapsulates what Arthur H. Williamson has identified as the 'apocalypticism' of Stuart imperial ideology.[2] Two things are important about this apocalypticism for the present chapter, which seeks to trace the beginnings of the literary and cultural traditions of Scottish Atlantic writing in the seventeenth century: first, the intertwinement of colonial thought with other ideological foundations of early modern Britain, including religion; and second, the worldly implication that, in order to establish 'a Church over all the earth' before Christian Judgement Day, the time to act is now. Although the poem portrays God as chief colonial agent, the implication is that it is up to Jacobean readers to bring God's work of converting the 'barbarous Realmes' to Christianity to perfection, and that they had better do it before it is too late.

Alexander's *Doomes-day* anticipates what will emerge as a central tenet of the Stuart imperial agenda: namely, the artistic framing of Atlantic colonialism as a method of reform. The Nova Scotia scheme was envisioned as an improvement scheme on at least two levels: on one side, it was intended to transform the North American territory, including its people, its nature and its culture; on the other side, it was meant to reform seventeenth-century Scotland, which was perceived, by some, to be lagging behind in terms of global trading patterns and international migration policies. This dual objective of making both the 'new' world and the 'old' world a better place is a key feature of the colonial utopian genre that developed in Scotland from the 1620s onwards and became a subgenre of utopian writing in the course of the seventeenth century. The following chapter adopts an argument Roland Greene makes about the interaction between early modern poetry and the rise of European colonialism. According to Greene, even seemingly detached discourses such as Petrarchanism interact meaningfully with colonial thought of the time through such tropes as conquest, unrequitedness and material desires.[3] In Scottish colonial writing of the seventeenth century, love themes are not a dominant aesthetic mode. Instead, *Scottish Colonial Literature* suggests that utopianism is a major generic interlocutor of Scottish colonial literature and that the links between these two traditions are frequently used to naturalise and popularise colonial ideas among readers. Colonial writing is not a genre set apart from other genres or literary traditions in early modernity. It is a generic hybrid that dialogues with different literary and cultural traditions and borrows from it some of its established images and tropes. Next to Petrarchanism, the utopian tradition is a vehicle for the emergent ideologies of settler colonialism, as writings about Scotland's attempt to establish a colony in Nova Scotia in the 1620s illustrate.

Table 2.1 provides a basic chronological outline of the Nova Scotia scheme that serves as reference point for the following discussion. Further figures and events are mentioned in the subchapters below.

Table 2.1 The Settlement of Nova Scotia and Cape Breton

– to present	Mi'kmaq and Maliseet populations inhabit the eastern coast of what is nowadays Canada
1605	The French lay claim to a region on the eastern coast of Canada, known as L'Acadie, which includes parts of Nova Scotia
1620	John Mason publishes *A Briefe Discourse of the New-Found-Land with the Situation, Temperature, and Commodities Therof, Inciting our Nation to Goe Forward in that Hope-full Plantation Begunne*, which mentions the idea of Scotland's participation in overseas colonialism
Sept. 1621	James VI and I grants Nova Scotia to Sir William Alexander
Nov. 1621	James VI and I grants Cape Breton to Sir Robert Gordon of Lochinvar
1622/1623	First Scottish expeditions to Nova Scotia return without having established a permanent settlement there
1624	Alexander publishes *An Encouragement to Colonies*
1624	James VI and I creates a new *Order* of *Knight Baronets* of *Nova Scotia* in order to promote the colonisation of Nova Scotia; the idea was to allow wealthy Scots- and Englishmen to buy a piece of land in the colony and, in return, earn the title of knight-baronet
1625	Gordon publishes *Encovragements, For Such as Shall Have Intention to Bee Vnder-takers in the New Plantation of Cape Briton, now New Galloway in America, By Mee Lochinvar*
1627	Alexander's son, also called William Alexander, establishes the first Scottish settlement in Nova Scotia
1629	Another group of settlers arrives on Cape Breton; a member of the expedition, Richard Guthry, writes a letter home, which is the only surviving first-person narrative by a Scottish settler of the 1620s
1631	Treaty of Suza negotiated to end the Anglo-French War; it determines that Nova Scotia should be returned to France
10 July 1631	Charles I orders Alexander to tell his son to destroy the settlement and leave Nova Scotia in order to fulfil Treaty of Suza
until today	Continuing use of the name, coat of arms and flag from the 1620s Nova Scotia scheme as official name, provincial flag and coat of arms of the Canadian Province of Nova Scotia

When is Utopia? A 'New' Scotland at Home and Abroad

In 1624, William Alexander, with whose poem *Doomes-day* this chapter began, published *An Encouragement to Colonies*. The volume,
printed in London, is one of the founding texts of Scotland's Atlantic
literary tradition after 1603. In it, Alexander promotes the colonisation
of Nova Scotia as a paradigm shift in Scottish history, one that will
propel Scotland into an age of modernity. Alexander writes that, just as
there is 'a *New France*, a *New Spaine*, and a *New England*', so the world
'might likewise haue a *New Scotland*'.[4] This new Scotland, he hopes,
will help old Scotland to move from a premodern into a modern –
that is, an Atlantic – age. A similar hope is voiced in Robert Gordon of
Lochinvar's *Encovragements, For Such as Shall Have Intention to Bee
Vnder-takers in the New Plantation of Cape Briton, now New Galloway in America, By Mee Lochinvar*, published in 1625.[5] Together with
two royal charters issued by James VI and I in 1621, and some other
sources that relate to Scotland's involvement with Nova Scotia in the
1620s, Alexander's and Gordon's texts constitute the main textual corpus for analysing Scotland's Atlantic imaginary in the Stuart era. Small
as this corpus may be, it offers evidence that Scotland's entry into the
Atlantic is construed by the authors as a paradigm shift that will instigate a wholesale reform of Scotland. This idea also becomes evident in
the Atlantic colonial texts issued by James VI and I.

On 10 September 1621, James VI and I issued a royal charter to
Alexander over Nova Scotia. In this charter, originally published in
Latin, the King says that he wants to 'give, grant, and dispose to the
aforesaid Sir William Alexander, his heirs or assigns' the territory of
'*Novae Scotae*'.[6] The text is titled *Carta Domini Wilhelmi Alexandri
Equitis Dominii Et Baroniae Novae Scotae in America*. In it, James
specifies the boundaries of Nova Scotia, which was to extend from
'Cap Sable' in southwest Nova Scotia to 'Cap Britton' (Cape Breton) in
the northeast of Nova Scotia.[7] In addition, the territory was to include
parts of what are nowadays New Brunswick, Quebec and Maine. On
8 November 1621, James VI and I signed another royal charter, this
time issued to Robert Gordon of Lochinvar, a Scottish aristocrat from
the country of Galloway, and granting him the right to colonise Cape
Breton. At that time, Cape Breton was still an island unconnected to
the mainland of Nova Scotia. It is likely that Alexander supported this
second royal charter because he may have hoped for a joint settlement
scheme with Gordon. Taken together, Nova Scotia and Cape Breton,
as outlined in the royal charters, were vast territories. As S. G. E. Lythe

notes, 'if it [the Nova Scotia colony] had been developed and held, [it] would at one stroke have elevated Scotland to the top rank of colonial powers'.[8] From a contemporary perspective, such a historical possibility of Scotland becoming a global imperial power in the early seventeenth century throws the conception of the early British Empire as being predominantly English into stark relief. With the signing of the royal charter in 1621, Alexander became 'the one Scotsman of the time who fairly bears comparison with the Sidneys and the Raleighs of Elizabethan England'.[9] Such a comparison to Sir Philip Sidney (1554–86) and Sir Walter Raleigh (c. 1554–1618) points to the stupendousness of the colonial territory, which Scottish authors sometimes framed as a sign of religious approval of their colonial undertaking.

In keeping with the religious tropes of *Doomes-day*, both Alexander and Gordon insist that the colonisation of the Americas is a God-given plan. Alexander writes that 'it hath pleased the Lord to locke it [the Americas] vp so long amidst the depths, concealing it from the curiositie of the Ancients, that it might be discouered in a fit time for their posteritie'.[10] Similarly, Gordon addresses the 'Gentle Reader' with a recourse to colonial settlements 'from the creation of the World vnto this time', beginning with 'Adam and Eva' and ending with 'the planting of Countries, and civilizing barbarous and inhumane Nations' in the sixteenth and seventeenth centuries.[11] In this religiously connoted history of settlement schemes, Gordon suggests, Scotland should now play its role, as 'the English, the French, the Spaniard, the Portugale' have already done.[12] The temporal urgency expressed in such calls to Scottish colonialism are an earnest sounding of the idea that Scotland is lagging behind in the early modern race for the Americas, and that the creation of an overseas colony may serve to instigate a paradigm change for both 'old' and 'new' Scotland.

If England came comparatively late to the colonial competition in comparison to other European colonial cultures,[13] then Scotland joined the competition over the Atlantic even later. Alexander and Gordon alert their readers to this temporal dimension of European empire-building and mark the present time as a historical moment of change for Scotland. Their hope is that Scotland will join the European colonial competition that was eating its way into global geopolitical structures in the early seventeenth century. Guided by the models of English, Spanish and French settlements abroad, Alexander and Gordon formulate the hope that Atlantic colonialism would help the transformation of Scotland's trade, its political strength and its pressing social problems, such as unemployment and overpopulation. Here is how one of Alexander's acquaintances, the Welsh colonist and author Robert Hayman, conceives of this paradigm shift in Scottish history. His laudatory poem, 'To the Right Honorable Knight, Sir William Alexander, Principall, and Prime Planter in New-Scotland: To Whom the King Hath Giuen a Royall Gift to Defray his Great Charges in that Worthy Busines' (1628), expresses the dual spatial and temporal dimensions of the Nova Scotia undertaking:

> Great Alexander wept, and made sad mone,
> Because there was but one World to be wonne.
> It ioyes my heart, when such wise men as you,
> Conquer new Worlds which that Youth neuer knew.
> The King of Kings assist, blesse yon from Heauen;
> For our King hath you wise assistance giuen.
> Wisely our King did aide on you bestow:
> Wise are all Kings who all their gifts giue so.
> 'Tis well giuen, that is giuen to such a One,
> For seruice done, or seruice to be done.
> By all that know you, 'tis well understood,
> You will dispend it for your Countries good.
> Old Scotland you made happy by your birth,
> New-Scotland yon will make a happy earth.[14]

The epic scale of the Nova Scotia undertaking, as envisioned by Hayman, comes out in at least three rhetorical devices. First, the comparison between William Alexander and Alexander the Great insinuates that William Alexander, in colonising Nova Scotia, brings to perfection a process of expansion begun by emperors of ancient times. The difference is that Alexander the Great was still limited by geographical restraints whereas William Alexander is unbound in his imperial desires because Europeans now also have the Americas to pursue their expansionist desires. Second, the repetition of the word 'King' stresses both the royal and the religious approval of the undertaking while the repetition of the word 'wise' in the same lines invokes the image of King Solomon as another ancient royal known for his peacefulness and prudence. Third, and most importantly for the present chapter, the play with anaphora and temporal opposition in the final couplet captures the dual temporal framework employed by authors for the Nova Scotia scheme. The vision is to make both 'Old *Scotland*' and '*New-Scotland* [. . .] happy'. Like other utopian narratives of early modernity, the Atlantic is envisioned as a paradigm shift that has both temporal and spatial dimensions. It was to work at two places: in North America and in Britain. It was also to work across time by propelling a Scotland that was perceived as premodern by some into an age of modernity. To appreciate how sharply this couplet expresses the twofold hope of Scottish colonists in the 1620s, and to see how it dialogues with the multiple temporalities of the utopian tradition, it is useful to turn to the historical context of the Jacobean period more fully and situate Atlantic writing in it.

It is no coincidence that Scotland's Atlantic enterprises began after James VI and I (1566–1625) succeeded to the throne of England and Scotland in 1603. Together with James, numerous Scottish court-iers went to England, thus effecting a more concentrated mixture of Scottish and English court cultures than before. This also had an effect on the literature written at the Jacobean court. Scottish authors, such as Alexander Craig (c. 1567–1627), Robert Ayton (1570–1638) and William Alexander, moved to the London court with James after 1603. Their works are frequently noted for interacting prominently with English literature at the time,[15] specifically for their use of English as a literary language instead of Scots.[16] James VI and I endorsed this development by encouraging Scottish authors to avoid Scotticisms and to anglicise their language.[17] The rise of Scottish Atlantic writing was another indicator of the interactions between Anglo-Jacobean court culture and Scottish literature in the Stuart reign. Analysis of Scottish literature from the 1620s indicates how firmly written documents about the settlement of Nova Scotia draw on the larger British traditions of early modern travel literature and utopian writ-ing. Partly, this is due to personal contacts between Scottish, English and Welsh colonists at the Jacobean court.

Alexander originally made his career at the Edinburgh court as a courtier–poet. He wrote both poetry and drama, as well as royal advice texts, and, later, worked on translations and rewritings of earlier works. Sometimes, he is associated with the Castalian Band, the group of poets known for their close connection to the Scottish court in the 1580s and 1590s. James VI and I was both a patron and a participating author in this literary circle. In 1584, he pub-lished 'Ane Schort Treatise, Conteining Some Revlis and cautelis to be obseruit and eschewit in Scottis Poesie', which indicates the importance he attributed to literary court culture at the Jacobean court.[18] After his move to London in 1603, James VI and I contin-ued to support the arts, but his emphasis on the kind of literature to be published changed. One indicator of this change is the use of English as the preferred language of publication. Like others who came to the London court with him, Alexander began to write pre-dominantly in English after leaving Scotland. His early years at the

English court were highly productive and indicate his close connection to the King. He is known, amongst others, for his 'A Paraenesis to Prince Henry' (1604), *An Elegie on the Death of Prince Henrie* (1612), the sonnet sequence *Aurora* (1604), the series of dramas *The Monarchicke Tragedies* (1603–7) and, together with James, the metrical verse translation of *The Psalms of King David* (1636). At the same time as publishing courtly literature, Alexander moved up the political ladder at the Jacobean court. He was knighted in 1609, was made Master of Requests in 1614 and, one year later, became a member of the Privy Council of Scotland.[19] The notorious Scottish satirist Thomas Urquhart (1611–60) depicted Alexander as someone who 'was born a poet, and aimed to be a king. Therefore would he have his royal title from King James, who was born a king and aimed to be a poet.'[20] The quotation is telling not only for its insight into later assessments of Alexander's high ambitions but also concerning the literary traditions in which Scottish colonial writing of the 1620s participated.

As a Scot in London, Alexander became part of the process of Anglo-Scottish rapprochement that James VI and I actively worked towards during his reign.[21] Although James's plans for a constitutional union between England and Scotland, which he had tried to put into effect after his succession in 1603, proved to be unworkable because of parliamentary resistance, there were other, less obvious, ways of gradually uniting the kingdoms of England and Scotland. One of those means was colonialism. Andrew D. Nicholls notes that 'inter-kingdom co-operation' was part of 'a means of extending central authority into remote regions of the British Isles' in the early Stuart reign.[22] The participation of Scottish settlers in the colonisation of Ulster and Munster was a case in point.[23] Ireland became a site where James VI and I sought to expand and stabilise his power, and to enact the markers of his newly unified kingdom: 'The systematic influx of England and Scottish settlers was designed to hamper any attempts by hostile Catholic powers to use Ireland as a back door through which they could invest the king's Protestant realms.'[24] In addition, the Atlantic became another sphere of colonial interest in which some Scottish individuals saw opportunities for Anglo-Scottish co-operation. Together with James VI and I, and Gordon, Alexander advanced this vision by promoting Nova Scotia as a colonial site that would help Scotland to become a prosperous, agriculturally advanced partner in the British union.

Alexander's *An Encouragement* reads like the story of a fresh, successful and wealthy Scottish nation. Nova Scotia features as a site that would help Scotland enter an age of prosperity and progress by means of Atlantic settlement and trade. The very epigraph of the printed work heralds this line of thought and the construction of the narrative along utopian lines. It is taken from Virgil's *Eclogues* and prophesies the birth of a child that will bring forth a new, golden age.[25] Alexander cites the following lines from Virgil's Eclogue 4: 'Alter erit tum Tiphis, & altera quæ vehat Argo / delectos Heroas,' which translates as 'There will be another Tiphys and another Argo that will carry / chosen heroes.'[26] Virgil was well known by early modern humanists, not only for his *Eclogues* but also for his *Georgics*, which had been a source of inspiration for English colonial writing on Ireland.[27] The *Georgics* continued to be of ideological value for colonists in later centuries, too. They praised 'incessant work and vigilance', whereas '[t]he apparently passive nature of pastoral life might be seen as akin to the indolence and sloth that Virgil felt led to social and cultural regression.'[28] In Alexander's *An Encouragement*, the *Georgics* are not directly mentioned. Still, Virgil's emphasis on work and vigilance as conditions of success operates as a leitmotif in the text. References to classical antiquity serve the means of situating the Nova Scotia scheme in line with Renaissance humanism. They manage to envision Scotland's glorious future, which is simultaneously a return to the past. Alexander's literary background shines through in such framing devices of the Scottish Atlantic tradition, which rhetorically fuse the ancient golden age with a new golden age for Scotland. Claiming dominion not only over geographical spaces but also over Scotland's future reveals the intersections of multiple topographies and temporalities in the colonial utopian tradition. The genre asserts power over both spatial and temporal aspects of the Atlantic and does so, at least partially, by framing it in utopian terms.

Like Jason and the Argonauts on their search for the Golden Fleece, so Scottish settlers feature as travellers who will enter a paradisiac future by crossing the Atlantic. Nova Scotia figures in *An Encouragement* predominantly as a place of bucolic abundance, where settlers find ample resources, simplicity and harmony with nature. The colony is framed as one of 'the most pleasant parts in the World', where 'very good fat Earth' awaits the settlers and 'new Fieldes and Riuers' provide plenty of opportunities for hunting and gathering.[29] There are also some references to the harsher realities of the North American climate and environment but, by and large, Alexander's narrative weighs towards a pastoral portrayal of Nova Scotia. Virgil's *Eclogues* come to mind when reading *An Encouragement*, which others have shown to share rhetorical and generic features with the tradition of early modern pastoralism.[30] According to David Parkinson, the

'Sidneian pastoral romance' serves as a generic interlocutor for such representations of a bucolic and simultaneously abundant landscape in *An Encouragement*.[31] The utopian literary tradition is another, previously overlooked, generic interlocutor of Scottish colonial writing about Nova Scotia and Cape Breton. In contrast to pastoralism, utopianism goes one step further by not only idealising rural life but adding an active power claim to the bucolic vision. It pictures the Atlantic as a holistic reform plan for seventeenth-century Scotland and, in so doing, uses the utopian mode as a vehicle for requesting an active role for Scotland in European expansion. Whereas the idea of the harmonious, benign and idyllic land in pastoral literature is sometimes seen as an escape from reality, the colonial utopian tradition seeks actively to change reality by tackling its problems. The rivers are said to be so full of fish and the bays so rich in 'Herrings, [. . .] Lobsters, Crabs, Cockles and Mussels' that Nova Scotia would be 'a very fit place for a Plantation'.[32] *An Encouragement* draws on earlier traditions of idealised worlds not to suggest that these times are gone. Instead, it carries a clear message that it is possible to retrieve the ideal world by means of crossing the Atlantic. The present time is presented, once more, as the moment of change. Utopia is accessible if people venture abroad and contribute to its realisation. In this vein, *An Encouragement* is not simply another Renaissance pastoral. It is neither a less poetic version of Philip Sidney's *Arcadia* (1590), which Alexander rewrote a few years before *An Encouragement*,[33] nor a rewriting of Virgil's *Eclogues*. Instead, it is a colonial utopia that uses pastoral aesthetics to locate its power claims simultaneously in the past and in Scotland's envisaged, Atlantic future.

In the following, I want to borrow some thoughts about the relationship between modernity and colonialism from Dipesh Chakrabarty in order to conceptualise the temporal dimension of the Nova Scotia scheme further and to suggest that this has particular relevance for Scotland's place in the early Stuart empire.[34] As Chakrabarty has shown in his study of European empire-building, the concept of 'historical time' became 'a measure of the cultural distance' between cultures.[35] In the colonial context, such temporal configurations usually divide the world 'between the West and the non-West', and they have been used as a means to 'legitimat[e] the idea of civilization' and, consequently, subjugation in European empire-building.[36] Scotland's position in the early modern colonial sphere has to be read in such terms of temporal configurations. The promotional texts by Gordon and Alexander, as well as those by authors and colonists of the time with whom they were acquainted show how the settlement of Nova

Scotia is envisioned as achieving a paradigm shift that will thrust Scotland into an age of modernity. Emphasising the promises over the potential problems, and invoking the belief that there is an ideal, rather than a midway, solution for Scotland's lack of supplies are where the discourses of colonialism intersect with the discourses of utopianism. Nowhere is the utopian force of Scottish colonial writing stronger than in the assurance that there are no drawbacks, no uncertainties and no compromises to be made when turning towards the Atlantic. At the same time, this utopian force of Scottish colonial writing shows how the teleology of progress not only cuts European and non-European cultures into half, as Chakrabarty suggests. It also divides those cultures within Europe that have entered the colonial age and those that have not, or at least not yet, such as Scotland. According to the cultural logic of colonial utopias, non-colonial cultures emerge as backward, whereas colonial cultures are presented as progressive. In the eyes of Alexander and Gordon, it was time for Scotland to make that leap, too.

It is clear from Gordon's and Alexander's texts that they did not consider Scotland a future-oriented culture in the 1620s. Otherwise, they would not urge their countrymen and women to enter the age of colonialism, which they equated with progress. Alexander, for one, imagines the overseas colony as having profound effects on Scotland's domestic economy and its trade. Whereas the past and present are troublesome, *An Encouragement* promises that the future holds the key towards wholesale social and economic transformation:

> And where the *Scottish* Merchants before had no trade but by transporting Commodities that might haue beene imployed at home, and oftentimes monie, to bring backe Wine from *France*, and Pitch, Tarre, and Timber from the Easter Seas. Now only by exporting of men, Corne, and Cattle, they may within a little time be able to furnish back in exchange these things before named. As likewise a great benefit of fishes, Furres, Timber, and Metals, drawing forth our people to forreine Traffique, wherewith they neuer haue bin accustomed before, and that to the great increase of the Customes, helping hereby to enrich that ancient Kingdome.[37]

Alexander's model of colonialism is meant to mark a change in the development of Scotland towards an age of modernity. It shows how Chakrabarty's temporal framework is prefigured in texts of the early seventeenth century, when colonialism became 'a measure of the cultural distance' between cultures.[38] In this case, it is a European culture that is assessed as lagging behind because it does not have a colony.

Alexander portrays Scotland as retrogressive and urges readers to move forward by entering the age of Atlantic colonialism. According to the excerpt, this move across the Atlantic would offer a means to solve Scotland's economic crisis by advancing 'forreine Traffiq' and 'helping hereby to enrich that ancient Kingdome'.[39] Progress is equated with material acquisition here, which becomes, for Alexander, a marker of 'historical time' as a measure of progress.[40]

Surely, Scotland is not alone in seeking Atlantic solutions to its domestic problems. Many British and European colonists went abroad for reasons of destitution, impending imprisonment or forced emigration.[41] Such emphasis on the socio-economic context of the migrants helps to unsettle narratives of British colonialism as a purely teleological process of creating a new world system. Many colonists were poor, desperate and unfree when they crossed the Atlantic. Charles I even suggested in 1629 that it might be possible to dislodge Highlanders and Islanders to Nova Scotia in order to get rid of what was perceived as some of the more troublesome inhabitants of his kingdom.[42] A similar scenario was envisioned by Alexander and Gordon, who framed the Atlantic as a relief plan for the poor and dispossessed, and who artistically shaped it as a site where Scotland could reform itself. As in other colonial texts of the time, overseas colonisation is depicted as a swift measure to bring relief to as many people as possible in as short a time as possible. In this way, the argument Alexander puts forward grapples with the same question that other utopian narratives of the time tried to answer: the question of supply.

Utopian narratives usually express some kind of desire. The genre, as developed by Thomas More, Francis Bacon, Gerrard Winstanley, Henry Neville and Margaret Cavendish, has to be read in terms of the needs and desires it expresses and how it negotiates solutions to dealing with these needs and desires. J. C. Davis identifies the supply of material needs as one key trope of utopian narratives:

> All ideal societies must solve the problem of relating the existing and changing supply of satisfactions, some of which are by nature limited in supply to the wants of a heterogenial group, the desires of which will be, in some respects, unlimited.[43]

This idea also transpires in Scottish colonial writing of the 1620s. The concept of infinite supply materialises in the praise of unlimited land, natural resources and trading patterns that would be available to Scottish merchants and individuals by entering the Atlantic sphere.

Alexander addresses those '*Scottish* Merchants' who 'before had no trade' and are now meant to increase their profits through the expansion of the colonial market into North America.[44] The opportunities are unlimited, according to Alexander, because Atlantic trade is also unlimited. The following quotation provides evidence for this point by imagining how even the indigenous populations will eventually become trading partners for Scottish merchants and, in this way, expand the colonial market even further:

> We here goe to cause preach the Gospel where it was neuer heard, and not to subdue but to ciuillize the Sauages, for their ruine could giue to vs neither glory nor benefit, since in place of fame it would breed infamie, and would defraud vs of many able bodies, that hereafter (besides the Christian dutie in sauing their soules) by themselues or by their Posteritie may serue to many good vfes, when by our meanes they shall learne lawfull Trades, and industries [. . .].[45]

The passage emphasises the economic advantages that the Atlantic settlement will have for Scotland in the long run. The indigenous populations are envisaged as future collaborators, which supports the idea that Nova Scotia can become a major new trading hub in the seventeenth-century Atlantic. Such discursive transformations demonstrate how, by the 1620s, the Atlantic was becoming a space of primitive accumulation. Mercantilism was increasingly imagined as a means to offset the feudal system that distributed land and material supply unevenly in early modern Europe, as Karl Marx and Friedrich Engels have shown. In their *Manifesto of the Communist Party*, they discuss the relationship between colonial trade and the rise of capitalism from the sixteenth century onwards:

> The discovery of America, the rounding of the Cape, opened up fresh ground for the rising bourgeoisie. The East-Indian and Chinese markets, the colonisation of America, trade with the colonies, the increase in the means of exchange and in commodities generally, gave to commerce, to navigation, to industry, an impulse never before known, and thereby, to the revolutionary element in the tottering feudal society, a rapid development.[46]

According to Marx and Engels, the hope for prosperity was a guiding principle in the rise of Atlantic colonialism, which in turn affected the development of mercantilism and, later, capitalism throughout Europe and the world. That this form of Atlantic mercantilism, which was seen as a means to disrupt aristocratic hierarchies, would forcefully dispossess those already living in foreign places is one of the paradoxes with which studies of early modern colonialism need to come to terms.

Reading Scottish Atlantic texts of the seventeenth century lays bare the ruptures in the aesthetic and ideological patterns of colonial writing. Later chapters will draw on Doyle's concept of the 'paradox of freedom'[47] to conceptualise how categories of race figure in the dichotomous relationship between utopianism and colonialism. The emphasis on trade in the excerpt above already offers an early sample of how conceptions of Western modernity developed vis-à-vis racialised power constellations in the Atlantic. Paul Gilroy reminds us that the 'liberal sensibilities' that frequently drove colonists into Atlantic waters 'were connected to struggles over race, slavery, and imperial rule'.[48] *Scottish Colonial Literature* addresses these paradoxes and asks how Scottish authors and colonists deal with the conception of liberty versus repression in the Atlantic sphere, as well as the tension between possession and dispossession. Accessing these ideological entanglements from the angle of the colonial utopian tradition is one means to understand that these paradoxes are part and parcel of early modern thinking about the Atlantic. In More's *Utopia*, there are slaves working on the island, just as there are people on Utopia who are driven away from their native land because they refuse to cultivate the soil in the manner King Utopus instructs them to. Such cases of unequal power relationships in *Utopia* do not merely remind us of the paradoxical nature of More's work; they highlight the structural and ideological similarities that exist between the early modern utopian and the early modern colonial tradition.

The desire for material possessions in Scottish Atlantic writing may stand in stark contrast to More's *Utopia* with its lack of private property. That said, physical satisfaction has been part of the utopian tradition from *The Land of Cokaygne* onwards. 'All visualisers of ideal societies are concerned to maximise harmony and contentment and to minimise conflict and misery.'[49] In Scottish colonial texts, this ideal of minimising misery takes on a special significance because of Scotland's economic position at the time. To strengthen the mercantile argument, both Alexander and Gordon outline how the imperial ventures of Spain, France, England and Portugal have helped to improve the economy of the respective countries.[50] The dream of economic improvement is a cornerstone in Alexander's and Gordon's narratives of modernisation, which crystallises into a belief of Atlantic colonialism as Scotland's nascent modernity. Alexander asks his readers to trust in the prospect of material accumulation, which also comes with the prospect of upward social mobility:

> Where was euer Ambition baited with greater hopes then here, or where euer had Vertue so large a field to reape the fruites of Glory, since any man, who doth goe thither of good qualitie, [. . .] being the first Founder of a new estate, which a pleasing industry may quickly bring to a perfection; [. . .] and so euery one of inferiour sort may expect proportionably according to his aduenture:[51]

Marx and Engels's comment about the interaction of mercantilism and colonialism offers a conceptual framework to think about Scottish Atlantic writing in the larger context of European economic and societal changes. *An Encouragement* wants Scotland to be part of the rising mercantilism across Western Europe. Other developments, such as the growing belief in individual agency, went hand in hand with this belief in mercantilism, and it is likewise present in utopian writing of the seventeenth century. Robert Appelbaum refers to this as the 'Cartesian moment of self-assertion' in the utopian tradition, which believes in the transformation of society based on agency: first, the agency of the utopian mastermind and, second, the agency of the people who follow the mastermind.

The heyday of utopian reformism had not yet arrived in the 1620s, with the reform writings of Samuel Hartlib, Gerrard Winstanley or John Drury printed in the mid-seventeenth century. Still, a text like Gordon's *Encouragements* or Alexander's *Encouragement* already calls readers to improve their individual situation and, with it, their home society by participating in overseas colonialism. For Gordon, 'everie man' ought 'to inlarge his patrominie, as that hee bee not chargeable to others', which would be possible 'in a lawfull plantation abroad'.[52] Heralding the ideas of John Locke, whose role in colonial discourses will be further discussed in Chapter 3, Gordon posits that individual agency and self-determination are key concepts in the process of overseas plantation, and that the Scottish people must learn to embrace these 'modern' values in order to be successful planters:

> The chiefe (then) and the farthest poynt that my intention shall seeke to arrive at; shall bee to remove that vnbeliefe, which is so grounded in the mindes of men, to discredite most noble and profitable endevoures with distrust: and, first, to shake off their colourable pretences of ignorance, and then, if they will not be perswaded to make their selfe-willes inexcusable; I shall make manifest the worthinesse of the

> cause to the mindes of such as are desirous to bee settled in a cer-
> taintie. [. . .] but knowing that the chiefe commendation of vertue
> consisteth in action, I haue resolved a practice [. . .].[53]

The passage is noteworthy for the emphasis it puts on the minds of
the people and on their 'self-willes', both of which support the idea
that individual agency was a central trope of seventeenth-century
colonial literature. The urgency with which Gordon calls his readers
to act and become part of the Atlantic passage goes hand in hand with
the temporal split of Atlantic modernity outlined above. Chakrabarty's 'historical time' as 'a measure of the cultural distance'[54] is calculated in terms of Scotland's reluctance to enter Atlantic settlement
schemes, which Gordon assesses as a marker of cultural backwardness. He believes this backwardness can be changed and Scotland
propelled into an age of modernity if people take their fate in their
own hands by investing their time, money and life in the colonisation of the Atlantic. Gordon calls fellow Scotsmen and women to
move from a premodern to a modern age by crossing the Atlantic.
The colonial utopian tradition of early seventeenth-century Scottish
writing is organised around this threefold temporality, which allows
the authors to bridge the gap between Scotland and North America
as much as the gap between Scotland's past, present and future.

What is Utopia? Framing the Early Stuart Empire

One aspect that deserves closer attention in the literary history of
utopian writing is the role that colonial literature, and especially
Atlantic writing, played in the late sixteenth and early seventeenth
centuries. Although it has been frequently acknowledged that John
Winthrop's sermon 'A Model of Christian Charity' (1630) and James
Harrington's *The Commonwealth of Oceana* (1656) are part of the
utopian tradition, and that *The Commonwealth of Oceana* actively
shaped parts of the Massachusetts constitution, as well as those of
'Carolina, Pennsylvania and New Jersey',[55] the mutual interdepen-
dence of colonial and utopian writing in the context of Atlantic
expansion still calls for further investigation. This particularly concerns the question of the utopian canon. Important work has been
done lately on opening up the canon of utopian writing to include
travel writing and reformist literature.[56] According to Amy Boesky,
the mid-seventeenth century saw a major shift in the development
of utopian writing from a fictional towards a reformist genre. Social

utopias, such as Gabriel Plattes's *A Description of the Famous King-dome of Macaria* (1641), the writings of Samuel Hartlib and Gerard Winstanley's *The Law of Freedom in a Platform* (1652), have become part of the canon of utopian reformist writing. They are prime speci-mens of a type of utopianism that questions how the social and eco-nomic situation of seventeenth-century society can be improved. Key concerns in this reformist tradition of utopianism are labour, econ-omy and industry.[57] Similarly, Houston observes in *The Renaissance Utopia* that a major shift in the utopian genre happened in the mid-seventeenth century and equally includes reformist writing and travel writing in the utopian canon. According to Houston, the seventeenth century is the first time in Western society in 'which the achieve-ment of the ideal human society genuinely appeared possible'.[58] Scot-land's colonial literature from the early seventeenth century provides a means to open up the canon of utopian writing further to include works written in a global, and especially in an Atlantic, context. It enters the debate on what counts as utopianism and how we as con-temporary readers relate to the moral and ideological ambiguities of early modern utopianism.

Scottish Colonial Literature offers glimpses of the wide spectrum of colonial utopian narratives that existed in the seventeenth cen-tury. Social reform utopias, such as those by Winstanley, Plattes or the Hartlib Circle, had significant precursors and intellectual inter-locutors in the Atlantic context. Scottish colonial literature from the 1620s is an example of how overseas settlements functioned as laboratory spaces for seventeenth-century reform literature, and how they pushed the utopian tradition in the direction of practical, sometimes propagandistic or didactic, writing. Even if we may ques-tion in retrospect the underlying purposes of the utopian mode they used, colonial authors framed their works as finding solutions for existing domestic problems by going abroad. Seen in this light, there were plenty of utopian texts published between More's *Utopia* and Bacon's *New Atlantis*. These texts are about the Atlantic as much as they are about domestic affairs. Scottish authors were not the first to initiate this tradition of colonial utopian writing, but they readily picked up on the aesthetic design of Atlantic literature and idealised the foreign sites to the point of fictionalising them.

In the texts discussed above, Gordon and Alexander open up a narrative familiar from reformist utopian writing. In the mid-seventeenth century, Boesky notes, the utopian tradition had devel-oped a strong quality of social reformism in which 'Idleness and poverty were argued to be interrelated.'[59] Several decades earlier, the same argument emerged in the context of Atlantic writing. Colonialism, for Gordon and Alexander, is a method of social reform, one that can restructure Scotland's social and economic system and thrust Scotland into an age of modernity. Gordon, being the more polemical writer of the two, asks his readers to assess Scotland's position in the European context critically and to look to the Atlantic as a means of improvement:

> Or bee wee so farre inferiour to other Nations, or our Spirites so farre dejected from our ancient Predecessoures or our minds so vpon spoyle, pyracie, or other villanie, as to serve the *Portugale, Spaniard, Dutch, French,* or *Turk,* (as to the great hurte of Europe too manie doe) rather than our GOD, our King, our Countrie, and our selves? excusing our idlenesse, and our base complaints by want of imployment? when heere is such choyce of all sortes, and for all degrees in this plantation.[60]

The emphasis on the communal effort in this passage through the repetition of the word 'our', as well as the reference to the inhabitants of rival imperial nations such as '*Portugale, Spaniard, Dutch, French,* or *Turk*', support the idea that Scotland's place in the early Stuart empire was considered a contested one. Gordon urges his readers to think back to their 'ancient Predecessoures' in order to recognise that Scotland must be willing to fight for its future well-being. For Gordon, this means that Scotland must expand its social and economic sphere to the Atlantic. Otherwise, it will suffer from 'spoyle, pyracie, or other villanie'. There is a utopian undercurrent in this praise of the Atlantic that might help contemporary readers understand why colonial thought gained such prevalence in the early seventeenth century. It prefigures certain features of the reformist tradition that took on further force in later decades. In the works of reformers such as Hartlib, Drury, Harrington or Winstanley, the idea that alternative societies in Great Britain could be achieved through the activism of the people is a common device. Some decades earlier, English and Scottish writers were already fathoming such alternative societies by imagining the Atlantic as a British reform space. In their writings, the idealism of the utopian tradition intersects with colonial discourses of oppression, exploitation and racial denaturalisation. Scotland's place in the early Stuart Empire is one reason why the colonial utopian tradition features particularly strongly in Scottish literature of the seventeenth century. Its authors continued to refer to Scotland's domestic situation and to advise readers to improve this situation by venturing abroad.

Like the rest of Western Europe in the sixteenth and early seventeenth centuries, England and Scotland felt the effects of the price revolution.[61] Prices of food and other goods escalated to the point of making them unavailable to large parts of the Scottish population. Numerous people starved because they could not afford to buy food. In the British Isles, the effects of the price revolution were further exacerbated by the declining demand for traditional trading goods on the European continent, such as cloth and wool.[62] In Scotland, the situation worsened because of repeated famines, as well as outbreaks of the plague in the sixteenth and seventeenth centuries.[63] Although Scotland's economy eventually improved during the relatively stable reign of James VI and I,[64] a large portion of people lived in poverty. Scottish colonial writers of the seventeenth century responded to these problems and envisioned the overseas settlement as a means to make the country more prosperous and secure. Despite differences between the fictional story of King Utopus and the real-life attempt to create an overseas colony in Nova Scotia, it is possible to see structural parallels between the idea of finding an ideal commonwealth abroad that provides answers to England's problems, as in *Utopia*, and the idea of establishing a transatlantic settlement that can be turned into a solution for Scotland's domestic problems, as in Scottish writing about Nova Scotia. More's *Utopia* structurally divides this dual aim of utopian literature, with Book I describing England's domestic problems and Book II presenting the solution to these problems abroad. As the previous section discussed, Scottish colonial literature usually merges these two sides of utopianism and explains in one breath the benefits of an overseas settlement for Scotland. Significantly, Scottish authors were not alone in envisioning the Atlantic as a solution to Scotland's domestic problems. There was a pan-British interest, at least among elite circles, to endow Scotland with more economic strength in the early seventeenth century and, in so doing, turn it into a stable partner for England in the united British kingdom.

The original idea for a Scottish overseas colony appears to have come from Captain John Mason (1586–1635), an English sailor and colonist who was appointed second governor of Newfoundland in 1615. David Armitage notes that the earliest document in which the idea of Scottish participation in the colonisation of the Americas occurs is Mason's *A Briefe Discourse of the New-Found-Land* from 1620.[65] There were, in fact, other documents that may have inspired Scotland's colonial undertakings prior to Mason's tract, including a letter written by Mason to Sir John Scott of Scotstarvet (1585–1670) from August 1617, in which Mason promises to produce a detailed map and account of Newfoundland in the future, probably with the intention of encouraging Scottish colonialism there.[66] There is also a letter from James VI and I to the Privy Council of Scotland from late 1617 or early 1618, in which he suggests sending disobedient Scotsmen to Virginia.[67] *A Briefe Discourse* remains, however, the most immediate source for the royal charter issued in 1621. Mason dedicated his treatise to Sir John, a Scottish noble and statesman, who was a privy councillor in the reign of James VI and I. *A Briefe Discourse* asks Scott in its dedication 'if you thinke it [the treatise; K. S.] may doe good by incouraging any of your Countrie to the interprise'.[68] Mason specifically refers to a Scottish colony, which he imagines to have positive effects on '[t]he great intercourse of trade by our Nation these threescore years'.[69] Mason's *A Briefe Discourse* is an open invitation to Scott, and Scotland, to partake in the colonisation of Newfoundland – an idea not taken up by Scott himself but by William Alexander, who met Mason upon the latter's return to England in 1621.

It is likely that, after having met Mason, Alexander approached James VI and I with the idea to plant a Scottish colony in North America.[70] On 5 August 1621, James wrote a letter to the Privy Council of Scotland, in which he expressed his support for the Nova Scotia scheme. He states that

> Wee haue the more willingly harkened to a motion made vnto vs by oⁱ trusty and welbeloued Counsellour SIR WILLIAM ALEXANDER knight who hath a purpose to procure a forraine Plantation haueing made choice of lands lying betweene our Colonies of New England and Newfoundland both the Gouernours whereof haue encouraged him thereunto.[71]

In this letter, James lists three major motives for his support of the colonial scheme. The first reason is the religious cause of 'the conversion of [Infidells] to the Christian faith'.[72] The second reason is the economic advantage that Scotland would gain by creating 'a new trade at this tyme when traffique is so much decayed'.[73] The third reason is to turn Scotland into an imperial nation, following the 'sundry other Kingdomes [. . .] of late' who have 'renued their names' by 'imposeing them thus vpon new lands'.[74] Taken together, these three motives – religious, economic and patriotic – are common strategies of legitimising and promoting early modern European colonialism, not only in Scotland but also in England and elsewhere. What is particular about the Scottish case is James's view of Nova Scotia as a possible solution to Scotland's domestic problems, specifically its lack of trade and its economic hardships. The utopian ethos of finding answers to domestic problems by venturing abroad is perceptible in passages such as the following by James:

> such an enterprise is the more fitt for that our kingdome that it doth craue the transportation of nothing from thence, but only men, women, cattle, and victualls, and not of money, and maie giue a good returne of other commodityes affording the meanes of a new trade at this tyme when traffique is so much decayed.[75]

Nova Scotia appears to promise James what the island of Utopia had embodied for Raphael Hythloday, the fictional traveller in More's narrative: a solution to domestic problems, which cannot be solved at home. James implicitly points to the poverty problem in Scotland by emphasising that the settlement scheme needs nothing else but people, animals and victuals, and that money and other commodities are unnecessary for establishing an overseas colony. Colonialism, as viewed by James, is a perfect solution to Scotland's hardships. It adds something to the country – trade – without the need to invest anything in it beforehand. Or so the theory goes.

There is a stark discrepancy between the utopian framing devices that Alexander, Gordon and James use in their texts and the reception of the Nova Scotia scheme by the majority of Scottish people. There is evidence to suggest that most Scottish people at the time were reluctant to participate in Atlantic settlement schemes. Both Gordon and Alexander lament the fact that their country's people are unwilling to go abroad to either Nova Scotia or Cape Breton. The very titles of their works – *An Encouragement to Colonies* and *Encouragements, For Such as Shall Have Intention to Bee Vnder-takers in the New Plantation of Cape Briton* – indicate that the authors sought to promote the transition of Scotland's international vision against all odds: from European to Atlantic trading patterns, from a premercantile to a mercantile age, and from continental alliances towards global political partnerships. At the outset, their efforts were met with little success. Whereas the London Company, which later merged with the Plymouth Company to form the Virginia Company, managed to gather almost 1,700 shareholders for their colonial efforts after an extensive promotion campaign in the early seventeenth century,[76] a similar result was unthinkable in Scotland. Alexander and Gordon were able to arouse the interest of merely a 'few hundred Scots' who went to Nova Scotia in the entire decade of the 1620s.[77] This includes

the several expeditions that Alexander financed to explore the overseas territory in 1623 and 1624, and the two settlement schemes in
Nova Scotia and on Cape Breton in 1627 and 1629.

We lack primary sources from the Scottish public relating to the Nova
Scotia undertaking, which makes it difficult to speculate about the reasons for the scarce support for Atlantic settlement schemes among the
larger Scottish population in the early seventeenth century. There are,
to the best of my knowledge, no sources authored by women, Scottish
tenants or manual labourers, Catholics or Highlanders and Islanders
concerning the Nova Scotia undertaking, let alone by children or other
parts of the public that are under-represented in literary sources of the
time. The same goes for sources authored by the indigenous populations
of Nova Scotia and Cape Breton, which would allow us insight into
their perspectives on Scottish settlements in the late 1620s. Corresponding to the general tendency in Scottish Atlantic writing outlined earlier,
the surviving sources about Scotland's involvement with Nova Scotia
were written by members of the Lowland elite, mostly by courtiers, aris-
tocrats, settlers and royalty. This exclusiveness of sources endorses a
point that Laura Stewart makes about the difficulties of establishing a
public sphere in the early modern British archipelago: 'Whether there
was any "popular" or "public" dimension to the creation of, and to
reactions against, a British ideology (or ideologies) has proven more
difficult to demonstrate.'[78] Scottish public opinion on Atlantic trade or
colonial schemes is difficult to come by, which is why references to public opinion in the texts must be treated with caution.

Most references to Scottish public opinion on the Nova Scotia
scheme come from the corpus and authors outlined above. Alexander,
for instance, complains that he cannot find sufficient people willing to
participate in an expedition to Nova Scotia. The passage is included
in William Vaughan's *The Golden Fleece*, in which the author quotes
a conversation with Alexander that addresses the question of why so
few Scots participate in the Nova Scotia undertaking. Alexander is
quoted as saying of his countrymen:

> Men for the most part are now become peruerse Pigmeyes in respect
> of their generous Ancestours. They are *better fed than taught*, faire
> without, and foule within, if not rotten like that *Spaniards apple*. [. . .]
> They are more heauie-spirited, dull-headed, and almost growne out
> of kind.[79]

It is telling that Alexander, as portrayed in Vaughan's text, uses nature
imagery to describe those Scotsmen and women who are unwilling

to go to Nova Scotia. The metaphor 'peruerse Pigmeyes' parallels the savage trope commonly used for the indigenous populations of North America, but also reflects earlier representations of Scotland, and particularly of Gaelic Scots, in the Anglophone literary imagination.[80] The striking thing about Alexander's text is that the rift does not run along any geographical or cultural lines. Instead, it divides different colonial attitudes. Those who support Atlantic colonialism feature as progressive in Alexander's version, whereas those who are hesitant about Atlantic colonialism figure as unrefined and regressive. This rhetorical rupture creates a division among the Scottish people that, despite its one-sidedness, has become the basis for some scholarly interpretations of Scottish colonialism prior to 1707.

Some historians have tried to gloss over the lack of primary sources by offering explanation models for the lack of interest in Scottish colonial schemes among the public. One of those models draws on conceptions of political and economic modernity. In *Scottish Colonial Schemes*, George Pratt Insh notes that the Scottish people in the early modern period were, by and large, more conservative than their English neighbours and that this conservatism explains Scotland's lack of overseas plantations before 1707.[81] Insh refers to a wide range of political, economic and social practices in Scotland, which he considers less progressive than English practices of the time and which also account, for him, for the different migration strategies of the English and Scottish people.[82] Insh mentions the adherence to traditional trading and fishing customs among Scottish merchants and fishermen, which led them to trade not with new overseas markets but with the English and Irish. He also relates how young Scottish soldiers preferred to pursue military careers in mainland Europe instead of going overseas, where Englishmen and women of the time were travelling more readily. Those Scotsmen and women who were migrating in the late sixteenth and early seventeenth centuries – and their numbers were significant – usually went to other parts of Europe, especially to the Netherlands or to Poland and Scandinavia.[83] Worthington estimates that 'somewhere between 60–80,000 Scots left for European destinations (excluding those who went to England, Wales and Ireland) between 1600–1650, with a further 10–20,000 doing the same between 1650 and 1700'.[84] For Insh, all of these are signs of Scotland's conservatism.

My reading of Scotland's place in the early Stuart Empire is more hesitant to accept such grand narratives. It seems as if Scotland's restraint towards Atlantic undertakings in the seventeenth century asks larger questions about the links between modernity and colonialism than Insh's explanation offers. One of these questions is the relationship between the idea of Atlantic modernity and European colonialism that this chapter has addressed with reference to Chakrabarty's conception of colonial temporalities. Another question is how to deal with the lack of sources that makes any profound understanding of public opinion about the Nova Scotia scheme seem impossible. Herein lies one of the central points that *Scottish Colonial Literature* intends to make: it is not only important to realise the diversity of early modern empire-building but also to reconsider the methodological approaches we take towards early modern Atlantic writing, especially when it comes to under-represented parts of society. The absence of colonial settlements does not necessarily mean the absence of progress or political modernity. Such an explanation model is tautological because it presupposes that colonialism is equal to progress. To offer alternative explanation models that evade such a tautology, scholars need to gain more and better insight into the diversity of perspectives on Scottish colonialism that co-existed in the seventeenth century. Here, as throughout this book, I am hoping that future research will disclose further sources that articulate the views or opinions of those hitherto under-represented in the corpus.

One of these groups is formed by the people of the Scottish Highlands and Islands, especially the Gaelic-speaking parts of the population. Their role in the early Stuart realm is sometimes considered to be close to that of other colonised cultures. Scholars have noted that the rhetoric of Jacobean Atlantic colonialism is rooted in James's political agenda concerning the Scottish Highlands and Islands.[85] Control over the Highlands and Islands had been a longstanding source of conflict within the British Isles. Under the government of James VI, measures were taken to centralise and homogenise those parts of Scotland that were most remote from the seat of government in Edinburgh. In his royal advice tract, *The Basilicon Doron* (1599), James advises his son to overthrow the Highland 'Ouer-lords, & the chiefs of their Clannes' in order to keep the Scottish kingdom safe and stable.[86] The Statutes of Iona (1609), according to which Highland chiefs were required to send their successors to Lowland Scotland for an education in Protestant, English-speaking schools, were one measure to gain better control over the Highlands and Islands.

An earlier policy was to create Lowland plantations in Kintyre and Lochaber, as well as on the island of Lewis, throughout the 1580s and 1590s. Through such plantations, James sought to change the traditional societies of the Highlands and Islands, something recent critics have described as 'Deculturalisation and Extirpation'.[87] James was particularly suspicious of clan structures with their decentralised form of power relations. *Basilicon Doron* depicts the people living in the 'Hie-lands' as 'alluterlie barbares'.[88] Lowland Scots are portrayed as responsible Scottish 'subjects', whereas the inhabitants of the Highlands and Islands are said to be 'stubborne' or 'barbarous' people.[89] By planting Lowland settlers in the Highlands and Islands, the Stuart King intended to change the political structures of the Gaelic communities gradually, together with their cultural and linguistic patterns: from Gaelic to Scots, from clan system to a more centralised monarchy, from Gàidhealtachd to something approaching Lowland culture. James's solution was to plant 'Colonies among them of answerable In-lands subjects, that within short time may reforme and civilize the best inclined among them; rooting out or transporting the barbarous and stubborne sorte, and planting ciuilitie in their rooms'.[90] Such a tactic, so went the political reckoning, should decrease the linguistic, cultural and political differences between Lowland Scotland and the Gàidhealtachd. Homogenising policies such as these were not unique to early modern Scotland, seeing as sameness meant stability, and stability meant a higher chance of an enduring claim to power. But the pattern shows that the Scottish elite, even before the Union of Crowns in 1603, was not exempt from expanding and centralising its power.

Ever since Michael Hechter's *Internal Colonialism: The Celtic Fringe in British National Development, 1536–1966* (1975), the concept of internal colonialism is frequently used in relation to Scotland and, more generally, Celtic communities in the UK.[91] Hechter's argument is that Celtic and Gaelic cultures at home underwent a form of internal colonisation that is different from overseas expansion but that nevertheless shares certain features with other forms of British empire-building. The Highlands and Islands particularly are often viewed as affected by Anglophone empire-building. Although Scotland's status as a postcolonial culture remains contested, there is a tendency in contemporary scholarship to situate Scotland in a postcolonial framework and to argue for its special role in the UK. Some critics view this tendency with suspicion and wonder whether it is suitable 'to borrow postcolonialism's fashionability in order to provide a wider audience for Scottish literary criticism'.[92] While many studies remain critical of the applicability of postcolonial criticism to Scotland, others argue in favour of including Scotland at least partially in the field of postcolonial studies. Colin G. Calloway, for instance, has written about the similarities between the destruction of tribal structures in the Highlands and the colonisation of indigenous populations in the Americas.[93] Although direct connections are difficult to draw between the experiences of groups so vastly different as Gaelic

Scots and indigenous populations of the Americas, there is an ongoing interest in exploring the possibilities of linking global cultures that are considered to be marginalised in their home countries in one way or another. One of the points that Calloway makes is that it is necessary to rethink the concept of colonialism in order to allow for more diverse studies to emerge about the Atlantic. According to Calloway, colonialism is 'not a one-size-fits-all concept'.[94] Scotland's place in the Stuart Empire emphasises the diversity of colonial thought and colonial practices, and shows that colonialism was an ambiguous concept in the 1620s. 'Colonial relationships did not always break down neatly into exploiter and exploited.'[95] Literary texts about Scottish colonialism before 1707 highlight this complexity and refuse any simple categorisation of coloniser and colonised.

To return to the utopian dimension of early Scottish colonial writing, it is possible to trace certain idealising patterns back to Jacobean rhetoric about the Highlands and Islands. James writes in *Basilicon Doron* (1599) that 'a good King (after a happy and famous reigne) dieth in peace, lamented by his subiects, & admired by his neighbours'.[96] The emphasis on harmony may have been propaganda to some extent. And yet, throughout his reign James cherished the idea of expanding his power in a peaceful way. When he succeeded to the throne of England in 1603, James carefully constructed his image as a British Caesar Augustus, as Paulina Kewes has shown.[97] One of Alexander's *Monarchicke Tragedies*, *The Tragedy of Julius Caesar* (1607), was part of this larger ideological and aesthetic narrativisation, which imagined James as both a peaceful and a successful ruler.[98] Like his historical predecessor, James intended to become known as a benign emperor who had managed to unite England and Scotland without blood. Ideally, James hoped that he would also be able to extend his reign into the Atlantic without any wars. Here is where the utopian tradition enters the scene again and joins with the colonial impetus of Scottish Atlantic writing.

Jeffrey Knapp reasons in *An Empire Nowhere* that More's narrative of conquering land and forming it according to the coloniser's ideas was a major influence on colonial thought from the sixteenth century onwards.[99] Even if *Utopia* warns of territorial expansions when recounting how the Achorians conquered another kingdom and then had trouble handling the expanded empire, the main narrative is one of conquest. Knapp goes so far as to call *Utopia* 'perhaps the first Tudor attempt to elaborate a theory of colonization'.[100] Like the idealistic portrayal of King Utopus's reign, many theorists of the early modern Atlantic presented colonialism as a benevolent alternative to ancient forms of empire-building.[101] Alexander, the initiator of the Nova Scotia scheme, thought of colonialism as 'a new mode of empire-building, one that could unite the pursuit of greatness with goodness'.[102] Ancient empires, such as the Roman, the Ottoman or the Byzantine, served Alexander as negative examples of expansion in his *Monarchicke Tragedies* (1603–7). In contrast, Jacobean empire-building was framed as being at once peaceful and flourishing, at once benevolent and prosperous. This is how Alexander describes Scotland's Atlantic expansion to James VI and I in utopian terms:

> By this meanes, you that are borne to rule Nations, may bee the beginner of Nations, enlarging this Monarchie without bloud, and making a Conquest without wronging of others, whereof in regard of your youth any good beginning in this (like your vertue upon which it doth depend) boding a speedie Progresse Time in your own time, doth promise a great perfection.[103]

Surely, such verses stand in the sycophantic tradition of early modern literature. And yet, they help us understand the idealism underlying the utopianism of Stuart empire-building. James is said to be 'borne to rule Nations' and 'bee the beginner of Nations'. Stuart expansionism figures as a natural process, almost like a birth, as the body metaphors imply. Alexander alludes to James's 'youth' and suggests that he may be 'enlarging this Monarchie without bloud', as if he were procreating in the political rather than the private realm. Such a dual function of the royal body is reminiscent of Ernst Kantorowicz's concept of *The King's Two Bodies*. According to Kantorowicz, for early modern people the royal body consisted of two parts: the body natural and the body politic.[104] The two interacted closely with one another, but while the prior grew old and eventually decayed, the latter remained eternally young because it was a spiritual body, endowed with divine qualities. For the passage quoted above, this division between the physical and the political body offers an explanation of why James could be called a youthful king in 1624, when he was in his fifty-seventh year and surely no longer youthful in physical terms. In fact, James VI and I died one year later, in 1625. Yet, his body politic could still be described as young and energetic in 1624. In fact, it was presented as so lively that it could produce new offspring around the world in the form of overseas colonies.

In reality, the colonisation of overseas territories was far from peaceful, neither in the Jacobean period nor before or afterwards. There was both direct and indirect violence against the indigenous populations around the world. There were forceful expulsions, unnumbered killings, the spread of alcoholism and diseases and, again, unnumbered deaths as a result of these diseases. There were frequent skirmishes with earlier colonisers from France, Spain or other European countries and, as always in the colonial arena, there was violence against nature with the cutting down of forests, the killing of pelted animals for the fur trade, the forceful manipulation of nature and the exploitation of natural resources such as oil, gold or turpentine. Ecocritical approaches remind us that '[t]he developing scope of European expansion during the Renaissance offered the opportunity for [. . .] obviously economic projects of early colonialism.'[105] Nature becomes part of the utopian conception of early modern colonialism because humans try to reorganise the relationship between land and people. Digging up gold in excessive amounts, clearing forested land in order to grow marketable products on it or introducing new crops in order to cater to the colonial market are attempts to dominate nature. Settlers become mini-models of King Utopus, who changed the entire island setting in order to make nature fit his needs.

The utopian tradition glosses over many of the less harmonious aspects of Atlantic colonialism. Instead, it portrays the Americas as a place where perfection can be achieved. The frontispiece of Alexander's *An Encouragement* conveys this utopian message of Scottish colonial writing, and brings in the Protestant work ethos that shaped literature about Nova Scotia (Fig. 2.1).

The man standing on the ship in the middle of the frontispiece looks as if he is determined to conquer new worlds. Two ribbons surround the male figure, one of them featuring the word 'PEACE' and the other 'PLENTIE'. These mottos indicate once more how important a non-violent vision was to Alexander in his conception of the Nova Scotia undertaking and also how materialism influenced the Stuart colonial agenda. A banner with the words 'FOR THOU SHALT LABOUR' surrounds the man and the ribbons. The partial quotation of the fourth biblical commandment – the whole of which reads 'Six days shalt thou labour, and do all thy work: But the seventh day is the sabbath of the LORD thy God' – highlights the intertwinement of material and religious motifs in a similar manner to the quotation from *Doomes-day* at the beginning of the chapter. 'PLENTIE' will come only to those who labour, or so the frontispiece seems to say. The religious narrative of the frontispiece is reminiscent of other colonial undertakings of the 1620s, including the settlements in New Plymouth and early Massachusetts, with Winthrop's 'Citty

Figure 2.1 Frontispiece. William Alexander, *An Encouragement to Colonies*. London: William Stansby, 1624. Reproduced with permission of the British Library.

upon a Hill' being perhaps the most famous motto that expresses European colonial ambitions in spiritual terms.[106] Not coincidentally, the frontispiece also recalls Alexander's long poem *Doomes-day* from a decade earlier, with its fusion of religious and economic language in 'those who will receive'.[107] As in other British colonial writings of the sixteenth and seventeenth centuries, Protestantism is repeatedly invoked as a legitimising discourse of Scottish colonialism and as a rhetorical tool against competing Catholic colonisers.

Any idea of the Auld Alliance is missing from Scottish colonial writing of the 1620s. Instead, Gordon and Alexander evoke a Protestant discourse that links their undertakings to the emergent sense of Britishness in the early seventeenth century. French colonisers in North America are allegedly 'lothing labor' and refuse anything that 'would impose more vpon them then was agreeable with the indifferencie of their affections and superficiall endeuours'.[108] Alexander claims that

French settlers show 'needlesse ostentation' and 'lazinesse',[109] which explains why Scottish settlers would be so much better colonisers in Nova Scotia than the French, at least in the eyes of Alexander. Denominational issues may be a pretext to condemn the colonial efforts of one's opponents. Still, it aligns with a new development of British nation-building in the seventeenth century that specifically addresses Protestant colonisers from England, Scotland and Wales. Alexander praises Protestantism at an age when it was already, at least officially, the leading denomination across Great Britain. James VI and I came to the throne of England, amongst other things, because he was a Protestant. Such emphasis on the advantages of Protestantism is surely not a singularity of Alexander's text. Colonists from all over Europe justified their actions by referring to their denominations and claiming the necessity of converting the native inhabitants to the denomination of their ruling monarchs. In *The Discoverie of the Large, Rich, and Bewtiful Empyre of Guiana*, Walter Raleigh disparages Spanish colonisers in South America as dissolute and corrupt before proudly proclaiming the victory of his Protestant troops over the Catholic competitors.[110] Conversely, French colonisers such as Pierre Biard condemned the alleged immorality of Protestant settlers in North America and decried their purported mistreatment of the native population.[111] What is particular about Scottish colonial writing from the 1620s is that Scottish colonists tried to emphasise the common goals of English and Scottish colonialism. They were keen to present Scotland as an especially powerful – because hardworking – kingdom to participate in the common British pursuits of Stuart empire-building. Here is how Alexander portrays his fellow Scottish inhabitants:

> When I doe consider with myselfe what things are necessarie for a Plantation, I cannot but be confident that my owne Countreymen are as fit for such a purpose as any men in the world, hauing daring mindes that vpon any probable appearances doe despise danger, and bodies able to indure as much as the height of their minds can vndertake, naturally louing to make vse of their owne ground, and not trusting to traffique.[112]

The Protestant work ethic is fully in play here, and it interacts with the body imagery of the passage. Scottish bodies are portrayed as enduring and strong, 'naturally louing' agricultural work. Such images function to strengthen the alignment of Scottish interests with European colonial pursuits and, in an inner British context, with the interests of English and Welsh colonists. In *Britons Forging the Nation 1707–1837*, Linda

Colley identifies colonialism as one of the forces that helped to meld a common British identity in a later period.[113] David Armitage makes a similar argument in saying that the concept of Britishness rose in relation to the processes of colonialism after the Union of Crowns.[114] According to Armitage, the Jacobean era helped to strengthen a common British identity, which was plural at all times, but which increasingly pursued comparable interests.[115] Colonialism allowed for certain class alliances and Atlantic trading networks that connected people across the UK and, also, continental Europe. The colonisation of Nova Scotia gestures towards this interaction between colonialism and the rise of Britishness in the early decades of the seventeenth century. At the same time, it illustrates how little effect this official narrative of unification seems to have had on those parts of the kingdom that were not part of the political and economic elite.

While Alexander and Gordon published advertising texts to arouse interest in their colonial schemes abroad, James VI and I tried to raise support for the Nova Scotia settlement by offering to bestow the title of baronet or knight on those willing to support the colonial undertaking financially. But even this effort proved to be in vain. The lack of public support for the Nova Scotia scheme lends support to Benedict Anderson's argument that, in seventeenth-century empire-building, 'the "spirit" of these conquests was still fundamentally that of a prenational age'.[116] Literary sources point to the split between the small group within the Scottish population that favoured Atlantic settlement schemes and the much larger part of the population whose reactions and perceptions have not been recorded. Given the representation of the Scottish public in the available sources, it seems unlikely that the Atlantic constituted a unifying force in 1620s Scotland. Colonial narratives sometimes suggest that national unity existed among the Scottish people, but in the end, such rhetoric must be read as part of the utopian toolbox that invented the Scottish Atlantic for a seventeenth-century audience.

Where is Utopia? Nova Scotia and the Virginia Company

For all we know, neither Gordon nor Alexander had ever been to the Americas. Neither of them was an experienced traveller, merchant or fisherman with Atlantic experiences. Compared to the activities of the East India Company, which had been founded by merchants in 1599 and had received a royal charter in 1600, Alexander and Gordon were in uncharted waters when it came to foreign trade or establishing colonial settlements abroad. Herein lies one of the keys to understanding their writings about the Atlantic and the entire Nova Scotia and Cape Breton scheme. If the previous sections showed how idealising rhetoric informs the temporal and economic conception of Nova Scotia literature, then the present section examines how intertextual links between Scottish colonial writing and earlier travelogues inform the geographical and spatial vision of the texts. As always, the utopian tradition is not far from this vision.

When Alexander and Gordon were writing about Nova Scotia and Cape Breton in the mid-1620s, the Virginia Company – formed by a fusion of the London Company and the Plymouth Company – was already flourishing. Its primary product was tobacco, but slavery, too, was a growing trade.[117] After the Jamestown Massacre of 1622, James VI and I decided to dissolve the company and turn Virginia into a royal colony. Well-known investors included Captain John Smith, Richard Hakluyt (junior) and Sir Oliver Cromwell, an 'uncle of the future Lord Protector'.[118] This prominence of the Virginia Company is important because it partly explains its role as textual interlocutor for the Nova Scotia scheme. Texts written about the Virginia Company are central intertexts for Scottish writings about Nova Scotia and Cape Breton in more than one way. They provide both structural and direct textual sources for the representation of Scottish colonialism in the early seventeenth century. For one thing, the owners and advocates of the Virginia Company 'presented colonization as a solution to domestic social problems in England'.[119] Alexander and Gordon ventured a similar rhetorical campaign for Scotland and partly organised their writings in line with this reasoning, as the previous chapters have shown. In addition, there are other insightful links between Scottish colonial writing and Virginia Company literature, some of which have previously gone unnoticed. These links help to illustrate how intertextual entanglements make any strict generic division between colonial literature, travel writing and utopian literature impossible and also how the fictional geographies of Virginia, Nova Scotia and Cape Breton merge in Scottish Atlantic writing of the 1620s.

Gordon's *Encouragements* is the most pronounced case of textual collaboration and geographical conflation between Virginia Company literature and Scottish colonial writing. For a long time, criticism read Gordon's *Encouragements* as the more scientific text in comparison to Alexander's *An Encouragement*. Insh claims that Gordon's *Encouragements* 'shows traces of [. . .] the exploits of the

Age of Discovery' because of 'the precision with which it sets out the shortness of the Atlantic voyage, the topography and the products of the Island'.[120] Indeed, when one reads Gordon's account of Cape Breton, one is struck by the amount of detail he is able to provide about the place and its fauna, flora and people. Note in the following excerpt the specificity of the natural products that Gordon lists and his apparent knowledge of the uses of these natural products, some of which do not exist in Europe:

> The ground it will yield us an admired varietie; some wee shal have that are merchantable, which, by the serving for ordinarie necessars of the planters & inhabitants, may yield a superplus sufficient, by way of traffick and exchange with other nations, to enriche our selves the provyders; such as flaxe, hempe, which the Soyle doth yield of it self not planted. For pitch, tarre, rozen and turpentine, there bee these kind of trees there, which yield them aboundantlie. Sassafras, called by the natives, winauk, a kind of wood of sweet smell, and of rare vertues in Physick. The Vine, it groweth there wild. Oyle there may be there of two sortes; one of walnuts; and another of berries, like the ackornes which the natives use. Furres of manie and diverse kinds; such as the marterne, the otter, the black foxe, the luzernes, Deere skins, bevers, wildcat, and manie others. Sweet gummes of diverse kinds, and many other Apothecarie drugges. Dyes of diverse sortes; such as shoemake, for black:[121]

For someone who had presumably never been to Cape Breton or, for that matter, to North America, this is an astonishingly detailed account of the place. To know exactly what kinds of animal live on Cape Breton, which oils can be produced there, what the indigenous name for a certain tree – sassafras – is and what the medical uses of this tree are: all this is remarkable information for someone who had never travelled across the Atlantic and lived in an age when intelligence about overseas places was not as easy to come by as in later centuries. The question is, then, where does Gordon get his information? An answer to this question has been partially provided by Andrew Fitzmaurice, who has shown that Gordon's *Encovragements* borrows extensive passages 'from Virginia Company literature', and it usually does so 'without acknowledgement'.[122] Fitzmaurice specifically refers to two Virginia Company texts, written by travellers to the English settlements on the North American east coast, including the anonymously published *A True Declaration of the Estate of the Colonie in Virginia* (1610) and John Smith's *The General Historie of Virginia* (1624). What seems to have been overlooked so far is that

Gordon also borrows extensively from a much earlier text about Virginia: to be precise, one of the founding texts of Virginia Company literature, Thomas Hariot's *A Briefe and True Report of the New Found Land of Virginia* (1588).

Thomas Hariot (c. 1560–1621), also spelled Harriot, was an English scientist and traveller. He accompanied the Roanoke expedition of Ralph Lane in 1585, which was funded by Walter Raleigh. Hariot was a gifted linguist. He learned the Algonquian language of Virginia's native inhabitants, which gained him access to different kinds of knowledge from the indigenous populations of the North American east coast. His *A Briefe and True Report* features this insider knowledge, which ranges from his acquaintance with North American herbs and spices to familiarity with the flora, fauna and culture of the indigenous peoples. The text was first published in 1588. It was reprinted in 1590 in Theodor De Bry's *America* (1590–1634), where it was accompanied by illustrations based on drawings by John White, the official artist and mapmaker of the Roanoke expedition under Richard Grenville.[123] Hariot's account is, in many ways, proto-ethnographic, but it has also been used for colonial purposes, both in his own time and by later authors. A comparison between Hariot's *A Briefe and True Report* and Gordon's *Encouragements* shows how this was the case in the Scottish context. Hariot's *A Briefe and True Report* is used in Gordon's *Encouragements* as an immediate source to imagine a quasi-utopian island of Cape Breton or, as Gordon names it, New Galloway.

Gordon copies, sometimes word for word, the list of natural resources from Hariot. He lists the 'pitch, tarre, rozen and turpentine' allegedly found on Cape Breton,[124] just as Hariot records the '*Pitch, Tarre, Rozen, and Turpentine*' in Virginia.[125] The '*Flaxe and Hempe*' cited by Hariot as being 'not planted as the soile doth yeeld it of it selfe'[126] find their way into Gordon's *Encouragements* as 'flexe, hempe, which the Soyle doth yeeld of it self'.[127] The 'Oyle', 'Furres of manie and diverse kinds', 'Deere skins', 'Dyes of diverse sortes' and 'Sweet gummes' that Gordon enumerates[128] are likewise reproduced from Hariot's report, where Virginia is said to be rich in 'Oyle', 'Furres', 'Deare skinnes', 'Sweete Gummes' and 'Dyes of diuers kindes'.[129] Such intertextual links suggest that the natural products listed in Gordon's *Encouragements* are not necessarily those of Cape Breton. They are those of Virginia, or at least of the Virginia as described in Hariot's text, which in itself is ideologically charged because of the colonial context in which it was written. From the perspective of Scottish colonial writing of the 1620s, the purpose of these detailed lists of natural resources seems to be to idealise the colonial space by presenting it in terms of material abundance. The list of natural products endows the picture of Cape Breton with a degree of authenticity that is typical of early modern travel writing. Such discourses of authenticity are meant to prove the truthfulness of the account and, in an Atlantic context, the value of the colonial territory. Ironically, the opposite is the case. New Galloway is reinvented by Gordon, who copies Hariot's narrative to make his version of Cape Breton sound economically attractive to readers. After all, all of the items that Gordon lists were desirable trading commodities on the early modern colonial market. Although the demand for furs was declining in early modern Europe,[130] iron and copper were increasingly valuable goods, which is also true for wood and timber, as well as the herbs and therapeutic plants that were used for apothecary supplies.[131] Gordon's description of Cape Breton's natural products plays into the commercial interests that were guiding principles of Scottish colonialism in the 1620s.

As seen earlier, the Nova Scotia scheme was intent on increasing Scotland's trade. The authors sought to reform Scotland's economy through 'a lawfull increase of necessary commerce'.[132] Likewise, King James imagined the colony as creating 'a new trade at this tyme when traffique is so much decayed' in Scotland.[133] Gordon's duplication of Hariot's list of natural resources may well have been meant to underpin this reformist agenda of Scotland's colonial efforts. After all, as Claire Jowitt has shown, '[t]he assessment of future markets for English goods was an important feature of the intended voyage.'[134] The same seems to have been true for Scotland. Only when sufficient commodities were envisaged as being available in the foreign place were people likely to be willing to invest time, money and energy into overseas travels. In the Scottish context, such appraisal of 'the potential local market'[135] may have been particularly relevant because the increase of trade was seen as a primary goal of overseas colonialism, and also because most Scotsmen and women had few resources to spare. Gordon's list, it appears, was meant to persuade those who were previously cautious about going to Cape Breton to overcome their hesitation. The rhetorical mode of persuasion is a central component of colonial literature.[136] Gordon's use of this mode partly works via intertextual collaboration and the spatial conflation of two Atlantic spaces into one.

Interestingly, Gordon never mentions Hariot in his text. This is curious because he does refer to other Virginia travellers such as Walter Raleigh, John Smith and Christopher Newport.[137] Whether or not Gordon actively tries to conceal his act of replication is impossible to say. What is clear is that the reproduction of the natural resources from Hariot serves as a literary strategy of promoting Atlantic trade by making it sound extremely profitable, well explored and safe for those who will go there. One could say that Gordon fictionalises Cape Breton to the point of making it a utopia. It is construed as a place where wine 'groweth [. . .] wild' and where the soil yields the natural products 'of it self not planted': that is, without the need for being cultivated.[138] It is possible that Gordon implicitly quotes Jacques Cartier here, who wrote in his *Voyages en nouvelle France* (1534–6), about Upper Canada, that it is 'loaded with grapes along the river that it appeared as if they had been planted by man rather than otherwise, but they are neither cultivated nor pruned'.[139] Such tropes of abundance are common not only in early modern colonial narratives but also in utopian narratives from *The Land of Cokaygne* onwards. In the latter, there are said to be 'satisfactions enough to satiate the grossest appetite'.[140] In *The Land of Cokaygne*, the main point is that all of this happens without the need for human effort because the land itself will yield what is necessary to live lavishly. For Gordon, the utopian dimension of overseas colonialism lies only partly in the abundance of the land. More importantly, this abundance, with its generous provision of natural resources, will enable and enhance the trading opportunities for seventeenth-century Scotland.

Related ideas about the Americas as a utopian space exist in texts written for and about the Virginia Company. Michael Drayton's 'Ode to the Virginian Voyage' (1610) praises the abundance of the place, its

> Fowle, venison, and Fish;
> And the fruitfull'st Soyle,
> Without your toyle,
> Three harvests more,
> All greater than you wish.[141]

It is not surprising, given this emphasis on abundance, that Gordon fictionalises Cape Breton to propagate the settlement to his readers. There was a long tradition of describing colonial territories as gardens, sometimes a Garden of Eden which needed tillage, but always as a garden that contains plenty of resources for people to prosper if the soil is adequately worked.[142] By the seventeenth century, the North Atlantic was commonly associated with the Garden of Eden: for instance, in the frontispiece, 'Adam and Eve', accompanying the foreword to Hariot's *A Briefe and True Report* in Theodor de Bry's reprint (1590).[143] In the image, the Garden of Eden figures not as a pastoral or bucolic place. Instead, there are labourers who need to work the field and a woman is shown nursing her infant while vultures (lions, tigers, snakes) are pictured in the surroundings. The Garden of Eden of the Americas needs labour and civilisation in order to make it a liveable, peaceful place. Gordon reproduces parts of Hariot's depiction of Virginia but shifts the emphasis from labour to the effortlessness of colonisation. In his epistle, he writes that 'Adam and Eva did first beginne this pleasant works to plant the Earth to succeeding posteritie.'[144] He continues to emphasise the pleasantness and easiness of the settlement: for instance, by reassuring his readers that the risk of violent encounters with the indigenous populations of Cape Breton is virtually non-existent.

Gordon describes the native inhabitants as 'harmlesse' people whose 'weapons [. . .] are onelie Bowes made of Hazell, and arrowes of reedes', but no 'weapons of yron'.[145] Here, as elsewhere in Gordon's *Encouragements*, the risks of Atlantic settlement are downplayed. The passage is again copied from Hariot's account of Virginia, which states that the indigenous populations of Cape Breton are 'hauing no edge tooles or weapons of yron or steele to offend vs withall, neither know they how to make any; those weapons y they haue, are onlie bowes made of Witch hazle, & arrowes of reeds'.[146] The reassuring message that Gordon tries to convey is that North America's indigenous populations are martially and technologically inferior to Europeans:

> If there shoulde fall out anie Warres betwixt vs and them, what fight coulde there bee, wee having advantages against them, so manie manner of wayes: it maye bee easilie imagined, by our discipline, our strange weapons, especiallie, our Ordinance great, and small.[147]

As to be expected, the passage is once again copied from Hariot's Virginia narrative. The original passage states:

> If there fall out any warres between vs & them, what their fight is likely to bee, we hauing aduantages against them so many maner of waies, as by our discipline, our strange weapons and devises els; especially by ordinance great and small, it may be easily imagined.[148]

A pattern emerges here in that Gordon reproduces those parts from Hariot's account that seem to be specifically appealing or reassuring to his readers, who are induced to think about Cape Breton as a safe, profitable and superior place. There is plenty of wishful thinking in colonial texts of the early modern period. Gordon's *Encouragements* is perhaps the most patent case of intertextual colonial utopianism because it imagines a foreign place as ideal by copying text passages from an earlier text. This earlier text refers to a different geographical region, which is how the spatial geography of the Atlantic becomes unstable. The Cape Breton Gordon describes never existed in the physical world. It is a projection of the author's wishes on to the Atlantic territory.

A similar point about the projection of authorial wishes on to the colonial space can be made with regard to the early modern colonial cartographic tradition. A look at the map included in Alexander's *An Encouragement* visualises the idea that Scottish colonists would be able to create a New Scotland at home and abroad (Fig. 2.2). As always in the colonial arena, naming and mapping are operating devices that serve the long-term establishment of imperial power structures.

Figure 2.2 'The mapp and description of New-England'. William Alexander, *An Encouragement to Colonies*. Reproduced with permission of the British Library.

The map 'is derived from the work of Samuel de Champlain (fl. 1612–1613), Johannes De Laet (1581–1649) and the previously unpublished cartography of John Mason (c. 1600–1672)'.[149] Alexander seems to have issued the map specifically for advocating his cause and visually introducing his readers to the territory he promoted for settlement. Cartographically, the map is

> notable for a number of first's [sic] including the first appearance of the term 'Cape Cod' on a map, the earliest mapping of Prince Edward Island, the first mapping of the French settlement of Kebec on an English map, and the first use of the term 'New Scotland' or 'Nova Scotia' on a map.[150]

On a theoretical level, the map evinces concern with the ideological function of maps in colonial processes, where they actively created spaces rather than merely representing them.[151] 'New Scotlande' is divided into two parts, the southern one called 'Caledonia' after the Celtic name for Scotland and the northern one 'The Prouince of Alexandria' after the chief coloniser, William Alexander. The island on the northeast shore of Nova Scotia is Cape Breton, here spelled '*C. Briton*'. The river 'Twede' on Alexander's map is today the St Croix River dividing Maine from New Brunswick. 'Twede' is a duplication of the River Tweed, which divides England and Scotland. Similarly, the Saint John River in Nova Scotia bears the name 'Clyde' on Alexander's map, which reproduces the name of the Scottish river that flows into the Firth of Clyde. Naming strategies such as these corroborate the larger argument about the twofold newness that Scottish colonisers hoped to achieve through the overseas territory. They also exerted power claims over the colonial territory.

Naming a colony or parts of it after one's home country is a common instrument of appropriation in the early modern colonial arena.[152] Alexander lists New France, New England and New Spain as examples that induce him to 'likewise haue a *New Scotland*'.[153] The map is a visual tribute to this desire for a new Scotland. Anderson theorises this dual dimension of colonial naming practices by showing how evocations of novelty in the colonial context differ from other invocations of novelty in so far as they do not suggest chronological replacements – a new item replacing an old one. Instead, they suggest the temporal simultaneity of the eponymous places: 'Vizcaya is there *alongside* Nueva Vizcaya, New London *alongside* London: an idiom of sibling competition rather than of inheritance.'[154] Anderson's reading not only supports the argument made throughout this book that verbal practices are vital instruments of power in the early modern colonial sphere. In addition, it endorses a reading of the colonial territories as utopian spaces where novelty features as a key trope. More's *Utopia* and Bacon's *New Atlantis* both stress the newness of their societies in their titles, More in the subtitle – *On the Best State of a Commonwealth and on the New Island of Utopia* – and Bacon in the main title: *New Atlantis*. Margaret Cavendish's *The Description of a New World, Called the Blazing World* equally emphasises the novelty of the narration in its title, as does Henry Neville's *New and Further Discovery of the Isle of Pines*. Taken together, this emphasis on innovation and originality in early modern utopian literature helps to delineate how the process of knowledge acquisition aligns with the familiar trope of utopian mastery. The imagined discovery of new geographical spaces, new forms of government and new liberties in More's, Bacon's, Cavendish's and Neville's texts gesture towards the supremacy of discoveries and knowledge production as a central precept of early modern utopianism.

Two years after the printing of Gordon's *Encouragements*, Bacon published *New Atlantis*. Although there is no direct link between these two texts, Bacon's utopia helps to theorise further the relationship between knowledge and power in early modern colonial writing. More than his essays 'Of Empire' (1612; rev. 1625) and 'Of Plantation' (1625),[155] *New Atlantis* captures the idea of exerting power over the world via the careful handling of information. The foremost symbol of this power relationship is the House of Salomon (or Solomon), which constitutes the island's temple of knowledge. The House of Salomon stores the knowledge the Bensalemites gather on their travels, but it refuses to share any information about the Bensalemites themselves.[156] The governor of Bensalem tells his visitors that 'we know well most part of the habitable world, and are ourselves unknown'.[157] From this knowledge springs a hierarchy because the rest of the world is left outside the model of knowledge acquisition that the House of Salomon practises. Hogan shows, in her reading of Bacon's *New Atlantis*, how this precept federates with colonial elements in early modern utopias: 'While Bensalem may not overtly model a violent, militarily aggressive empire of direct domination, it is certainly a fantasy of empire where natural knowledge becomes a vehicle for and a product of mercantile exploitation.'[158] In most utopias of the time, there is an uneven relationship between the enclosed space of the idealised society and the rest of the world, which is not so privileged and blessed with knowledge as the utopian society. According to Hogan, *New Atlantis* can be read as a text that 'negotiates anxieties about a burgeoning world system by allowing Bensalem to benefit from global relations without actually participating in them'.[159] A similar hierarchy is at work in early modern colonial literature, where Europeans are gathering information about foreign places and cultures, and using this information to gain power over these places. Scottish writing of the early seventeenth century follows this logic of knowledge as something to be produced, and used, for colonial purposes. The crux is that neither Alexander nor Gordon had first-hand knowledge about the colonial places they envisioned in their writings. They consulted earlier travel narratives to conceive of their own, idealised, image of Nova Scotia and Cape Breton, and to envisage new forms of mastery in which Scottish merchants and colonists would join the group of leaders. The Atlantic, with its ongoing redistribution of power, patterns of trade and strategic importance for European rulers, offered a space to fulfil such a fantasy of Scottish and British mastery. To print a map of North America with Scotland's and Alexander's names inscribed on it provided a visual space for this narrative of mastery.

It would be useful to know more about the conception of the map reprinted here, such as who exactly gave orders to divide the territory into the different parts, who named the rivers and who conceived of the name 'Province of Alexandria'. Without such knowledge, one can only speculate on the role that Alexander or the cartographer played in this process, and the gestures of power implicit in these acts of naming. What is clear is that the mapmaking fits the overall strategy of European cartographic appropriation of the time. According to Alfred Hiatt, 'the territorial expansion of Europe from the twelfth to the fifteenth centuries (and beyond) both brings about, and is made possible by, changes in mapping practices'.[160] What is particular about the New Scotland map is that, in all likelihood, the territory was never surveyed, mapped or mathematically calculated by any of the Scottish colonists who wrote about it. The mapmaker appears to have copied the earlier maps of de Champlain, de Laet and Mason, and added the Scottish names to it, perhaps on behalf of Alexander or whoever paid him. This practice of relying on other people for the creation of Scotland's Atlantic vision of the 1620s is part of a larger argument that can be made about Scottish colonial writing of the seventeenth century: namely, its tendency towards collective authorship. Literature about Nova Scotia relied heavily on literature about Virginia, just as later authors writing about Darien relied heavily on travelogues by Lionel Wafer and William Dampier to convince their readers of the profitability and alleged effortlessness of the Darien

Scheme, as Chapter 4 illustrates. To point out these practices of collective authorship does not mean to discredit the authors or to charge them with plagiarism. Copying, rewriting and intertextual references were common practices of early modern writing. In colonial literature, though, they take up a peculiar role because they partly seem to stand opposed to the primacy of knowledge and factual reliability that authors often claimed in the processes of colonisation.

Perhaps Gordon actually thought of Virginia and Cape Breton as similar. As Knapp points out, 'Renaissance writers generally assumed that the same latitude meant the same climate, and the same climate was all one country needed to produce the same commodities as another country.'[161] It is possible, therefore, that Gordon believed in the likeness of Virginia and Cape Breton and that he wanted to share his conviction of the place's abundance with his readers. Truth, in early modern travelogues and colonial literature, is frequently an unreliable discourse rather than a source of factual information. Sometimes, information was added that turned out to be inaccurate. At other times, information was withheld from potential settlers in order not to thwart the colonial enterprise. We know, for instance, that 'colonists in Virginia were [. . .] eating leather boots and serpents' in order to survive in the first decade of the seventeenth century: 'One man killed his wife, chopped her up, and salted her for food; others dug up corpses from graves and ate them.'[162] These conditions in the Virginia Company were likely to be not altogether unknown to those interested in Atlantic colonialism, nor were the drastic death rates of Virginia colonists, whose chances of surviving the first two years abroad were about one in nine. Of 535 settlers, only 60 survived over a period of two years.[163] The careful handling of such information by English and also Scottish authors, who may or may not have been aware of the details of the Virginia settlement, was one literary strategy to create a utopian setting for the colonial narrative. Scottish colonial writing conflates different spatial settings and creates new Atlantic geographies through literal and aesthetic intertextualities.

Whose Utopia?

Every utopia contains the seeds of dystopia. From Ashcroft's postcolonial perspective on utopias, as well as Mannheim's and Ricœur's conceptualisation of utopias as outlined in the Introduction, Scotland's Atlantic literature of the 1620s reveals the evident biases of the colonial utopian tradition. What is a utopia for some is a dystopia for others. In the colonial context, this Janus-faced nature of utopias materialises most strongly in the relationship between different groups involved in the process of colonisation. The indigenous populations of the colonial sphere and others who were forced participants of European colonialism are surely not the ones whose desires are expressed in colonial utopian writing. The utopias studied in this book are Eurocentric utopias. Doyle has written about the co-formation of the concepts of liberty and race in early modern empire-building. For Doyle, race was a key factor in the development of the concept of freedom as a marker of modernity. This modernity was also strongly Eurocentric.

> Failure to be autonomous can mark one as a member of an inferior race, or it can authorise expulsion from the dominant race, or at least threaten loss of race protection and privilege. Conversely, the enactment of self-supporting, individual *autonomy* ratifies one's membership in the race community.[164]

The texts by Gordon and Alexander illustrate how this discourse of race circulated not only in English writings of the time but also in Scottish texts. Scotsmen and women, so Gordon argues, can make the transition towards an age of modernity and, to borrow Doyle's words, become 'member[s] of this race-empire of freedom'.[165] This is part of the narrative of liberty and freedom that was sung across Europe in the seventeenth century, and which some Scottish individuals hoped to spread in Scotland by promoting colonialism. Utopia, as a genre, acquired fresh political purposes in the hands of writers such as Alexander or Gordon. Their works, together with similar texts by English and Welsh colonists, sought to propel Scotland into an age of liberty. At the same time, and through the marking of liberty as Eurocentric, they helped to create a vision in which other parts of the world population were structurally excluded from the pursuit of liberty.

In Scottish colonial literature, as in other colonial texts of the time, the pursuit of colonial desires frequently goes hand in hand with the dispossession of non-European agents. This is a recurrent topic in Scottish Atlantic writing from the early to the late seventeenth century. In the colonial 'contact zone'[166] of the Atlantic, this pertains above all to the indigenous populations of the Americas, as well as to enslaved people. As the excerpt from Gordon's *Encouragements* in the previous section has shown, indigenous peoples are subordinate figures in the Stuart colonial ideology. Alexander describes the native

Mi'kmaq[167] as 'brute beasts' who 'runne like beasts after beasts, seeking no soile, but onely after their prey'.[168] Although James hopes that there will be 'peace, alliance, friendship and mutual conferences, help and communication with those wild Aborigines and their chiefs', he also allows for the possibility that the colonisers need to exert their 'rule and power over them', if needed by 'taking up arms against them, whereby they may be reduced to order'.[169] Some of the later settlers were endowed with both weapons and military experience to prepare for such a possibility of warfare with the Mi'kmaq.[170] Despite its constant emphasis on kindness, Stuart colonialism is built on the structural hierarchies that settler colonialism has endorsed from the early modern period onwards.

Although it is true that role allocations in the colonial context were frequently more fluid than the dual conceptions of coloniser and colonised suggest, the hierarchical structures of the European-dominated colonial sphere remained in place even centuries after the original schemes. In 1921, Nova Scotia celebrated the 'three-hundredth anniversary of Sir William Alexander's 1621 charter' with a plaque that honoured Alexander's role in the settlement of Nova Scotia.[171] Such acts of public commemoration are part of a larger cultural commemoration of European settler history in the Americas. Patrick Wolfe makes a crucial point about such continuations of colonial ideologies even centuries after the original colonial acts. According to Wolfe, settler colonialism is a 'structure not an event'.[172] What Wolfe means by this is that the patterns of thinking and acting that are initiated in a settler colonial context frequently remain in place long after the actual colonial undertaking has ended. This is true not only for Scottish colonialism but for most kinds of settler colonial practices around the globe and across the centuries. Scottish colonialism in Nova Scotia is an example of the structural longevity of settler colonialism. Its patterns have been naturalised in Nova Scotia's cultural history. The name of the province is the first of several examples that show how this process of naturalisation works.

Like other European kings and queens, James took it for granted that he could bestow an overseas territory on one of his courtiers. He also took it for granted that he could name the colonial space and, in this way, exert his power over it. He writes in the royal charter issued to Alexander:

> Which lands aforesaid, in all time to come, shall enjoy the name of Nova Scotia, in America, which also the aforesaid Sir William shall divide into parts and portions, as to him may seem meet, and give

names to the same, according to his pleasure; together with all mines, as well royal of gold and silver, as other mines of iron, lead, copper, brass, tin, and other minerals whatsoever, with power of digging them, and causing them to be dug out of the earth, of purifying and refining the same, and converting and using them to his own proper use, or to other uses whatsoever, as to the said Sir William Alexander, his heirs or assigns, or those whom it shall have happened that he shall have established in his stead, in the said lands, shall seem meet.[173]

Nature is a resource in this vision of Scottish settler colonialism, which James VI and I develops together with Alexander and Gordon into a narrative of economic success. While France and Great Britain famously fought over the question of ownership of Nova Scotia throughout the seventeenth and eighteenth centuries, the basic tenets of settler colonialism have remained in place from the time of the first European settlements onwards: land can be owned, and European settlers have the right to claim this ownership. These structures partly remain in place throughout the world today. Although there are clear signs of change throughout Canada and North America, as well as other parts of the globe, the struggle over land and land ownership remains a conflict-ridden issue for indigenous communities across the Americas. This aligns with the patterns and epistemologies of space established about 400 years ago.

The settlers who arrived on Cape Breton Island in 1629 'carried a hefty supply of guns, ammunition, and heavy artillery, and were evidently prepared to take an aggressive stance from the time they arrived'.[174] Both Alexander's *Encouragements* and Gordon's *Encouragements* signal a willingness for imperial aggression in their texts: for instance, by referring to the indigenous populations of Nova Scotia and Cape Breton as 'Sauages', 'beasts' or 'the People'.[175] Remembering that neither Gordon nor Alexander had ever travelled abroad is instructive for understanding the distanced, anonymous image they create of the Mi'kmaq. Gordon describes them as 'so poore, so base, so inciuile, and so savage' that they can hardly be considered a danger in the colonial territory.[176] Where Montaigne's idea of the noble savage subtly criticises the Eurocentrism of early modern travellers by stating that his traveller to Brazil found nothing 'that is either barbarous and savage, unless men call that barbarisme which is not common to them',[177] Scottish colonial texts of the seventeenth century come closer to More's version of conquest in *Utopia*, where King Utopus encountered 'rude and wild people' and transformed them into peaceful and cultured citizens.[178] Alexander claims that 'the Land' in Nova Scotia is 'either wanting Inhabitants, or hau-ing none that doe appropriate to themselues any peculiar ground'.[179] This alleged lack of land ownership – *terra nullius* – leads Alexander to contend that Nova Scotia is free for Scottish settlers to take. He promises that

> any man, who doth goe thither of good qualitie [. . .] shall haue as much Bounds as may serue for a great Man, wherevpon hee may build a Towne of his owne, giuing it what forme or name hee will, and being the first Founder of a new estate, which a pleasing industry may quickly bring to a perfection, may leaue a faire inheritance to his posteritie, who shall claime vnto him as the Author of their Nobilitie there [. . .].[180]

Apart from corroborating the argument about the mercantile spirit of the Scottish colonial imaginary, the quotation displays the growing desire for land in early modern Britain. Since land was rare and oppor-tunities to inherit land were mostly restricted to the first-born sons of a land-owning family, a class of aspiring young men were attracted by the opportunity to purchase property in the overseas colonies. Around 1485, the King of England alone held about 5 per cent of all land in England, the nobility another 5–10 per cent, and the landed gentry roughly 25–30 per cent.[181] It is easy to see from such numbers why the possibility of acquiring land abroad plays such a central role in early modern Scottish writing. Settler colonialism developed partly as a theory of land acquisition for those who did not own any. With land, they hoped to increase their social status and the availability of material supplies. If these goals could be achieved without open war-fare, then early modern political theory could peacefully solve one of its main problems: land supply. Yet, what solves the problem for one creates a problem for others.

It is commonly acknowledged today that Europeans and the indigenous peoples of the Americas had vastly different outlooks on the question of land ownership when they met in the early modern period. As Urs Bitterli explains with regard to the period of the first encounters between European settlers and the indigenous popula-tions of other continents and places:

> In America, Asia and Africa, misunderstandings frequently arose from the fact that the Europeans who wished to acquire land did not understand, and did not want to understand, the cultural conditions governing such transactions. Noticing that, by European standards, the natives did not cultivate their land at all intensively, the colonists

assumed that the natives had more land than they knew what to do with and lacked any definite concept of ownership. The natives, on the other hand, had never entertained the notion that land could be handed over to people of alien origin, and in concluding agreements and treaties with the white men they thought they were only temporarily transferring the right of cultivation.[182]

No matter whether the land was called Virginia, Nova Scotia or East New Jersey, herein lies one major source of the conflict that has continued to shape cultural relations in the Americas until today. James bestowed on Alexander the right to divide and sublet Nova Scotia according to his needs and wishes. The Mi'kmaq and Maliseet, who had lived in the region, had in all probability a very different understanding of land and people's right to live on it without ownership. According to James, Alexander may use all the natural resources of the colony 'according to his pleasure'. Alexander reassures his readers that land ownership in Nova Scotia could be achieved 'without dispossessing of others'.[183] He makes a similar claim when he promises James VI and I that the colonisation of Nova Scotia is a means to 'enlarg[e] this Monarchie without bloud, and making a Conquest without wronging of others'.[184] Here, as elsewhere, Alexander denies the native inhabitants of Nova Scotia and Cape Breton any right to their land. The Mi'kmaq of Nova Scotia and Cape Breton are portrayed as so innocent that they pose no threat to the European settlers. Alexander writes that the 'Plantations in *America* doe approch neerest to the puritie [. . .] of the first age' in which the native inhabitants live, like Adam and Eve, 'in the infancie of the first age'.[185] For all the differences between a Christian paradise and the Nova Scotia settlement, settlers are promised that the colonial passage across the Atlantic is a journey back in time, just as it is a journey into the future. The golden age may be an ideal in the cultural sphere. In foreign politics, paradise can come into existence again by turning America into a superior version of early modern Europe.

The very name Nova Scotia is an example of the longevity of Scottish settler colonial structures there. James VI and I first mentions the name in his *Carta Domini Wilhelmi Alexandri Equitis Dominii et Baroniae Novae Scotae in America* and says it should 'be called by the aforesaid name of Nova Scotia, in all time to come'.[186] Even if very few people probably think of this colonial context when uttering the name Nova Scotia today, the name reiterates, albeit implicitly, the colonial aspirations of early modern Scotland. Some refer to the region as L'Acadie or as Mi'kma'ki, but the official name is Nova Scotia or, in French, La Nouvelle-Écosse. However one views this continuing use of colonial names in the present, it is telling that the Scottish name, rather than the French or Mi'kma'ki one, stuck with the region. The longevity of Scottish settler structures is perhaps nowhere more evident than here. John Reid has pointed to the strategic reinvention of Nova Scotia by British imperial forces after the Siege of Port Royal, also known as the Conquest of Acadia, in 1710.[187] Part of these efforts was a renewed emphasis on the name 'Nova Scotia', which British imperialists used in order to arouse interest in the region as a potential settlement site.[188] This is where the early history of Scotland's settlement scheme in Nova Scotia connects with the later migration waves of Scottish settlers to Nova Scotia in the eighteenth and nineteenth centuries.[189] Beneath the naming history of the province lies a story of colonial power and the effort to secure British dominion over Nova Scotia, both imaginatively and demographically. Scottish and, later, British imperial agents endowed Nova Scotia with a name that they thought would epitomise their claim over the province. The ongoing use of the name Nova Scotia bears witness to the naturalisation of Europe's imperial history in the Atlantic. An inquiry into Scottish colonialism can help to heighten awareness of the sublime ideologies that are still at work across the Atlantic. Following such a trajectory of thought, it is likewise possible to see the long-term structures of settler colonialism in Nova Scotia in the continuing use of the flag and the Armorial Achievement from the 1620s, both of which are the basis for Nova Scotia's flag and Coat of Arms today (Fig. 2.3).

The Armorial Achievement abounds with images that conceive of a powerful Scottish nation and, at the same time, a friendly relationship with the indigenous populations of the Americas. Its message is utopian because it envisions peace and domination as working together. The ideological thrust is clearly colonial. The unicorn stands for strength, liberty and the uniqueness of the colonial undertaking. The highly aestheticized, though scarcely armed, figure of the Mi'kmaq echoes the depiction of the First Nations in Gordon's and Alexander's texts, as it suggests the possibility of an easy victory over the indigenous populations. This is reinforced by the shaking hands above the crown. These visually embody the idea of unity between settlers and the First Nations. Similarly, the laurel and the thistle support the vision of Scotland as a congenial colonial country. The Armorial Achievement visually taps into the central narratives of Stuart empire-building, which is to reconcile conquest and peace, moderation and greed, philanthropy and

Armorial Achievement of Nova Scotia

North American savage supporter as depicted by armorial artists. Edinburgh
early 17th Century

Figure 2.3 Armorial Achievement of Nova Scotia. *Transactions of
the Royal Canadian Institute* No. 31, Vol XIV, Part 1, 1922, p. 73.
Reproduced with permission of the Royal Canadian Institute.

power. The Latin phrase printed above the crest supports the utopian
dimension of the colonial scheme: '*Munit haec et altera vincit,*' Latin
for 'One defends and the other conquers.' This motto is another way
of imagining colonial power relations as harmonious and yet clearly
ranked. Coming back to Wolfe's argument about the longevity of settler
colonialism, the longevity of Nova Scotia's name, its flag and its coat
of arms attests to the strength of colonial power structures once they
have been established in a given region, even if the original settlement
lasted for only a short time. Ian McKay and Robin Bates connect this
ongoing use of Scottish insignia to the larger movement towards forging a collective identity in Nova Scotia, one that is particularly intent on
creating the 'Scottish Myth of Nova Scotia'.[190] McKay and Bates show,
in line with Eric Hobsbawm and Terence Ranger's concept of invented
traditions,[191] how a particularly Scottish history and cultural identity
were invented for Nova Scotia, which present the province's alleged
Scottishness as a natural product when, in fact, it is an invented tradition that serves particular economic and political purposes. A focus on

early seventeenth-century colonial writing helps to emphasise how this invention of a Scottish tradition for Nova Scotia uses fragments of earlier narratives and turns them into a fully-fledged mythology.

So far, my analysis has focused on writing by Scottish authors who had never been to Nova Scotia. There is, however, one surviving eyewitness account from the settlement in Nova Scotia, written by the settler Richard Guthry (fl. 1629), which partly disrupts the hierarchical language used for the representation of the indigenous populations in Scottish promotional pieces. Guthry participated in the attempt to establish a settlement at Cape Breton, near what is now Louisbourg, under Lord Ochiltree in 1629.[192] In his letter home, he includes a less aggressive portrait of the indigenous populations than either Gordon or Alexander, which deserves to be mentioned because it further complicates the narratives of Scottish settler colonialism before 1707. Although Guthry's thrust remains Eurocentric, the representation of the native population offers images of mutuality that are, perhaps, indicative of the initial possibilities of the 'contact zone',[193] even if they later turned into clear hierarchical relations. A longer passage from Guthry's text helps to make this point:

> The 10 day came tuo Salvages in a canow, the ribbs of it of small firre knit in with wicker, curiously wrought, and lyned with the barke of trees, tuo oares, like tuo peeles for pasties. In rowing infinitely swift, with there wifs and children there riches a few kettels, dishes of rynds of trees, plenty of dogges which they hunt with, and in want feed upon them, of a foxe kind, naked people with mantles, either of beaver, blanket, or deere leather curiously wrought, tyed over there left shoulder with a poynt, without Shirts, with clouts covering there secret parts. There parents inhabite the head of the river as they say; they seemed to be (as we found indeed) of the beggerly sort, comely and personable bodies, long blacke hair, cutt to length afore Easter the fashion of the Court of England, blacke, of a long life, verry healthfull, neither blacke nor tanny but swarthish, caused of creasie ointments, wherwith dayly they anoint them-selves, infinitly loving to there wyves and children, and one to another; feasting when they meet, till all there store be gone so every day serves it selfe. There language not copious, long words, marred with the Basques language, subtill in their truckings, and nimble fingered, fair cariaged a people among whom people may live verry weel. continuall eaters and drinkers of the best if they have it. At the first beginning they beginne by giving of gifts which they call Garramercies, and yet expecting gifts again when they cannot have any trucke according to

there minds, they will come with garramercies, knowing they shall have meat, drink and other necessaries. There habitation is under a tree, covering themselves with boughes and rynds of trees. They are able to fast 3 ore 4 dayes, great mourners for there dead, some times ten dayes.[194]

The author relays the moral uprightness of the natives' lifestyle, which is honest, respectable and kind despite their alleged simplicity. For all its Eurocentrism, Guthry's account searches for similarities rather than differences between the settlers and the indigenous populations. Guthry compares the haircuts of the Mi'kmaq, rather ironically, with 'the fashion of the Court of England' before Easter. Guthry also commends the way they treat their 'wyves and children' as 'infinitly loving', and he praises the fondness of the Mi'kmaq for food and festivities as signs of their good-naturedness. He writes that the locals are 'a people among whom people may live verry weel'. Guthry's depiction of the friendliness of the Mi'kmaq is consistent with other accounts of the indigenous populations in the region, who frequently supported European settlers in their explorations and provided them with food. Jacques Cartier (1491–1557) features a similarly benevolent account of the indigenous populations of Eastern Canada, and so do the narratives of the French explorer and clergyman Pierre Biard.[195] Again, there is no question about Guthry's colonial energy. However, judging from a generic perspective, there is a clear difference between, on the one hand, the narratives of the colonial theorists Alexander and Gordon and, on the other hand, Guthry's eyewitness account. Where the two armchair travellers resort to stereotypical images to assure their readers of Europeans' superiority over the Mi'kmaq, Guthry replaces myth with personal encounters and stresses peacefulness over colonial aggression. Different genres produce different colonial narratives. Eyewitness accounts are not always more benevolent than non-eyewitness accounts, but in Scottish Atlantic writing of the 1620s the actual encounter with Nova Scotia's indigenous populations seems to have produced a narrative that is less focused on hierarchical relations than it is on co-operation.

As mentioned earlier, there are no written sources from the seventeenth-century indigenous populations of Nova Scotia and Cape Breton. Their viewpoints can only be speculated upon. Scholars assume that the majority of tribes at the time were Algonquian-speaking peoples with mainly Mi'kmaq and some Maliseet living in Nova Scotia and on Cape Breton.[196] Even without written records, it is easy to imagine that they had very different conceptions of inter-cultural exchange and land ownership from the Scottish colonists of the 1620s. While critics debate the pros and cons of including Scotland in the field of postcolonial studies,[197] Mi'kmaq and Maliseet are still fighting on different fronts for equality, such as fishing rights or resolution of the structural inequalities they face because of the legal rights system.[198] It is worth repeating that seventeenth-century Scottish settlers were not the only ones, and arguably not the dominant ones, to have contributed to the establishment of settler colonial structures in Canada. And yet, they were part of a system of enduring power claims. Some Scottish agents were so actively involved in colonial politics before 1707 that their efforts still continue to live on four centuries later in the name and hereditary symbols of Nova Scotia.

Notes

1. Alexander, *Doomes-day* 50; italics in original.
2. Williamson, 'Britain and the Beast' 23.
3. Greene, *Unrequited Conquests.*
4. Alexander, *Encouragement* 32; italics in original.
5. Gordon, *Encouragements.*
6. Qtd in Fraser, *Nova Scotia.*
7. Qtd in Fraser, *Nova Scotia* 27–9.
8. Lythe, *The Economy* 72.
9. Lythe, *The Economy* 71.
10. Alexander, *Encouragement* 40.
11. Gordon, *Encouragements* 10.
12. Gordon, *Encouragements* 11.
13. Dandelet, *The Renaissance of Empire* 261.
14. Hayman, 'To the Right Honorable Knight, Sir William Alexander'.
15. Lindsay, *History of Scottish Literature.*
16. McDiarmid, 'Some Versions' 32–5.
17. Kastner and Charlton, 'Introduction' xiii–xv.
18. James VI and I, 'Ane Schort Treatise' 41–3.
19. Perceval-Maxwell, 'Sir William Alexander' 15–20.
20. Urquhart, *The Jewel* 168.
21. Kewes, 'Julius Caesar' 165.
22. Nicholls, *A Fleeting Empire* xviii.
23. Ó Ciardha and Ó Siochrú, 'Introduction' 8.
24. Ó Ciardha and Ó Siochrú, 'Introduction' 8.
25. Virgil, *The Eclogues* 21–4.
26. Alexander, *Encouragement* no page.

27. Montaño, *The Roots*.
28. Montaño, *The Roots* 51.
29. Alexander, *Encouragement* 40; 35; 43.
30. Parkinson, 'Arcadia' 252–65.
31. Parkinson, 'Arcadia' 252.
32. Alexander, *Encouragement* 18; 35.
33. Alexander set out to rework Mary Herbert's *The Countess of Pembroke's Arcadia* (1593), which is itself a reworking of Philip Sidney's unfinished revision of *Arcadia* (1586). Upon Sidney's death, his sister, Mary Herbert, Countess of Pembroke, combined the earlier work with the unfinished revision. Alexander set out to rework this combined version with the intention of smoothing over its irregularities. Alexander's co-authored version first appeared in 1621.
34. Chakrabarty, *Provincializing Europe*.
35. Chakrabarty, *Provincializing Europe* 7.
36. Chakrabarty, *Provincializing Europe* 7.
37. Alexander, *Encouragement* 39; italics in original.
38. Chakrabarty, *Provincializing Europe* 7.
39. Alexander, *Encouragement* 39.
40. Chakrabarty, *Provincializing Europe* 7.
41. Linebaugh and Rediker, *The Many-Headed Hydra*.
42. Cowan, 'The Myth of Scotch Canada' 53. See also Stroh, *Gaelic Scotland*.
43. Davis, *Utopia* 19.
44. Alexander, *Encouragement* 39; italics in original.
45. Alexander, *Encouragement* 37–8.
46. Marx and Engels, *Manifesto* Chapter 1.
47. Doyle, *Freedom's Empire* 3.
48. Gilroy, *Darker than Blue* 57.
49. Davis, *Utopia* 19.
50. Alexander, *Encouragement* 6–45; Gordon, *Encouragements* B2v–B2r; C2v–C3r.
51. Alexander, *Encouragement* 42–3.
52. Gordon, *Encouragements* C3v–C3r.
53. Gordon, *Encouragements* B2r–B3v.
54. Chakrabarty, *Provincializing Europe* 7.
55. Kumar, *Utopianism* 69.
56. Boesky, *Founding Fictions*; Houston, *The Renaissance Utopia*.
57. Boesky, *Founding Fictions* 87–90.
58. Houston, *The Renaissance Utopia* 12.
59. Boesky, *Founding Fictions* 90.
60. Gordon, *Encouragements* C2v–C2r.
61. Ramsey, *The Price Revolution*.
62. Moran, *Inventing Virginia* 6.
63. Lythe, *The Economy* 15–23; Withers, 'Emergent Nation' 146–7.

64. Lythe, *The Economy* 253.
65. Armitage, 'Making' 50.
66. Armitage, 'Making' 50.
67. Armitage, 'Making' 50.
68. Mason, *A Briefe Discourse* no page.
69. Mason, *A Briefe Discourse* no page.
70. For an overview of earlier colonial activities in North America and specifically the Atlantic region, see Nicholls, *A Fleeting Empire* 3–35.
71. Qtd in Laing, *Royal Letters* 12.
72. Qtd in Laing, *Royal Letters* 12.
73. Qtd in Laing, *Royal Letters* 12.
74. Qtd in Laing, *Royal Letters* 12.
75. Qtd in Laing, *Royal Letters* 12.
76. 'The Virginia Company of London' no page.
77. Landsman, 'Introduction' 22.
78. Stewart, 'Introduction' 714.
79. Vaughan, *The Golden Fleece* 8.
80. Stroh, *Gaelic Scotland* 153–4.
81. Insh, *Scottish Colonial Schemes* 4–26.
82. Insh, *Scottish Colonial Schemes* 4–26.
83. Insh, *Scottish Colonial Schemes* 4–26.
84. Worthington, 'Introduction' 1.
85. Armitage, 'Making' 56–7.
86. James VI and I, *The Basilicon Doron* 71.
87. Cowan, 'Land and Freedom' 135–43.
88. James VI and I, *The Basilicon Doron* 71.
89. James VI and I, *The Basilicon Doron* 71.
90. James VI and I, *The Basilicon Doron* 71.
91. Hechter traces the concept of the internal colony back to V. I. Lenin and Antonio Gramsci. It is also used frequently in Latin American studies. See Hechter, *Internal Colonialism* 8–9.
92. Connell, 'Modes of Marginality' 47.
93. Calloway, *White People*.
94. Calloway, *White People* 13.
95. Calloway, *White People* 14.
96. James VI and I, *The Basilicon Doron* 57.
97. Kewes, 'Julius Caesar' 155–86.
98. Kewes, 'Julius Caesar' 155–86.
99. Knapp, *An Empire Nowhere* 24–5.
100. Knapp, *An Empire Nowhere* 21.
101. Sandrock, 'Ancient Empires' 346–64.
102. Sandrock, 'Ancient Empires' 361–4.
103. Alexander, *Encouragement* no page.
104. Kantorowicz, *The King's Two Bodies* 7–25.
105. Grove, *Green Imperialism* 4.

106. Winthrop, 'A Model' 33.
107. Alexander, *Doomes-Day* 50.
108. Alexander, *Encouragement* 36.
109. Alexander, *Encouragement* 36.
110. Raleigh, *The Discoverie* 166.
111. Biard, 'Biard to the Provincial' 535.
112. Alexander, *Encouragement* 38.
113. Colley, *Britons Forging*.
114. Armitage, 'Making' 34–62.
115. Armitage, 'Making' 44–7.
116. Anderson, *Imagined Communities* 90.
117. Romaniello, 'Through the Filter' 914–37.
118. Wolfe, 'Virginia Company of London'.
119. Linebaugh and Rediker, *The Many-Headed Hydra* 15.
120. Insh, *Scottish Colonial Schemes* 97.
121. Gordon, *Encouragements* unpaginated recto page following C3.
122. Fitzmaurice, *Humanism and America* 96.
123. Hadfield, 'Afterword' 62.
124. Gordon, *Encouragements* unpaginated recto page following C3.
125. Hariot, *A Briefe and True Report* B2r; italics in original.
126. Hariot, *A Briefe and True Report* B2v; italics in original.
127. Gordon, *Encouragements* unpaginated recto page following C3.
128. Gordon, *Encouragements* unpaginated recto page following C3.
129. Hariot, *A Briefe and True Report* unpaginated recto page following B3.
130. Moran, *Inventing Virginia* 115–16.
131. Moran, *Inventing Virginia* 112–19.
132. Alexander, *Encouragement* no page.
133. Qtd in Laing, *Royal Letters* 12.
134. Jowitt, 'The Uses of "Piracy"' 118.
135. Jowitt, 'The Uses of "Piracy"' 118.
136. Spurr, *The Rhetoric of Empire*.
137. Gordon, *Encouragements* B2v–B2r.
138. Gordon, *Encouragements* unpaginated recto page following C3.
139. Cartier, *A Shorte and Briefe Narration* 51–8.
140. Davis, *Utopia* 21.
141. Drayton, *The Works*.
142. Montaño, *The Roots* 60–3.
143. Hadfield, 'Afterword' 66.
144. Gordon, *Encouragements* B.
145. Gordon, *Encouragements* D2v–r.
146. Hariot, *A Briefe and True Report* E2v.
147. Gordon, *Encouragements* D2v.
148. Hariot, *A Briefe and True Report* E2r.
149. Geographicus Rare Antique Maps.
150. Geographicus Rare Antique Maps.

151. Greenblatt, *Marvelous Possessions* 82.
152. Greenblatt, *Marvelous Possessions* 82.
153. Alexander, *Encouragement* 32; italics in original.
154. Anderson, *Imagined Communities* 187.
155. Bacon, *Francis Bacon: The Essays*.
156. Bacon, *New Atlantis* 177–83.
157. Bacon, *New Atlantis* 159.
158. Hogan, 'Of Islands' 40.
159. Hogan, 'Of Islands' 36.
160. Hiatt, 'Mapping' 49.
161. Knapp, *An Empire Nowhere* 142.
162. Linebaugh and Rediker, *The Many-Headed Hydra* 12.
163. Linebaugh and Rediker, *The Many-Headed Hydra* 12.
164. Doyle, *Freedom's Empire* 11; italics in original.
165. Doyle, *Freedom's Empire* 11.
166. Pratt, *Imperial Eyes* 6.
167. Mi'kmaq is the most common spelling today. Other spellings include Micmac, Mi'gmaq or Mìgmaq.
168. Alexander, *Encouragement* 44; 37.
169. Qtd in Fraser, *Nova Scotia* 35–7.
170. Nicholls, *A Fleeting Empire* 132.
171. McKay and Bates, *In the Province of History* 267.
172. Wolfe, *Settler Colonialism* 2.
173. Qtd in Fraser, *Nova Scotia* 29–31.
174. Nicholls, *A Fleeting Empire* 132.
175. Alexander, *Encouragement* 44; 37; Gordon, *Encovragements* D2v.
176. Gordon, *Encovragements* D2v.
177. Montaigne, 'Of the Caniballes' no page.
178. More, *Utopia* 50.
179. Alexander, *Encouragement* 37.
180. Alexander, *Encouragement* 42.
181. Bucholz and Key, *Early Modern England* 24–5.
182. Bitterli, *Cultures in Conflict* 30–1.
183. Alexander, *Encouragement* 37.
184. Alexander, *Encouragement* no page.
185. Alexander, *Encouragement* 37, italics in original.
186. Qtd in Fraser, *Nova Scotia* 45.
187. Reid, 'The Conquest of "Nova Scotia"' 39–59.
188. Harper and Vance, 'Myth' 14–48.
189. Harper and Vance, 'Myth' 14–48.
190. McKay and Bates, *In the Province of History* 287.
191. Hobsbawm and Ranger, 'Introduction: Inventing Traditions' 1–14.
192. All quotations from Guthry's letter are taken from Griffiths and Reid, 'New Evidence on New Scotland, 1629' 500–8. An independent publication of Guthry's text does not yet exist.

193. Pratt, *Imperial Eyes* 6.
194. Guthry, 'A Relation' 506.
195. Biard, 'Biard to the Provincial' 533–6.
196. Reid, *Acadia* 3; Griffiths and Reid, 'New Evidence on New Scotland' 498, note 30.
197. See Introduction.
198. Coates, *The Marshall Decision and Native Rights*.

Chapter 3

Scotland's Atlantic Visions, 1660–1691

John Bunyan's *The Pilgrim's Progress: From This World to That Which is to Come* (1678–84) maps a narrative of religious quest that shares central elements with the utopian tradition of the seventeenth century. It imagines a symbolic space where all earthly difficulties will be overcome, and where those who have risen above the world will enjoy both spiritual and material pleasures. Echoing earlier literary depictions of a perfect Christian dwelling place, such as 'Dante's *The Divine Comedy* (c. 1321) and Milton's *Paradise Lost* (1667)',[1] *The Pilgrim's Progress* is based on a dual time-scheme that is well known from the utopian literary tradition: it envisions an ideal place that 'lay not only in the past but also in the future'. Here is how Bunyan's main figure, allegorically named Christian, imagines the Celestial City that is the geographical embodiment of the narrative's religious quest motif:

> *Christian*: There is an endless kingdom to be inhabited, and everlasting life to be given us; that we may inhabit that kingdom forever. [. . .]
> *Christian*: There are crowns of glory to be given us, and garments that will make us shine like the sun in the firmament of Heaven. [. . .]
> *Christian*: There shall be no more crying, nor sorrow; for He that is owner of that place, will wipe all tears from our eyes.[2]

Perhaps it is no coincidence that Bunyan has a background as a reformer with ties to the utopian movements of the mid-seventeenth century. Several years before writing *The Pilgrim's Progress*, he was a committed 'roarer, ranter, swearer, and bell-ringer himself, affected by the ideas of the Ranters, Diggers, and Levellers before being converted by a poor woman, which led him to preaching, the Baptist Church, and jail'.[3] The images of spiritual gratification in *The Pilgrim's Progress* interact meaningfully not only with the domestic utopian tradition but also with Atlantic visions of ideal settlement sites. There is a distinct tradition from the 1620s onwards, which envisages North American settlement sites as places 'of renewal, repatriation, and reunification'.[4] This tradition dialogues with the ideal of Christian rebirth and restoration in Bunyan's allegory. Pilgrims went abroad and settled on the North American east coast, especially in the New England region, in order to found settlements according to their own religious ideas. Winthrop's 'Citty upon a Hill' comes to mind once more as a famous example of such spiritual utopianism.[5]

Scottish colonial activities of the second half of the seventeenth century, too, have frequently been conceived of as partly or predominantly driven by religion.[6] Religious rhetoric is one of several trajectories that the following chapter pursues in its exploration of Scotland's Atlantic visions between 1660 and 1691. Other patterns of thought and rhetorical devices in the Scottish Atlantic tradition between 1660 and 1691 include an emphasis on law and order; the aesthetic primacy of land; and the ambiguous role of Scottish settlers vis-à-vis the indigenous populations of the Americas and the Atlantic slave trade. These themes also emerge in Scottish domestic drama from the 1660s onwards. Because it is a previously understudied field, this chapter opens with an investigation of Scottish drama from the 1660s to the early 1690s with a particular view to Atlantic and Black Atlantic imagery. Later parts of the chapter draw on material written in relation to the settlement of East New Jersey, which is why Table 3.1 offers a chronological account of the Scottish settlement history there.

Scottish Drama and the Atlantic

In his study *The Black Atlantic* (1993), Paul Gilroy establishes a link between the rise of Western modernity and the Atlantic slave trade.[7] According to Gilroy, the modern socio-cultural and political formation of the nation state is largely informed by the history of European colonialism, especially by the plantation system in the Americas and by the Atlantic slave trade that came to dominate the moral and material economy of the Atlantic from the early modern period onwards. Not only was slavery an integral 'part of the ethical and intellectual heritage of the West as a whole' but, Gilroy shows, the narrative of the

Table 3.1 The East New Jersey Settlement

- to present	Six Nations – the Mohawk, the Oneida, the Onondaga, the Cayuga, the Seneca and the Tuscarora – live along the US American and Canadian east coast, including the territory that is nowadays New Jersey
1664	English troops invade the Dutch-claimed New Netherlands (parts of which later become East New Jersey); Charles II grants the New Netherlands to his brother, the Duke of York
June 1664	The Duke of York grants New Jersey to John Berkeley and George Carteret, who divide it into East and West New Jersey
1682	George Carteret sells East New Jersey to twelve Quakers, six of whom are Scottish
1682	Scottish Quaker Robert Barclay becomes governor of East New Jersey
1684	First two ships leave Scotland for East New Jersey from Montrose and Aberdeen; among the settlers is George Keith
1685	George Scot publishes *The Model of the Government of the Province of East-New-Jersey in America: And Encouragements for such as Designs to be Concerned there. Published for Information of such as Are Desirous to Be Interested in that Place*
1693	George Keith and others publish *An Exhortation & Caution to Friends Concerning Buying or Keeping of Negroes*
1702	Return of East New Jersey to the British Crown
1703	Return of West New Jersey to the British Crown; afterwards, East and West New Jersey are united again as New Jersey

'intellectual and cultural achievements of the black Atlantic populations exist partly inside and not always against the grand narrative of Enlightenment and its operational principles'.[8] Scotland's role in this history of the Black Atlantic has been repeatedly addressed over the past decades. Historians have brought to the fore the numerous connections, direct and indirect, between Scotland, Africa, the Americas and the Caribbean, while also negotiating Scotland's role in the abolitionist movement of the eighteenth and nineteenth centuries.[9] What has been less frequently discussed is the role of Scottish literature and particularly seventeenth-century drama in the context of the Black Atlantic. My analysis of Scottish drama from the Restoration period adds to research on the manifold connections between Atlantic slavery and Scotland in the seventeenth century by highlighting the role that literary culture played in the naturalisation and popularisation of the Black Atlantic. Scottish drama offers some salient examples of how Atlantic colonialism and slavery became part of the aesthetic repertoire of Scottish domestic literature between the 1660s and the early 1690s. My focus is on Thomas Sydserf's *Tarugo's Wiles: Or, the Coffee-House. A Comedy* (1667) and Archibald Pitcairne's *The Assembly; Or, Scotch Reformation: A Comedy* (1691).[10] The utopian impetus of Scottish dramas may be less overt than that in political pamphlets or colonial advertisement. Yet, the subtle idealisation of Atlantic trade, slavery and colonial consumer culture in the plays is all the more powerful because it is part of an entertainment culture targeted at both private and public audiences of seventeenth-century Scotland and England.

Heather Wells recently argued for a reconsideration of Scottish drama after the Restoration. Specifically, she calls for renewed attention to the 'literary and theatrical traditions' in Scotland after 1660, which were long considered absent or ignored compared with the more powerful traditions of English Restoration drama.[11] Scottish theatre from 1660 onwards remains an understudied field, partly because 'there was no professional theatre in Scotland to revive after the Commonwealth period' and partly because 'the Presbyterian church (and its opposition to such creative expression) was very influential in Scotland both before and after the Restoration'.[12] The result was a limited performance culture in mid- to late seventeenth-century Scotland and, in scholarly terms, a lack of research on the period's theatrical culture. This research gap is closing slowly, thanks to renewed interest in the period.[13] A tennis court theatre opened in Edinburgh in 1667. Other plays 'were circulated in manuscript form as closet drama, where plays were read in private homes, either collectively or individually, rather than produced by theatre companies'.[14] The following analysis seeks to open up debates about seventeenth-century Scottish drama and theatre culture further by turning towards the Atlantic. While Anglo-Scottish relations remain by all means core to Scottish theatre and literary culture from 1660 onwards, the Atlantic is another, hitherto understudied, geospatial interlocutor that shaped Scotland's artistic productions in the Restoration period.

In Sydserf's *Tarugo's Wiles* and Pitcairne's *The Assembly*, tropes of slavery, colonial commerce and overseas travel are part of the plays' aesthetic repertoire. Colonial imagery in both plays operates at the interface of other discourses of power, such as religion, politics, gender or race. The overlapping dynamics of these discourses can best be looked at through the lens of intersectionality with its focus on the junctures of different axes that lead to social division and inequality. As Felicity A. Nussbaum has shown in her discussion of English texts of the time, 'drama incorporated colonial encounters onto the skins, gestures, and dialogue of white actors at once to fabricate the representation of racial difference, to celebrate and worry it, and finally to grant it a recognizable reality'.[15] A similar argument can be made for Scottish drama of the 1660s and 1690s. Even if none of the authors discussed was an active coloniser, and even if none of the plays openly supports Atlantic empire-building, the imperial characters, metaphors and references they contain indicate that Atlantic imagery gained prominence in the course of the seventeenth century. Literature participated in a process of naturalising colonial systems such as the slave trade or the commodification of colonial goods. Even though the parts of the population that actively participated in colonialism were small in seventeenth-century Scotland, the effects on society were nevertheless weighty, as the coffee-house location and slavery tropes in *Tarugo's Wiles* suggest.

Thomas Sydserf's (fl. 1668) *Tarugo's Wiles: Or, the Coffee-House. A Comedy* was first performed in London in 1667. This 'mak[es] Sydserf the first Scot to have a play premiered there'.[16] Further performances took place in 1668 in Edinburgh, where Sydserf was manager of the Theatre of Holyrood from 1667 onwards.[17] The author's name is sometimes also spelled Sydserff, Sydserfe, St Serfe or St Serf. The play is, above all, a critique of early modern social conventions, especially the patriarchal family system and its strict social and cultural norms in seventeenth-century society. The critique centres on the figure of an over-protective brother, Don Patricio, who keeps his sister, Lavinia, from marrying the honourable Horatio. Eventually, Don Patricio is tricked into giving his consent to the marriage, which is achieved through the figure of Tarugo, the eponymous hero of the play. As fitting for a comedy, *Tarugo's Wiles* ends with Lavinia being allowed to marry Horatio. Don Patricio, too, is restored to virtue in the dramatic universe of the play when he recognises his mistakes and is rewarded for his repentance by gaining the love of the admired Sophronia. The stage history, with its premiere in London, signifies on a performative level the transregional scope of the drama, which also features in its textual history. *Tarugo's Wiles* is 'a free adaptation of the Spanish comedy, *No puede ser el guardar una mujer* (It's impossible to be a woman's guardian) by Agustin Moreto y Cabaña (1618–1669)'.[18] Its Spanish origins may partly explain why the text features numerous references to South American settings and foreign travels, and also why Atlantic imagery enters Western European cultural history as part of its entertainment culture.

As in the Spanish original, Tarugo is a traveller who has recently returned from London to his home town of Seville. In London, Tarugo came across a more tolerant, free-thinking lifestyle. This tribute to London is part of the drama's celebration of Britishness and participates in the colonial utopian tradition of idealising liberalism, upward social mobility and wealth. The play features various images, characters and concepts that relate to overseas travels in general and to Atlantic colonialism in particular. First, there is the image of Tarugo dressing up as a tailor in order to gain access to Lavinia's quarters. She is imprisoned by her brother, Don Patricio, but Tarugo tricks the guards into letting him inside her chamber by putting on the disguise of a foreign tailor and pretending he wants to customise some clothes for her. He claims to have learned his trade in 'the West-Indies'.[19] Tarugo enters the private quarters of Lavinia. He is apparently able to do so because a foreign-looking tailor is not considered a threat to the patriarchal order, which is a tellingly gendered conception of the foreign figure itself. Once inside the chamber, Tarugo tries to convince Lavinia of his abilities as a tailor with a fake travel story. He says he was 'carri'd Captive, being taking by a *Muscoviter* Man of War, going to *Alexandria*' and finally being 'brought [. . .] to the Southern parts of *America*, where to the Queen of the *Amazons* Taylor I was barter'd for an old Petticoat'.[20] Again, the scene is a gendered form of comic relief but it helps to establish the global consciousness of the drama. References range from Moscow to Alexandria to the South Americas and to Amazon tribes. Not unexpectedly for a comedy, Tarugo's account of his travels is wildly concocted. The humorous function of the scene materialises, amongst others, in an exchange between Tarugo and Lavinia, in which the former is pressed to explain why, according to his account, the Amazon Queen has the Christian name of Fatima:

> Liv. How, *Dona Fatima*? that's a Christian-name.
> Tar. It is, Madam, for so was her Mother call'd, who being a Frenchwoman became Renegado upon a point of curiosity to try the difference 'twixt Circumcision and Uncircumcision, and to that effect by way of Love Errantry she travel'd till she arriv'd to the Kingdom of the *Patagoones*, where she brought forth this Lady *Fatyma*, who now swayes the *Amazonian* Scepter.[21]

On a theatrical level, the humour of the exchange adds to the comedy of the play. Underlying the humour, Tarugo's sexually laden fantasy gestures towards the mobility of colonial utopian thought in seventeenth-century literature. There is no apparent ideological agenda, no outward sign of colonial exploitation in Tarugo's description of a Frenchwoman going to South America and giving birth to the future Queen of Amazones. The allusions are more subtle, and weightier, in their understated praise of European expansion, encoded in the Christian name of the Amazon Queen and her French origins. Sexual fantasy and imperial desire intertwine in Tarugo's remarks on the practices of circumcision, which apparently led Dona Fatima to travel the world and to found a new feminist tribe in Patagonia. The passage may be, above all, a parody of patriarchy. For all its proto-feminism, though, it simultaneously lends itself to an allegorical reading of a dream of European procreation that is reminiscent of Neville's *Isle of Pines*. In the latter, the protagonist George Pine founds several new tribes on a previously uninhabited island by reproducing with four women after being shipwrecked on the island. At the time of his death, Pine has 1,789 descendants who people the island and attest to his reproductive ability.[22] In *Tarugo's Wiles*, the Eurocentric fantasy is differently gendered, as it is a woman who goes to the Americas and founds a tribe there that is derived from a European, Christian background. Audiences may laugh at the passage, which is part of the play's ironical take on gender hierarchies. Yet, the underlying idea of European superiority is a powerful trope that pervades *Tarugo's Wiles* and uses the satirical mode to naturalise colonial utopian thinking.

Elsewhere in the drama, too, Atlantic imagery reveals how actively *Tarugo's Wiles* employs colonial themes. In one scene, two 'Scholars' and several 'Customers' speak about non-European locales and include a number of place names that appear rather familiar to them. They speak about '*New-England*', 'the *West-India*-Divines', '*Africa*', 'the *South-pole*', 'the *Atlantick* Ocean' and 'the Mountains of *Tartussely* in *America*', as well as 'the large Coast of *Terra Australis incognita*'.[23] London and Edinburgh playgoers of the 1660s may not have been familiar with all of these names, or may only have had a vague idea of where they are located and what Great Britain's relationship to them might be. Yet, the mere inclusion of such names in a drama meant to entertain audiences in London and Edinburgh suggests that some place names were probably known to the audiences and that the other names at least sparked interest in playgoers looking for entertainment. Later in the play, a letter from Peru arrives and the character who receives it reads it without too much surprise at receiving a note from such a distant part of the world.[24] The foreign has partly become familiar to Restoration audiences, if not through personal travels then through an increased number of oral and written stories about these places and their repeated inclusion in public forms of entertainment. The same is true for imagery that concerns the Atlantic slave trade and the proliferation of colonial goods, which Sydserf seems to have been intent on emphasising in his play.

As others have shown, Sydserf's drama expands on the Spanish original by adding 'the prologue and the coffeehouse scene of Act 3'.[25] The latter addition is particularly interesting for this chapter because it links *Tarugo's Wiles* to the increasing commercialisation and aestheticisation of Atlantic trading goods, especially coffee, in Europe and Great Britain. Coffee houses became part of British intellectual culture from the seventeenth century onwards, and they were a topic in copious literary works.[26] They were known as places where customers exchanged ideas about politics and social reforms, as well as legal and religious issues. They were also frequently satirised, especially from the 1660s onwards, because of the particular clientele they attracted and their increasing function as spaces where public opinion was being formed.[27] Markman Ellis includes *Tarugo's Wiles* in his study of coffee house imagery in British drama of the long eighteenth century, where it features alongside works such as Elkanah Settle's *The New Athenian Comedy* (1693), as well as Charles Johnson's *The Generous Husband: Or, the Coffee House Politician* (1711).[28] Coffee houses feature as places where British people consume goods traditionally associated with Atlantic trade, such as coffee, chocolate, tobacco, sugar products or rum. Through such consumables, the Atlantic becomes a storehouse of European desires, even without people travelling there directly:

> Metropolitan residents consumed the products, ideas and knowledge of the far reaches of empire, even if they did not directly encounter indigenous peoples. What needs to be stressed, to a greater extent, is the way in which imperialism became a significant constitutive element in British identities.[29]

In their material dimension, then, coffee houses are spaces where colonialism is institutionalised in British society. The consumption of colonial goods turned into a lifestyle of the elite, who may have discussed issues of social reform in the coffee houses at the same time as they accepted, or perhaps even promoted, the establishment of new social hierarchies around the globe in the form of international trade conglomerates and European colonialism.

In Scotland, the first coffee house opened a couple of years after Sydserf's comedy premiered. It opened 'near Newgate during the 1670s',[30] when colonial goods had already become established items on the luxury market of Europe. Consumers in Europe may or may not have known or consciously reflected upon the production of these goods, which were part of the triangular system of slavery, trade and enforced labour.[31] Likewise, *Tarugo's Wiles* does not openly address the fact that the institution of the coffee house is linked to the mass enslavement of people from Africa and to the enforced labour of children, prisoners, outcasts, the dispossessed and other involuntary migrants from different parts of the world.[32] Colonial labour is never an open issue in the play. It surfaces, though, in the existence of a servant figure in *Tarugo's Wiles*, who enters the stage as an enslaved labourer and, as such, references the Black Atlantic as part of European domestic culture.

In one scene, a '*Negro*-wench' is 'Playing and Dancing' in the kitchen, where she is apparently meant to labour for a Spanish family.[33] In a second scene, 'A little *Negro*-wench' is said to 'pass through the Garden to *Tarugo*'s Chamber'.[34] The character combines several features traditionally linked to the Black Atlantic. The '*Negro*-wench' is black, female and probably an enslaved labourer. As such, she becomes a symbol of the 'restructuring of political and economic relations' that became a norm of Western modernity with the rise of the Atlantic slave trade.[35] From a contemporary viewpoint, it is telling that the character is not explained to the rest of the dramatis personae. It is simply clear, from the stage instructions and character constellation, that white Europeans are the masters and the '*Negro*-wench' the slave, as it is common in the colonial utopian tradition. The term '*Negro*-wench' itself indicates the sexual and racial configurations of the Black Atlantic: it can refer to either a young woman or a female servant, or, archaically, to a mistress.[36] In a third scene, the same character reappears, this time with the sexual connotation of the term being made explicit. A male character calls to 'bring out the *Negro*-Girl', which is followed by the stage instruction '*They Dance, where Pugge at the corner of the Stage imitates with the* Negro-Girl.'[37] The sexual imagery of the stage instruction shows how slaves primarily had 'material value' for Europeans and functioned 'as labor supply', as well as as sources of sexual gratification.[38] Although there are no details on the cast of seventeenth-century performances of *Tarugo's Wiles*, it is likely that the actor who played the '*Negro*-Girl' would have been a white actor with a blackened face, as was frequently the case with non-white figures in domestic drama until the early nineteenth century.[39] From a seventeenth-century perspective, the scene may have added comic relief to a play that criticises traditional gender roles and offers a proto-feminist conclusion to its plot. From a postcolonial perspective, it illustrates how Black Atlantic imagery and ideas are fetishised in Scottish drama of the 1660s and how black female figures are excluded from the otherwise gender-critical ideas of the play. The split between black and non-black female figures in the play showcases once more how the colonial utopian tradition replaces one set of social hierarchies with another but always remains within a Eurocentric framework. Examining the role of non-white figures in plays such as *Tarugo's Wiles* 'provides a means to re-examine the problems of nationality, location, identity, and historical memory'[40] that are often overshadowed by a focus on Anglo-Scottish relations in the seventeenth century.[41] Atlantic imagery in *Tarugo's Wiles*, and seventeenth-century Scottish drama more generally, opens up questions of transnational identity-building and its relationship to Scottish domestic culture.

Another Scottish drama that attests to the prevalence of colonial imagery in the seventeenth century is *The Assembly; Or, Scotch Reformation: A Comedy* (1691) by Archibald Pitcairne (1652–1713), or Pitcairn. The play was originally known, and is sometimes relabelled today, as *The Phanaticks*.[42] The drama was circulated in 'handwritten copies' and not performed, 'not even published until 1722'.[43] Wells includes *The Assembly* among the tradition of closet dramas that is part of the Scottish drama tradition of the seventeenth century, but which has frequently been left out of theatre studies because of their private performances: 'Pitcairne based his characters on well-known Presbyterian individuals in Scotland who would have been recognizable to those who came across the play in its original form.'[44] According to the most recent editor, John MacQueen, it is likely that Pitcairne worked together with other authors when writing the play, probably with David Gregorie and perhaps Bertram Stott.[45] The main theme of *The Assembly* is Scotland's social and political transformation in the aftermath of the Revolution of 1688. In particular, the oath of allegiance plays a role, as does the movement towards prohibition and Presbyterianism, which are all satirised in the drama and may well have been the reason why it became part of the closet drama tradition rather than being performed on stage: 'Pitcairne successfully highlights the hypocritical abuse of religion. This success, however, was the play's undoing, for it was considered too scurrilous to be performed in Pitcairne's lifetime.'[46] The religious satire mostly works through a domestic plot. The young, liberal characters Frank and Will are eager to convince a staunch Presbyterian widow, named Old Ladie, that they should be allowed to marry her nieces, Violetta and Laura. Frank and Will achieve this by dressing up as Presbyterian ministers and giving the Old Ladie so much religious claptrap that she is persuaded of their 'good' faith. The widow ends up being the fool of the play, whereas the sly acts of Frank and Will are sanctioned through the happy ending and the promise of marriage.

Another thread running through the play is its Atlantic imagery. A few years earlier, Aphra Behn had published her prose novel *The History of Oroonoko, or the Royal Slave* (1688), which, with its account of Prince Oroonoko of Coramantien, is one of the foremost testimonies of the literary attention that was paid to colonial themes in late seventeenth-century British literature. In Scottish literature of the time, such themes are not quite as central, but they are also part of the cultural imagination, as *The Assembly* illustrates. The play opens with a scene in which a traveller, Frank, has lately returned to Edinburgh. He meets his old friend, Will, who tells Frank about the changes that have occurred during the latter's absence. The setting of the play is Edinburgh, but through the figure of the traveller, Frank, *The Assembly* features an insider–outsider view of Scotland that draws on Atlantic imagery. Frank tells Will how alienated he feels upon his return to Edinburgh by employing a colonial metaphor: 'I have walked the streets since six, encompassed with so many strange faces, that I imagined myself cast upon some new plantation on the other side of the globe, for they look not like the inhabitants of this world.'[47] The geographical location is unspecific, but the use of the words 'new plantation' suggests an American context, where European and British settlers were involved in settler colonial activities from the sixteenth century onwards. Frank uses the image to express his sense of newness and apprehension about the changes he notices in Scotland since he left for his travels. In the same conversation, Frank tells Will that he feels as if some people perceived him as 'some American monster' when walking the streets of Edinburgh.[48] The metaphor expresses estrangement but it also shows how commonly Atlantic imagery is used for domestic comparisons in Scottish drama of the time. MacQueen suggests that the reference to the monster is 'probably to a native North American clad in feathers and war paint, put on exhibition as part of a travelling show'.[49] It may be true that Frank knew about the indigenous populations of the Americas through travelling exhibitions, which had toured Europe ever since

Amerigo Vespucci brought back West Indian inhabitants from his travels. It is, however, equally likely that Frank himself travelled the world in his time abroad, and that he is familiar with plantations 'on the other side of the globe', as well as with some of the indigenous people to whom he refers.[50] Either way, a pattern emerges in *The Assembly* in which domestic affairs are clothed in metaphors deriving from overseas contexts and used to express newness and estrangement. Although *The Assembly* does not use the figure of the traveller primarily to tell stories about the Americas but rather to criticise Scotland through references to global affairs, the imagery is based on the colonial tradition that sees Atlantic expansion primarily as a means of fulfilling European desires, if necessary at the cost of suppressing the desires of others.

Following the internal logic of the drama, Pitcairne's play warns of a sinister future for Scotland and does so by using colonial images. One character has the ominous foreboding that the country might become 'famous for [. . .] producing monsters, like the Indies' if it continues to develop in the political and religious direction it is currently doing.[51] The reference to foreign monstrosity is a stock image of early modern literature. In *The Assembly*, it is not used primarily to explore the Atlantic connection but rather to criticise the present moment and to envision, in line with the colonial connotations of the Caribbean, a monstrous future for Scotland. A phrase such as Indian 'monsters'[52] may primarily function to satirise the Presbyterian characters that are at the heart of the play's criticism, but it simultaneously reveals the racial anxieties underlying Atlantic thought in seventeenth-century drama. *Tarugo's Wiles* and *The Assembly* participate in the transculturalisation of domestic literature and in the manifold processes by which racial and colonial thought entered European modernity. Scottish drama of the 1660s and 1690s may not be the foremost proponent of colonialism, yet it, too, participated in the naturalisation of colonial imagery and drew on Atlantic images for entertainment purposes. The fact that both plays are comedies shows how much the Atlantic becomes part of a positive narrative in Western Europe. In both private and public performances, the history of colonisation is conceived of as a success story that opens up opportunities for fulfilling the desires of European travellers and consumers. Enslaved labour, racialised misogyny, the consumption of colonial goods and the fear of the Other have become part of seventeenth-century entertainment culture, thus showing how deeply ingrained the colonial utopian genre has become in Scottish domestic culture.

Atlantic Visions: Law, Order and Land

Between the 1630s and the early 1680s, the Atlantic activities of Scottish groups or individuals were scarce. So were Scottish literary productions referring to Atlantic settlements at that time. Some scholars mention that 'a small Scottish community was resident in Barbados from 1625',[53] which is probably connected to the Scottish trading networks that existed in the Caribbean prior to 1707. In 1636, the Guinea Company of Scotland tried to establish trade with West Africa, but shortly after a single voyage on which one of two ships was captured by Portuguese forces, the company ceased to operate.[54] Scottish trading networks also operated in New England and in some parts of the Dutch Atlantic colonies in the seventeenth century.[55] Others note that there were negotiations for a Scottish colony either in Florida or on the island of Dominica in the 1670s, as well as endeavours by Scottish agents to establish a trading hub on the island of St Vincent in the Caribbean.[56] Apart from these trade-oriented activities, it was not until the 1680s that Scots participated in further fully-fledged Atlantic settlement schemes. Reasons for this may include the large number of Scotsmen who went abroad during the Thirty Years' War (1618–48), which has been said to constitute a 'Scottish diaspora in Europe'.[57] This may have left little manpower for other overseas activities. Further reasons may include the political upheavals of the mid-seventeenth century and the effects of the Civil Wars, the Interregnum and the Protectorate on Scotland and Great Britain,[58] which stand in close relationship to the utopian movements of the mid-seventeenth century.

In 1682, a group of Scottish individuals became co-proprietors of East New Jersey. This led to increasing numbers of Scottish settlers in the so-called Middle Colonies. These included what is nowadays Delaware, New Jersey, New York and Pennsylvania. Literature about the Middle Colonies provides the main source of primary material for Scottish settler writing in the 1680s and early 1690s. There was also a short-lived attempt to create a colony in South Carolina by Scottish settlers in 1682, when Sir Cochrane of Ochiltree and Sir George Campbell of Cessnock bargained for land in South Carolina with the aim of providing space for a Scottish settlement there. In 1684, Scottish settlers arrived in South Carolina, but the settlement was destroyed by Spanish colonisers from St Augustine two years later, in 1686.[59] The most prominent, and literarily productive, settlement site remains East New Jersey in the Middle Colonies.

Scottish Atlantic literature in the seventeenth century spreads across genres as different as drama, poetry, orature, royal documents, life writing, religious documents, legal sources, advertisement texts and political pamphlets, as well as maps, cultural artefacts and naming strategies. As the seventeenth century progressed, colonial writing became an established part of British literary history. With the development of the British Empire, 'a flood of chapbooks, plays and pamphlets' emerged from the colonies.[60] Many of these documents 'extolled the virtues and profits of overseas settlement',[61] which indicates that most of them were written with a clear, colonial purpose in mind. Unsurprisingly, idealising strategies emerge once more as dominant aesthetic tools in Scottish colonial writing of the 1680s. In addition, and unknown in the Nova Scotia literary tradition, texts relating to the settlement of East New Jersey indicate other rhetorical elements known from the utopian tradition, including the drive towards order and regulation. This drive towards regulation is one of the most pronounced characteristics of Scottish Atlantic writing of the 1680s, and it shares central features with the utopian genre.

Most of the texts published in relation to East New Jersey stress the desire for law and order. Documents such as George Scot's *The Model of the Government of the Province of East-New-Jersey in America: And Encouragements for such as Designs to be Concerned there. Published for Information of such as Are Desirous to Be Interested in that Place* (1685) or the collection of documents in *The Grants, Concessions and Original Constitutions of the Province of New-Jersey* (1758)[62] envision the colonial space as a highly regulated zone of social stability and control. Whereas, in a medieval utopia such as *The Land of Cokaygne*, the abundance of nature leads to quasi-anarchy, many early modern utopias conceive of ideal societies not through the change of nature but through the change of social regulations.[63] More's Utopians are said to be satisfied not because the island is a land of milk and honey. They are said to be satisfied because life on Utopia is well regulated, from early childcare to education to the regular changing of houses and the number of working hours. Even nature is regulated. The geography of Utopia is changed in order to make it fit human needs: 'King Utopus, [. . .] even at his first arriving and entering upon the land, forthwith obtaining the victory, caused fifteen miles space of uplandish ground, where the sea had no passage, to be cut and digged up.'[64] Once the geographical setup is deemed perfect, the rest of society also needs to be controlled. Every digression from the ordered path receives more or less severe punishment in *Utopia*. This severity points to one of the underlying paradoxes of the utopian genre. Although there seems to be liberty at first, society is actually characterised by the absence of liberty.

As Stephen Greenblatt remarks, life in Utopia 'begins with almost unlimited license and ends with almost total restriction'.[65] Similarly, literature about East New Jersey in the second half of the seventeenth century frequently attempts to pursue the idea of liberty by creating a world of order. The sheer abundance of legal documents about East New Jersey and the Middle Colonies indicates how settlers sought to regulate the colonial body and how the Atlantic was seen as a space to be reformed and controlled in order to turn it into an ideal settlement site.

Just as Winstanley's *The Law of Freedom* ends with ten pages of specific laws to govern the ideal commonwealth he describes,[66] so East New Jersey settlers devise regulations for all kinds of possible scenario. *The Grants, Concessions, and Original Constitutions of the Province of New-Jersey* contains more than 600 pages, most of which specify the colonial rules and regulations. While not all of these pertain to East New Jersey, and while there are also some letters contained in these pages, the numerous revisions, rewritings and modifications of the constitution offer ample evidence that colonial life in New Jersey was meant to be highly regulated, and that the genre of legal writing became a major tool to implement this aspiration in the Atlantic sphere. There are, among many other laws, 'An Act to encourage the killing of Wolves', 'A Bill for the more regular Ordering of Fences' and 'A Bill to regulate Abuses in taking up Horses'.[67] The exhaustive number of acts, concessions, oaths, directives, laws, messages, notes and other legal documents passed under the different governments in New Jersey between 1664 and 1702 reveals the concerns of settler colonists to eradicate any untidy elements of colonial life. There is 'A bill for the orderly keeping of Swine', 'An Act for due Regulation of Executions' and 'An Act against Trading with Negro Slaves'.[68] In cases like these, the repeated emphasis on order and regulation in the very titles of the acts exhibits the anxiety of the settlers to make colonial life as safe and orderly as possible. This does not mean that the texts necessarily reflect reality. On the contrary, the utopian literary tradition teaches us that the emphasis on regulation stems from a perceived absence of order, which the new society tries to amend radically. Such literary insights fit in with the historical context of post-Civil War Britain and help to illuminate why order is such a central structuring device in Atlantic writing of the mid- to late seventeenth century.

The Civil Wars, the Commonwealth of England (1649–53) and the Protectorate (1653–9) left many people disappointed with the political and social elites of the time. In addition, many felt insecure about their place in society after the attempts to rework the governmental and constitutional organisation of England, Ireland, Scotland and Wales. The utopian movements of the 1640s and 1650s – from the Levellers to the Diggers, from the Ranters to the Fifth Monarchy Men – are indicators of the many unfulfilled needs and desires in British society of the mid-seventeenth century. There was a tendency to bestow a new kind of order on a world in which different political, cultural and societal forces were competing against each other. Many social reformists rejected 'weak governments with limited aspirations' and sought instead a powerful leadership and administrative command that could restore order after the upheavals of mid-seventeenth century Britain: 'Into this world of chaos, confusion, irregularity and incipient disorder the utopian injects images of a total and rational social order, of uniformity instead of diversity, of impersonal, neutrally functioning bureaucracy and of the comprehensive, the total state.'[69] Corresponding to these developments in the domestic sphere, the Atlantic became a space on to which colonists and reformers projected their desire for law and order. Interestingly, they frequently did so by blending narratives of orderliness with narratives of freedom.

At the same time as the governors of East New Jersey pursued an ideal of law and order, the regulations were intent on granting certain kinds of liberty to the settlers. People were free, for instance, to choose their own denomination and also to work towards their social position instead of being born into a prearranged feudal system. Land in the colony was meant to be available to everybody, regardless of their background or occupation.[70] This paradox indicates that early modern utopias are not about freedom per se. They are as much about safety, order and material satisfaction as they are about liberty. This becomes apparent in the trope of land acquisition and division that is the subject of a large number of laws pertaining to the settlement of East New Jersey. To a certain extent, this emphasis on territorial issues can be explained by the primacy of land in the settler colonial imagination.

In *Settler Colonialism: A Theoretical Overview*, Veracini marks out the differences between settler colonialism and other forms of migration or imperial expansion.[71] According to Veracini, most instances of settler colonialism pursue a particular kind of vision or ideal, according to which the newly settled site is supposed to be shaped: 'Settlers, unlike other migrants, "remove" to establish a better polity, either by setting up an ideal social body or by constituting an exemplary model of social organization.'[72] There is a utopian element to such an understanding of settler colonialism. Although the outcomes were frequently different, many of the original intentions of settlers were based on principles of improvement and societal advances, which overlooked or deliberately ignored the systems of stewardship developed by indigenous populations earlier and instead sought to implement European agricultural traditions that they considered beneficial. Gould coined the term 'settler colonial aesthetic' for literary works written from and about settler colonial sites.[73] The term draws attention to the 'aesthetic dimensions of settler colonialism' and how these are inherently connected with the 'political project' of settlement,[74] though not always in a straightforward manner. While some settler colonial texts use artistic strategies to support the politics of expansion, others use aesthetic choices to 'transfor[m] structures of domination into spaces of critique'.[75] *Scottish Colonial Literature* enters this discussion about the relationship between the aesthetic strategies and political purposes of settler colonial writing by exploring how tropes of poverty and desire come together in depictions of Scottish versus colonial land. Whereas the one was framed as unproductive and useless, the other was presented by most settlers as bountiful and sufficient.

There was a lively debate about the amount of land Scottish settlers could obtain if they volunteered to go abroad. While one settler, David Mudie from Montrose, Scotland, said he 'got 500 Acres' as soon as he moved to the colony and that others received the same amount,[76] some refuted such information and claimed that 'there is hardly any good Land untaken up'.[77] The debate illustrates how land ownership is a primary concern of settlers going abroad, and that reliable information on how much land was to be taken up on arrival was desirable among readers. Some settler narratives played into the trope of abundance, with the above-mentioned David Mudie stating that 'The Province is a third larger then ever it was represented in *Scotland*.'[78] Again, others contested such claims and added a more cautious note to the land ownership debate.[79] In another instance, a letter from John Forbes to 'Mr. James Elphingston of Logie Writter to His Majesties Signet, in Edinburgh, in Scotland' makes the connection between land ownership and material comfort obvious by naming the produce of the country as a source of physical comfort:

> *Strawberries grow very thick upon the ground amongst the Trees; so that some places of the Woods are in Summer as it were covered with a red cloath. As I am certainly informed, Fruit Trees advance at a great rate in this place, for a Man may have an Orchard within a few years after the Planting, that may yeeld him a great quantities*

*of Cydar, which is the chiefest of their drink in this Province, even
amongst the meanest of the Planters; So that this Countrey is well
improved, may make a fine place; for Nature has been defficient in
nothing to it, either for pleasure or fruitfulness of the Soyl; So that
a man being once settled two or three years in it, and having Corn,
Cattle, and all things necessary for the use of man within himself.*[80]

Food and drink serve as motifs of material comfort in this passage,
which is connected to the land trope. Strawberries, apples and other
goods are said to grow on the land, even if the subclause '*As I am certainly informed*' creates a sense of ambiguity about the truthfulness
of the account. Despite this ambiguity, the message of the passage
seems to be that future settlers can profit from the abundance of land
and the natural products that this land supplies. Settlers, it is implied,
will be able to provide for their own well-being if only they are willing to go abroad. The only things that are needed are land and the
stamina to make it cultivatable. Once the work has been done, there
will be a steady level of economic welfare, which is symbolised in the
passage by the mentioning of apple cider as a drink '*even amongst
the meanest of the Planters*'. Similarly, Peter Watson writes in a letter
from August 1684 to John Watson in Selkirk that '*it is a very good
Countrey, indeed poor men such as my self, may live better here then
in Scotland if they will but work*'.[81] Watson especially recommends
migration to East New Jersey to '*young men, who have no trouble,
they will do better to come and serve some years here then to serve in
Scotland*'.[82] The author does not deny that colonisation is hard work,
the '*hardest work that is here, is clearing of the Ground, and felling
of Trees, and the like*'.[83] He states, '*the first year is the worst, till they
be accustomed with the work of the Countrey*', and afterwards settlers will have plenty '*of Land, and have it planted with Indian Corn,
and Indian Beans, and Tobacco for our own smoaking*'.[84] In passages
like this, the emphasis on labour is simultaneously a promise of territorial possession and, with it, material supplies. Further letters and
constitutional writings from East New Jersey confirm the intersections between order, territorial possession and utopianism.

The Scottish settler Patrick Falkconer states that East New Jersey
is 'a good Countrey, for men who resolve to work hard for the first
two or three years, till they get a little Ground cleared'.[85] Falkconer
repeats towards the end of his letter that 'this is not a Countrey for
idle people, but such as will be at pains, they need not doubt but to
get Bread here in plenty'.[86] Labour is directly linked to the cultivation
of land, which turns into 'a new kind of British conquest particularly

suited to bourgeois colonialism and the history of British imperialism in America'.[87] As in More's *Utopia*, conquest is imagined to be peaceful and benevolent, with farming and labour being the strongest weapons the colonists have. Almost every story narrated in the letters of Scottish settlers in East New Jersey features the tropes of territorial acquisition via labour, which leads to the idea that an allegedly disorderly world can be turned into an orderly one via work. There is no better metaphor to illustrate this point than the one Robert Herdle uses in his letter to John Hardie. Herdle writes about East New Jersey that *'the Land is an brave and plentifull Land'*.[88] The personification of the land not only exemplifies the idealising narrative underlying colonial literature. It also suggests that colonists living there are equally brave: *'believe me, this is an brave Land, and any who will be Industrious, may live very comfortably here'*.[89] Both the land and the colonists are heroic in Herdle's version because the land is becoming domesticated, territorially divided and legally controlled. For many Scottish settlers of the mid- to late seventeenth century, this was an ideal.

Western epistemologies of space are central to the creation of what settlers deemed to be orderly societies. The importance of land as something that can be owned, allocated and divided already shows in the settlement history of East New Jersey. New Jersey had originally been Dutch and was known as New Netherlands. In 1664, English forces under the leadership of Richard Nicolls invaded the New Netherlands. James Stuart, the Duke of York and later James VII and II, supported Nicolls and possibly sponsored the latter's invasion of the New Netherlands. New Amsterdam fell and English troops claimed the territory for the British crown, thereby laying the foundation for English and Scottish settlements in New Jersey. In 1682, East New Jersey was sold to twelve Quakers, six of whom were Scottish. These six set the cornerstone for Scottish colonialism in East New Jersey, which James II authorised in 1685.[90] The proprietors' names were John Drummond, Robert Barclay, David Barclay, Robert Gordon, Gawen Lawrie and Arent Sonmans.[91] All of these Scottish proprietors were of established social and economic status in Scotland, and some of them never went to the Middle Colonies but governed through deputy governors. The map in Figure 3.1 shows East Jersey and West Jersey between 1674 and 1702. After 1702, East and West New Jersey became the joint colony of New Jersey again.

Processes of spatialisation are part of the regulating drive of settler colonialism, not only in the Scottish context but elsewhere, too. According to Veracini, 'settlers move across space and often end up

Figure 3.1 'Middle Colonies 1620–1702'. Florida Center for
Instructional Technology, map #03864. Reprinted from David B.
Scott, *A School History of the United States, from the discovery of
America to the year 1880* (New York: American Book Company,
1884). Reproduced with permission of the Florida Center for
Instructional Technology, College of Education, University of
South Florida.

permanently residing in a new locale', which they inhabit 'with the
aim of permanently securing their hold on specific locales'.[92] This
means that they try to establish spatial structures that would allow
them to permanently keep their newly acquired land. The creation of
spatial borders and land ownership rules was one means to achieve
these goals. According to Walter D. Mignolo, early modern colonialism was the main accelerator for the spread of European spatial epistemologies around the world and especially in the Americas.
Whereas large parts of the world population had lived without ideas
of territorial borders prior to colonisation, settler colonists and their
administrations were intent on mapping the spaces they sought to
control and on dividing the land according to property laws they
brought to the Atlantic from Europe: 'the connection of the Mediterranean with the Atlantic through a new commercial circuit, in

the sixteenth century, lays the foundation for both modernity and coloniality. [. . .] the Americas, contrary to Asia and Africa, are not Europe's difference but its extension.'[93] Settler colonialism and Atlantic trading networks operated with territorial paradigms based on European epistemologies of space, which they tried to impose on the newly settled territories. Legal and political writing of the Scottish settlers yields insight into these processes of implementing European spatial patterns on North American land.

In both textual and visual sources, settler colonists in East New Jersey attempted to change the spatial structures of the Americas and impose Western conceptions of space on to it. They did so partly to fulfil their desire for land and, with it, material and physical safety. For many people in mid- to late seventeenth-century Scotland, this was lacking. Like other tropes of colonial writing, spatial imagery in Atlantic writing can be linked to the domestic situation in Scotland and the UK. Whereas the Great Britain of the sixteenth and early seventeenth centuries was still very much a feudal society, the Civil War era sharpened the call for new societal and agricultural laws, which eventually led to the legal abolition of feudalism in England with the Tenures Abolition Act 1660. As to be expected, this change did not lead to sustained improvement for all. Both England and Scotland witnessed population increases in the course of the sixteenth and early seventeenth centuries. Both experienced food shortages and, resulting from that, the impoverishment of many people, but especially of the tenantry and non-privileged parts of society. In England, these problems were met with diverse measures, including giving access to newly cultivatable land, the introduction of novel agricultural methods, and the development of different kinds of crop that weathered the English winter better.[94] Literature discussing strategies to reform land use in Great Britain includes Gerrard Winstanley's *The True Levellers Standard* (1649) and *The Law of Freedom in a Platform* (1652), which are today commonly read as part of the utopian literary tradition.[95] Winstanley's catchphrase that '*True Commonwealth's Freedom lies in the free Enjoyment of the Earth*'[96] snarls at the restrictive territorial laws of seventeenth-century Britain and calls for a radical restructuring of ownership regulations. In Scotland, poverty and food shortages remained a key problem for the population throughout the seventeenth century. Scottish Atlantic writing offered an alternative vision of property acquisition, one in which land ownership would no longer be restricted to first-borns, landed families or otherwise privileged people. Instead, Scottish migrants could acquire land in East New Jersey in the lots that were, in orderly practice, reserved for them.

From the early 1680s onwards, a bill divided the land of New Jersey into English and Scottish lots. Each lot was assigned individually to the proprietors so as to eradicate, at least theoretically, the possibility of territorial conflict among the settlers. Again, the main objective of land distribution was order. The council under Gawen Lawrie, who was governor of East New Jersey from 1683 to 1686, drafted a document that ordered how land should be divided among Scottish and English settlers:

> And to the end there may be no jealousy of design or unequal dealing, we give this positive order, that no tract of land above forty-eight thousand acres be sold out in two lotts, viz. twenty four thousand acres each, which will make two thousand acres for a propriety, and that the next tract or neighbouring land on the English side, be appointed for the Scots lot; and the next tract or neighbouring land to the Scots side, be appointed for the English lot; and so *toties quotis*, as land is set out for the Proprietors:[97]

The order may have arisen out of internal strife among the proprietors, seeing as Lawrie's administration was suspected of secretive dealings and English proprietors especially were concerned about financial and legal transactions on site.[98] My interest in the bill arises from the spatial regulations it introduces into the colony as one way of trying to achieve order and control over the land and its inhabitants. Utopianism is based on the idea that 'spatial perfection requires boundaries, control, limits and direction'.[99] Similarly, the quotation echoes the desire for order and regularity, especially because it indicates the nervousness of settler colonial officials about spatial jurisdiction. The size of private properties and the question of proprietorship both need to be measured and legally divided in order to control the most prized asset of settler colonialism: land.

Officially, colonists were supposed to purchase land from the indigenous peoples in the Middle Colonies. 'A Letter from *Samuell Groome* Surveyour General in *East-New-Jersey*' from August 1683 specifies the procedure for purchasing land. If the colonists wanted land, they went '*to treat with other* Indians'.[100] In one specific instance, they went '*to buy other tracts of choice Meadowing, and Up-land that lyeth about 12. or thirteen myles up into the Countrey*'.[101] If they wanted more land, they set out to buy it from the indigenous populations '*as we may see occassion to purchase (presently) in order to a setlement there*'.[102] From the perspective of the settlers, the practice of land acquisition seems to have been a simple commercial transaction. The colonists bought land from the Five Nations and henceforth deemed themselves sole proprietors of the land. Phrases such as '*to treat with other* Indians', '*to buy*' and '*to purchase*' indicate that Western conceptions of liberty and free choice determine the practices of territorial acquisition.[103] In such passages, there are echoes of the idea that colonialism is a benevolent undertaking that will not harm others. From a European viewpoint, though probably not from an indigenous perspective, the Five Nations were considered partners in the settlement history of the Middle Colonies. The patent to Scottish proprietors states that '*this Collony may be founded in Justice, and without anything of Oppression, as all that is already Planted, it is truly Purchased from the* Indians, *so there is a great deal more of the Province cleared by their consent*'.[104] The emphasis on the lack of '*Oppression*' and the '*consent*' of the indigenous agents in this passage highlights the complicated role that Scottish settlers inhabited in the seventeenth-century Atlantic. They intended to satisfy their needs by means of territorial expansion, and the aesthetic emphasis on benevolence and justice supported the idea that everything was legal and orderly. In the long run, though, these processes of land acquisition were a decisive factor in creating the structural hierarchies that have led to the mass extinction and expropriation of the indigenous populations across the Americas. This brings me to the difficult question of how to deal with the relationship between Scottish settlers and the indigenous populations of East New Jersey and the Middle Colonies.

Internal and External Colonialisms

The indigenous populations of seventeenth-century East New Jersey largely belonged to the Five Nations: the Mohawk, the Oneida, the Onondaga, the Cayuga and the Seneca. In 1722, the Five Nations became the Six Nations when the Tuscarora joined the league. In the seventeenth and eighteenth centuries, this League of Nations from the Iroquois and Haudenosaunee People was the most powerful confederacy of indigenous tribes in North America. Its sphere of influence extended from the St Lawrence river to what is nowadays North Carolina. The Five Nations occupied a central role in the development of Dutch colonialism in the region and in British colonialism in subsequent periods because of the powerful commercial networks which they ran and in which they participated. Members of the Five Nations sold much-wanted furs and skins to European merchants and settlers, who subsequently traded them to European markets.[105] In exchange, they received axes, rifles and other weapons, which they could use to defend themselves against other indigenous Nations, as well as against French settlers. Alcohol was also a common trading good. Such a trade system suited the government of the New Netherlands and attracted numerous European settlers to the region, especially Swedish and Finnish migrants[106] but also German and Jewish settlers. By the 1680s, when Scottish settlers arrived in New Jersey, there was a multicultural trading community in the Middle Colonies based on the so-called Covenant Chain, which regulated trade between Europeans and the Five Nations. The specific terms of the covenant remained flexible, but they helped to turn the Middle Colonies into a place known for its economic prosperity and, due to the largely peaceful relations between Europeans and the indigenous populations, into what was perceived by Europeans as a site of colonial safety.[107] For Scottish settlers to enter these Atlantic trading networks meant to become part of a system that worked with partnership, but also with systems of possession and dispossession that are repeatedly negotiated in Scottish colonial writing.

To focus on the relationship with indigenous populations and, in the subsequent section, with enslaved workers in Scottish colonial literature means to open up a Pandora's box of questions about Scotland's role in the Atlantic. Ever since Michael Hechter's *Internal Colonialism: The Celtic Fringe in British National Development, 1536–1966* (1975), there has been a lively debate about Scotland's role in colonial and postcolonial studies. Essentially, this debate revolves around the question of whether or not it is possible to view Scotland in a postcolonial framework or whether colonial activities on the part of Scottish individuals and groups over the centuries prohibit such approaches.[108] While some argue that 'Scottish culture [. . .] [is] constantly threatened by the infection of the parochial' in a similar manner to how other cultures and countries are affected by the former British Empire,[109] others view the tendency to situate Scotland in a postcolonial framework as a means 'to borrow post-colonialism's fashionability in order to provide a wider audience for Scottish literary criticism'.[110] *Scottish Colonial Literature* enters this debate via Scotland's historical role as a colonising culture and the discussion of its conflicting power struggles in the Atlantic sphere. It argues that the competing narratives of possession and dispossession constitute a central dichotomy in the Scottish Atlantic literature of the seventeenth century. This dichotomy is partly continued in contemporary discussions about Scotland's position in colonial and postcolonial studies. The main questions posed in the contemporary debate equally revolve around the moral ambiguities of power, possession and dispossession in the colonial sphere. To focus on Scotland's Atlantic colonial activities before 1707 means to lay emphasis on the ambiguities of Scottish settlers, many of whom felt oppressed at home but nevertheless, or because of their experience of domestic oppression, entered repressive relationships with other actors abroad. Literary texts about East New Jersey yield insight into these relationships and complicate the narratives Scottish colonists told about themselves. Some background on Scotland's position in post-Civil War Britain helps to pave the way for the argument that the feeling of dispossession at home frequently led to rhetorical and material practices of subjugation abroad.

The period of the Civil Wars profoundly changed the nature of inner British relations. Oliver Cromwell's Protectorate had ambivalent effects on Scotland. As others have shown, Cromwell's army virtually conquered Scotland, and numerous Scotsmen and women were deported as prisoners to Virginia in the 1650s.[111] At the same time, the inclusion of Scotland in the Navigation Acts from 1651 onwards led to growing prosperity among some Scottish merchants.[112] Thus, while many Scottish and Irish people suffered under Cromwell's regime and were forcefully removed across the Atlantic,[113] others, above all Scottish merchants, could sell their goods not only to England but also to England's overseas dominions without additional taxation. This trade agreement ended with the restoration of the monarchy in 1660.[114] From that time onwards, Scottish merchants and businesspeople had to pay taxes again when trading with English dominions abroad. Of course, the restoration of the English trading monopoly was not always obeyed and illegal trade with English colonies, as well as trade via continental connections such as the Netherlands or Hamburg, flourished in Scotland during the second half of the seventeenth century.[115] By the mid-1680s, the Atlantic offered some Scottish migrants a potential alternative to the lack of economic prospects at home. Similar to the Nova Scotia scheme, texts relating to East New Jersey promote ideas of economic improvement, material comfort and upward social mobility. Such tropes are inseparable from the question of power relationships in the colonial sphere. Many Scottish migrants imagined settler colonialism as a means of improving their situations while accepting, consciously or not, the dispossession of others in the Atlantic sphere.

The colonist Gabriel Thomas writes in his *Historical and Geographical Account of the Province and Country of Pensilvania and of West-New-Jersey* (1698) that the willingness to work is the only precondition for a successful life in the Middle Colonies. His appeal to 'the Poor, the Idle, the Lazy, & the Vagabonds of these Kingdoms and of *Wales* to hasten thither, that they may live plentifully and happily' is not addressed to Scottish migrants specifically, but elsewhere in the text Thomas names Scots as part of the desired group of settlers. He concludes his preface with the wish that his report should be

> sufficient Encouragement to the Idle, the Sloathful, and the Vagabonds of England, Scotland, and Ireland to hasten thither, where besides this, they have a fair prospect of getting considerable Estates, at least of living very Plentifully and Happily, which Medium of Life is far better than lingering out their Days so miserably Poor and half Starved.[116]

The excerpt works with a series of antitheses to create a vision of the Middle Colonies as a land of happiness, prosperity and agency. It contrasts the lack of these prospects in England, Ireland and Scotland with those who live 'Plentifully and Happily' in the Middle Colonies. The final emphasis on the 'miserably Poor' and the 'half Starved' reinforces the point that, in terms of material welfare, the Atlantic is a solution to the material scarcity from which people suffered at home.

Whereas More's *Utopia* promotes the abolishment of private property, Scottish Atlantic literature gains much of its energy from the promise of land ownership and personal enrichment. An excerpt from Scot's *The Model of the Government* offers evidence for the material interests that underlie the East New Jersey vision:

> *you may easily consider, what an interest* Scotland *might have had in* America, *had all these who have gone from their native Countrey in queast of Honor and Fortunes, to these places, steered their course to this Airth; there is hardly any noble family in* Scotland, *or Gentlemen of any note, but ere this time should have some interest in* America; *If these had all settled in one place, it should have been a very considerable Collony ere this time;* Women also of our own Nation would not have been wanting to these Men, *by which the foundation of a very flowrishing Collonie should have been laid;*[117]

Upward social mobility and material possessions emerge as central forces of Scottish migration, expressed here in the '*queast of Honor and Fortunes*'. Now that East New Jersey belongs to Scottish proprietors, a space exists to establish '*a very flowrishing Collonie*' for Scottish migrants. According to the excerpt, most families in

Scotland were interested in Atlantic settlements by the 1680s. Many families allegedly already had relatives living abroad. Whether or not this is an exaggeration is difficult to say. In contrast to the lack of support for Nova Scotia, there actually seems to have been some interest in the undertaking throughout Scotland. Insh claims that the letters that were sent back home by Scottish colonists in East New Jersey were 'widely read' by their families and friends,[118] which would mean that Atlantic writing had a considerable readership in late seventeenth-century Scotland. In terms of numbers, though, it is difficult to talk about a national enterprise. Only two ships left Scotland in 1684 for East New Jersey, 'one from Montrose the other from Aberdeen'.[119] Following the original ships from Aberdeen and Montrose, other Scottish settlers went to East New Jersey on various vessels. None of these journeys was '*official*' in Anderson's use of the word, 'i.e. something emanating from the state, and serving the interests of the state first and foremost'.[120] Instead, the interest of the settlement scheme was mostly private and individual. The Scottish proprietors of East New Jersey 'encouraged more than a hundred of their countrymen to invest in East Jersey, purchasing about half of the proprietary interest, and Scots quickly became the most active force in colonization'.[121] Landsman calculates that between the 1680s and 1765, 'about 3,000 persons of Scottish descent inhabited the central Jersey corridor'.[122] The higher proportion of this number probably went in the eighteenth century after the proprietors surrendered the colony to Queen Anne in 1702. The main reason for their surrender was that the government proved unpopular among the settlers. There were repeated riots that the proprietors, many of whom did not live in New Jersey but in Great Britain, could not easily quell from afar. In return for their surrender of the colony, the proprietors received the guarantee that they could 'keep their hold on valuable proprietary property throughout the province'.[123] Land ownership, as always, turned out to be the decisive factor for the proprietors to surrender the colony, just as it had been the decisive factor for their investment in it.

Many settlers who went to East New Jersey were educated and belonged to the professional classes. They included 'merchants, officers, ministers, medical men, and professional persons of other sorts'.[124] And yet, the emphasis in colonial literature is not on professional skills but on land and agricultural work. A letter from Charles Gordon to his brother, 'John Gordon, [. . .], *Doctor of Medicines at Montrose*', from March 1685 indicates as much.[125] Writing from East New Jersey, Charles urges his brother to give up the medical profession in Scotland

and to come to the colonies instead: 'if you design to come hither your self, you may come as a Planter, or a *Merchant*, but as a *Doctor of Medicine* I cannot advise you'.[126] Following Gordon, doctors are not needed in East New Jersey because he 'can hear of no deseases here to cure but some Agues, and some cutted legs and fingers; and there are no want of *Empericks* for these already'.[127] Thomas's emphasis on the need for non-professional settlers in the Atlantic may be welcome news to those who have no education or special training at home. Other reformist movements of the seventeenth century may have privileged education as the most important basis for socio-economic improvement: for instance, the writings of Hartlib and Drury. The Atlantic vision of Charles Gordon and other settlers, in contrast, states that a professional education at home is not only not necessary but superfluous when coming to East New Jersey and starting a new life there.

Most migrants seem to have gone voluntarily to East New Jersey, though there was also some involuntary migration in the form of prisoners.[128] Many of these prisoners perished on the voyage when one of their ships sank.[129] It was common practice by the mid-seventeenth century to send 'convicts, prostitutes, debtors, vagabonds, escaped slaves and indentured servants, religious radicals, and political prisoners' to the North American colonies.[130] Linebaugh and Rediker have written, with regard to the Virginia Company, about the practice of sending 'forced labor overseas', which included 'thousands of children [. . .] between the ages of eight and sixteen', many of whom died on the voyage to Virginia while others were forced to work overseas.[131] No self-authored documents survive from these enforced labourers, neither in Virginia nor in East New Jersey. In the Scottish context, as in many others, 'the history of the Atlantic proletariat of the seventeenth, eighteen, and nineteenth centuries'[132] remains largely unwritten. And yet, one of the arguments this chapter makes with regard to the history of the Atlantic is that many settlers shared attributes of proletarian history in so far as they were 'lacking property, money, or material riches of any kind', and that this poverty was one reason why they became '*mobile, transatlantic*'.[133] Mobility itself is a sign of certain privileges, of course, then as now. In Atlantic literature of the time, these privileges are part of the structural hierarchies between European and non-European agents, but they are frequently de-emphasised to give priority to narratives of lack. The only prerequisite, so colonial authors state, is the ability to work and a willingness to acquire a piece of land from the indigenous populations on site. Here, as elsewhere in Scottish Atlantic writing, Mannheim's idea of a power struggle taking place in utopian movements resonates strongly with the hierarchical structures established in the colonial sphere. In literary works of the time, though, this power struggle is euphemistically framed in terms of friendly relations.

Throughout the literature relating to the colonisation of East New Jersey, authors stress the allegedly friendly relations between the settlers and the Five Nations. Peter Watson writes in a letter to John Watson from August 1684: '*the Indian Natives* [. . .] *are not troublesome any way to any of us, if we do them no harm, but are a very kind and loving people*'.[134] He stresses their innocent nature when relating how

> *the men does nothing but hunts, and the women they plant Corn, and works at home; they come and trades among the Christians with Skins or Venison, or Corn, or Pork; and in the Summer time, they and their Wives come down the Rivers, in their Cannoas, which they make themselves of a pice of a great tree, like a little Boat, and there they Fish and take Oysters.*[135]

Similar depictions of the indigenous populations can be found in literature relating to West New Jersey, where the picture of a congenial relationship between the Five Nations and European settlers equally exists.[136] And yet, despite the professed intentions of amicable relations between settlers and the indigenous populations of East New Jersey, many sources indicate that there were profound fissures in the vision of harmony and peace. It was generally acknowledged, for instance, that European commodities such as weapons or alcohol had negative effects on the indigenous populations of the Americas. Trade of these goods was forbidden in East New Jersey,[137] and the 'Bill for Regulating of Trade with the Indians' lists the exact products and procedures that it is lawful to trade with the indigenous populations.[138] Given the details of these bills, it is easy to imagine that such laws were regularly broken on both sides. The same seems to be true for regulations regarding the acquisition of indigenous land.

The language used in East New Jersey literature suggests that land acquisition procedures did not always go without conflict. Drummond writes in *An Advertisement Concerning the Province of East New-Jersey* concerning a piece of land '*about* Barnagate, *where there is also a River,* [. . .] *already cleared of the* Indian *incumbrance, enough to accommodate* hundreds of Families'.[139] The phrase 'Indian incumbrance' not only indicates the underlying attitude towards the indigenous populations but, combined with the verb '*cleared*', gives reason to assume that property purchases were not necessarily on mutual terms, even if official regulations said so. Other sources advise the settlers in East New Jersey to build 'fortifications [. . .] in every town of this Province [. . .] for securing of women and children, provision and ammunition in case of eminent danger by the Indians'.[140] Such protective measures are far from the idea of harmonious relations between settlers and the indigenous populations. There are evident cracks in the utopian vision of harmonious relations in East New Jersey. The settlement is only superficially ideal as long as members of the Five Nations comply with the settlers and their colonial vision. One writer, John Reid, laments that 'Its pity to see so much good land as I have been over in this province lying wast, and greater pity to see so much good and convenient land taken, and not improven.'[141] Reid's use of the word 'pity' appeals to a sense of moral judgement that legitimises the dispossession of indigenous people. Such rhetoric not only underlines the conflicts between settlers and native populations; it also prefigures John Locke's ideas about land ownership being essentially linked to agricultural cultivation.

John Locke (1632–1704) significantly contributed to the writing of the *Fundamental Constitution of Carolina* (1668). Between 1669 and 1675, he was Secretary to the Lords Proprietors of Carolina.[142] From 1673 onwards, he was also Secretary to the Council of Trade and Plantations in England. The president of the latter institution was Locke's close acquaintance, and proprietor of Carolina, the Earl of Shaftesbury.[143] As others have shown, Locke's *Essays on the Law of Nature* (1664) had a decisive influence on the intellectual history of the British Empire, specifically the idea that labour legitimises the spatial dispossession of the indigenous populations in the Americas.[144] Similarly, in *Second Treatise of Government* (1690), Locke formulates what became a consensus in large parts of the Atlantic – namely, that property goes hand in hand with European ideas of agriculture and spatial possession:

> There cannot be a clearer demonstration of anything than several nations of the Americans are of this, who are rich in land and poor in all the comforts of life; whom Nature, having furnished as liberally as any other people with the materials of plenty - i.e., a fruitful soil, apt to produce in abundance what might serve for food, raiment, and delight; yet, for want of improving it by labour, have not one hundredth part of the conveniences we enjoy, and a king of a large and fruitful territory there feeds, lodges, and is clad worse than a day labourer in England.[145]

Such assessments of indigenous agricultural practices reveal the fundamental conflict underlying Western conceptions of the Atlantic in the seventeenth century. European epistemologies of space clashed with the traditions of indigenous populations across the Americas. Once European settler colonialism took on force in the Americas, land was distributed according to European rather than indigenous epistemologies of space. According to Gilroy, Locke's 'doctrine of the *vacuum domicilium* (vacant land waiting to be settled and cultivated)' was 'fatal to the indigenous inhabitants of any territory judged empty or insufficiently worked'.[146] For Locke, the indigenous peoples of America forfeit their right to own land if they leave it untended.[147] The effects of such rhetorical and spatial dispossession are still felt by indigenous peoples across the Americas until this day. Land redistribution, as well as the material, economic and cultural inequalities that arose out of these land redistribution practices, is part of the long-term structure of settler colonialism in the Atlantic, in Wolfe's conception of the term.[148] This long-term objective of settler colonialism also emerges in monogenesis theories that concern the relationship between the indigenous populations and the settlers, which offers a noteworthy twist to the relationship between European settlers and the indigenous populations of East New Jersey.

Colonial writing from the second half of the seventeenth century sometimes promotes the idea that the indigenous populations of North America are related to European settlers through Adam and Eve. These so-called monogenesis theories postulated that all humans derive from the same biblical origins. They may inhabit different parts of the world but, in the end, everything and everyone were considered to be created by God, so even the indigenous populations of the Americas must be related to Europeans somehow. The way to explain this relationship was through biblical stories, with either the story of Adam and Eve or that of Noah featuring as prominent models for the spread of the world population: '*GOD* [. . .] *separated the Sons of* Adam, *and set the bounds of their habitation*' in different parts of the world.[149] Monogenesis theories were popular among mid-seventeenth-century thinkers, and they proved to have an influence on Atlantic writing, too. In *British Identities before Nationalism*, Colin Kidd traces how the explanation model, according to which Noah's offspring peopled the world with different races, influenced Atlantic writing.[150] Monogenesis theories conceptualised a 'collapse of time and space whereby ethnography recapitulated prehistory – to leave Europe was to travel back in time'.[151] In colonial literature, monogenesis theories give rise to the idea that Europeans are at a superior developmental stage and can 'help' their relatives in the Americas to reach the same stage through colonisation.

Various colonial writers of the 1680s suggest that all humans are related. Gabriel Thomas writes that 'The first Inhabitants of this Country were the *Indians*, being supposed to be part of the Ten dispersed Tribes of *Israel*.'[152] Similarly, Scot's *The Model of Government* mentions one of the most famous monogenesis theorists of the time, who explains the existence of diverse kinds of people with the biblical flood. The reference is to 'Judge Hales':[153] that is, Sir Matthew Hale (1609–76). Hale's work, *The Primitive Origination of Mankind Considered and Examined According to the Light of Nature* (1677), theorises the global dispersal of mankind. Part of the theory is that all people in the world derive from Adam.[154] Echoing the writings of Hale, *The Model of Government* states: '*the* Americans *had their Original from the Inhabitants of* Europe, Asia, *and* Africa, *that Transmigrated into that Continent, either intentionally or Casuallie, or both*'.[155] The estimated time of their arrival was sometime after '*the Flood, now above 4000. years ago*'.[156] This leads the author to speculate upon the routes of migration from Europe to North America, which could have been via either Asia or Greenland or Australia and the Philippines.[157] There is much knowledge of geography in Scot's speculations about the genesis of the Five Nations in the Middle Colonies. The underlying trajectory remains one of European power claims over North America. The Five Nations may be trading partners and, following monogenesis theories, brothers and sisters to the settlers. Yet, Scot's *Model* also makes clear that settlers must watch that they do not lose their alleged superiority, which is one of the anxieties expressed in settler colonial writing of the time:

> *where a Colony comes and keeps it self in a Body as the* Roman *Colonies did; and the Plantations in* Virginia, *and* New England *do; and the* New Accessions *incorporat and joyn themselves unto that Body, Custom, both Religious and Civil, And the Original Language are kept intire, but where the* Accessions *are but thin, and spairing and scattered among the Natives of the Countrey, where they come, and are driven to conform themselves unto their Customs, for their very substance, safety and intertainment; it falls out that the very first Planters doe soon degenerate in their habits and Religions, as a little wine poured into a great vessell, loseth it self; but if they escape a totall assimilation to the country where they thus are mingled; yet the nixt Generation in such a mixture, is quickly assimilated to the corrupt manners, and customs of the people, among whom they are thus planted; so that it is no wonder, if [. . .] The third Generation forgot their Ancestors, and the Customs, Religions and languages of these people, from whom they were first derived;*[158]

The author seeks to explain why the indigenous inhabitants differ so much from European settlers, despite their common descent from Adam. The passage is fraught with anxiety about European cultural superiority and the particular effects that colonialism had on the settlers if they did not preserve their authority. By using ancient settlement schemes as an example of how planters could '*degenerate in their habits*', the author warns colonists not to adjust to their new surroundings but to keep their borders – cultural and spatial – intact.[159] Everybody can become '*barbarous*', according to Scot's *Model*, as the '*Degeneration*' of North American Nations has shown.[160] Barbarity is not the Other. Barbarity is a potential part of the self, so it is important to preserve difference by means of social and cultural boundaries. Fear of downward social mobility shines through such passages with their emphasis on the intergenerational bond of families, as expressed in the repetition of 'Generation'. Where progress is possible, the opposite may also occur, the passage suggests: an allegorical movement back in time. The question of how the indigenous peoples had migrated from Adam via the Ten Tribes of Israel to the Americas continued to concern theologians until well into the nineteenth century.[161]

It may or may not be a coincidence that such an attempt to explain the origins of the scattered world population is known from earlier utopian literature. Both Bacon's *New Atlantis* and More's *Utopia* try to rationalise why previously unknown parts of the world are inhabited by humans. *Utopia* states that the native inhabitants of the island 'took their beginning of the Greeks, because their speech, which in all other points is not much unlike the Persian tongue, keepeth divers signs and tokens of the Greek language in the names of their cities and of their magistrates'.[162] In Bacon's *New Atlantis* the existence of an unknown part of the world and the indigenous populations therein is explained with 'the universal flood', meaning the biblical flood:

> For the poor remnant of human seed which remained in their mountains peopled the country again slowly, by little and little; and being simple and savage people, (not like Noah and his sons, which was the chief family of the earth), they were not able to leave letters, arts, and civility to their posterity.[163]

Both models, the classical and the biblical one, seek commonalities between the inhabitants of the globe. At the same time, they do not eradicate differences but insist on certain cultural hierarchies. This is especially apparent in Bacon's conception of Europeans as the most educated and civilised members of the world population. Henry Neville's *The Isle of Pines* (1688) endorses such an idea of European superiority in its allegorical rendering of the story of Noah. With its obvious sexual imagery, *The Isle of Pines* can be read as an allegory of English superiority that advocates the active reproduction of Britishness around the world.[164] Scottish colonial writing of the late seventeenth century testifies to similar concerns over racial and cultural superiority, and expresses anxieties over the potential loss of self-control in the Atlantic, which would have been contrary to Western ideals of temporal and spatial self-improvement.

Religion, Slavery and the Paradox of Freedom

In her book *Freedom's Empire: Race and the Rise of the Novel in Atlantic Modernity, 1640–1940* (2008), Laura Doyle examines the paradox of freedom in British writing about the Atlantic with a particular focus on race and literary culture. According to Doyle, the promises of liberty and freedom are not equally available for everyone in the Atlantic world. Instead, the pursuit of freedom and happiness is reserved for white Europeans, whereas people from other parts of the globe are, more often than not, denied what settlers searched for in the Americas:

> To be white is to be fit for freedom, and the white man's burden is to lead others by forging the institutions and modelling the subjectivities required to practice proper freedom, even if along the way this requires enslaving, invading, or exterminating those others who may not (yet) be fit for freedom. [. . .] in Atlantic modernity, freedom is a race myth.[165]

The following discussion of Scottish colonial writing draws on the concept of the 'race myth' and reflects on how narratives of religion and slavery in works about East New Jersey and the Middle Colonies relate to it. Many of the ambiguities that emerge in Scottish Atlantic literature parallel those of other British settlers. Authors seek to escape repression at home but, in the process of doing so, become part of a structural hierarchy that sees them at the more powerful end. Like the focus on the indigenous populations of East New Jersey, a focus on the Black Atlantic raises serious questions about Scotland's place in the emergent British Empire.

The quest for religious liberty features strongly in colonial narratives about the Middle Colonies. This is true, above all, for legal and propaganda writings about East New Jersey. *A Brief Advertisement Concerning East-New-Jersey, in America* (1685) stresses the promise of religious freedom that awaits settlers in the colony. It states that the roughly 300 Scottish planters who went to East New Jersey in July 1684 are able to '*freely enjoy their own principles, without hazard or the least trouble; seeing there are Ministers of their own perswasion going alongst*'.[166] Moreover, the text emphasises that it is one of '*the fundamental Constitutions of that Countrey,* [that all people; K. S.] *are allowed the free Exercise of their Ministry*'.[167] Religious freedom becomes a rhetorical pull-factor in the propagation of the settler community. Settlers living in New Jersey must in 'no way be molested or prejudged for their Religious Perswasions and Exercise in matters of Faith [. . .] nor shall they be compelled to frequent [. . .] any Religious Worship, Place or Ministry'.[168] The only requisite to enjoy this religious freedom is that everyone who wants to be a member of the colonial administration must be Christian, but of which denomination is unimportant: 'no Man shall be admitted a Member of the Great or Common Council, or any other Place of publick Trust, who shall not profess faith in *Christ-Jesus*'.[169] Just as More's *Utopia* rules out the existence of people on the island who do not believe in God,[170] so the East New Jersey administration wants to ensure that it remains a Christian colony:

> Libertie *in matters of* Religion *is established in the fullest manner. To be a* Planter *or* Inhabitant, *nothing is more required but* the acknowledging of One Almighty GOD, and to have a Share in the Government, A simple profession of faith of Jesus Christ, without descending into any other of the differences among Christians, only that Religion may not be a cloak for disturbance, who ever comes into the Magistrature, must declare they hold not themselves in conscience obliged, for Religions sake, to make an alteration, or to endeavour to turn out their partners in the Government, because they differ in Opinion from them, *and this is no more then to follow that great Rule,* To do as they would be done by.[171]

The governors use biblical language to call for liberty within certain bounds in the colony. 'To do as they would be done by' is the 'Golden Rule' of the New Testament, which is written down in Matthew: '*To do to others what we would have others do to us*'.[172] The belief in the principle of Christian equality may have held a special appeal for Quakers and other religious groups whose position was threatened in sixteenth- and seventeenth-century Scotland.

Various religious groups suffered from discrimination throughout Great Britain in the seventeenth century. These included Presbyterians, Lutherans, Independents, Catholics and Jews,[173] Covenanters and members of the Presbyterian Church, as well as the relatively recently founded Society of Friends, commonly known as Quakers.[174] There is some debate regarding the exact status of Quakers in Restoration Britain. Pomfret, for one, states that 'During the Restoration more than 15,000 Friends suffered imprisonment in England, and several thousand more in Ireland and Scotland.'[175] Such historical detail has led some scholars to view Scottish Atlantic settlements in the 1680s as primarily religion-driven: South Carolina is considered a Scottish Covenanter colony, whereas East New Jersey is viewed, at least predominantly, as a Quaker settlement.[176] In contrast, Insh argues that there was no such thing as an 'active persecution [of Quakers; K. S.] by the central government in Scotland'.[177] According to Insh, the personal accounts of the colonists offer little evidence to support the theory of religion-driven migration. Although there are letters in which Scottish settlers write to people at home that more ministers should come to East New Jersey, these references are brief and without any denominational specifications.[178] According to Insh, 'there is no trace either of Quaker sentiment or of Quaker phraseology' in the 'letters from Scottish settlers in East Jersey'.[179] Still, Insh concedes that discrimination against Quakers by local authorities took place, and that a general sentiment of repression may well have been a push-factor for migration among Scottish Quakers to the Americas.[180]

Legal and administrative documents support a nuanced reading of religious narratives in East New Jersey's colonial imaginary. A look at the different versions of the colonial constitution does not solve the debate about how far Quakerism influenced the colonial agenda, but it does demonstrate the centrality of religious liberty as a settler trope. Religious freedom features in different versions of the constitution, ranging from the 1660s to the 1680s. The 1664 text, when New Jersey was still under British control, says *'That no person as aforsaid within the said* Province *at any time shall be any wayes molested, punished, Disquyeted, or called in question for any* Difference in Opinion, *or* Practice in matters of Religious Concernments.'[181] The date of the proclamation points to the pan-British quality of the dream of religious freedom in the Middle Colonies. The particular importance of the promise for Scottish Quakers began only after 1682, when Robert Barclay became governor of the colony.

Barclay had converted from Catholicism to the Society of Friends in 1667. From that time onwards, he became a leading Quaker apologist and published numerous texts in favour of the Society of Friends. His most famous publications include *A Catechism and Confession of Faith* (1673)[182] and *An Apology for the True Christian Divinity, as the Time Is Held Forth, and Preached by the People, Called in Scorn, Quakers* (Latin 1676; English 1678).[183] Barclay was governor of East New Jersey from 1682 to 1688, administering the colony through several deputy governors while never visiting it himself. Almost surprisingly, given his religious background, Barclay did not write about the colony he governed in religious terms. Yet, it is not unreasonable to argue that his administration influenced other religious figures to adopt a central role in East New Jersey during the 1680s, such as the Scottish-born evangelist George Keith.

George Keith (c. 1638–1712) was perhaps the best-known agent of Quakerism in East New Jersey during the decade of Barclay's governorship. Keith was born in Peterhead, Scotland. He grew up in the Presbyterian Church but eventually grew dissatisfied with some of their teachings.[184] In the 1660s, Keith joined the Society of Friends and evangelised on their behalf. At the same time, Keith criticised the Society of Friends from within. One of his most famous works is *Help in Time of Need from the God of Help: To the People of the (so called) Church of Scotland* (1664).[185] The dissatisfaction with the Society of Friends back home led Keith to turn to the Middle Colonies for a more radical understanding of Quakerism. He left for North America in 1684 and started to write about Quaker theology there. *The Christian Faith of the People of GOD, called in Scorn, Quakers in Rhode-Island* (1692)[186] and *An Account of the Great Divisions, Amongst the Quakers, in Pensilvania* (1692) specifically address Quakers in the North American colonies and set out the special role Keith imagines for the Atlantic in the recreation of what he considers a true Christian faith.[187]

Keith resided for several years in New Jersey and its neighbouring colonies until returning, in 1694, to Great Britain. In his work, he urges the members of the Society of Friends to '*agree to draw up some Principles and Doctrines of Faith in the most necessary things, to qualifie our Church-Members, and distinguish Believers from Unbelievers*'.[188] In passages such as this one, Keith's religious vision concurs with the well-ordered tendencies of Scottish Atlantic literature. Both show the need for clearly set boundaries and social regulations, which are meant to turn the colony into an ideal space. As in other utopias of the time, the method of choice is the forming of laws or, in Keith's religious language, '*Doctrines of Faith*'. Like others of the time, Keith believed that 'the coming of Christ's rule could be helped on its way through human actions, and not just the actions of kings and rulers, but those of normal people'.[189] Religious reformation is a matter of public concern for Keith because religious reform is simultaneously social reform. Only a highly regulated, standardised doctrine could, in Keith's view, ensure that Quakers could unite and realise the religious utopia he had in mind for the Atlantic. Eventually, Keith left the Society of Friends and joined the Church of England. In 1702, he was ordained as priest in the Anglican Church. Yet, his earlier writings must be viewed in the context of eschatological perceptions of the Americas as a place for Christianity's rebirth.

There was a widespread belief that the Americas were a space for Christians to change both their own lives and the institution of the Church from within. As Mircea Eliade writes:

> The colonization of the two Americas began under an eschatological sign: people believed that the time had come to renew the Christian world, and the true renewal was the return to the Earthly Paradise or, at the very least, the beginning again of Sacred History, the reiteration of the prodigious events spoken of in the Bible.[190]

When Keith challenges and condemns the Quaker community as infested with inappropriate Presbyterian practices, then his criticism interacts with a vision of the Americas as a sacred space. Nothing old, nothing impure must enter the religious utopia of Keith's Quakerism. The Protestant Reformation was, for people like Keith, only the first step in a development leading to the wholesome reformation of the Christian Church. North America is the earthly paradise in which such reform is still possible. Keith's vision of religion as a public utopia participates in the eschatological narrative of the British Atlantic as a holy site, in which the paradise once lost can be regained. One thing that did not conform to Keith's vision of a paradise regained was the practice of slavery among settler colonial Quakers.

The slave trade was introduced into the British Atlantic in the first half of the seventeenth century. Bristol was one of the trading centres for the forced labour market, which developed into 'the city's greatest source of wealth by the end of the seventeenth century'.[191] While Bristol is not in Scotland, the connections between Scottish settlers and the Black Atlantic have become a focus of historical research lately.[192] As the discussion of Scottish domestic drama at the beginning of this chapter has illustrated, the connections between colonial trade and slavery were not unknown in Scotland. By the seventeenth century, slaves had become a reality in virtually all European colonies.[193] Their

work was the foundation for the riches accumulated by European settlers, and their lives and cultures shaped the history of colonisation
in economic, cultural, material and intellectual terms. My discussion
of the subject is informed by Gilroy's concept of the Black Atlantic as a hybrid space that is formed by African, American, European
and Caribbean elements together: 'cultural historians could take the
Atlantic as one single, complex unit of analysis in their discussions of
the modern world and use it to produce an explicitly transnational
and intercultural perspective' on 'black American cultural and political histories'.[194] Although sources from non-white agents are unfortunately absent from the corpus of East New Jersey literature from
the 1680s and 1690s, it is significant to recognise that slaves, and
especially enslaved Africans, were an integral 'part of the ethical and
intellectual heritage of the West as a whole'.[195]

Investigating Scottish colonial literature about East New Jersey
offers ample evidence that the prosperity of the Scottish settlers in
the Middle Colonies is based on slavery and on trade commonly
associated with the Black Atlantic. One author writes that East New
Jersey needs further 'Merchants here to export the product of the
Countrey to *Barbadoes*, and the *West-Indies*, and to Import *Rumm*,
Malasses, *Suggar* and *Cotton*, &c.'[196] Such export 'would do a great
deal of good to this Countrey',[197] the author states. Similarly, James
Cockburn states, in a letter from March 1685, that '*I am very well
in this land of* America; *We lake neither wild nor tame to eat; the
most part of our drink is* Rumm, Cyder, *and* Beer; *such as have these
to sell, drives a very good Trade.*'[198] Both texts confirm the role of
Black Atlantic trading networks in the increase of wealth among
settler colonists. Neither author mentions enslaved labour directly,
but both refer to locations and commodities that are unmistake-
ably associated with the Atlantic slave trade. Barbados, the West
Indies, rum, sugar, molasses and cotton, as well as the references
to 'export' and '*good Trade*', delineate the routes and commodities
that dominate the rise of the Black Atlantic.[199] While the authors do
not make any religious references in their texts, the links between
Quakerism and the Black Atlantic have been established as part of
North American settler colonial culture. Landsman describes how
economic growth in the Middle Colonies depended on enslaved
labour. He uses the example of 'the Free Society of Traders', which
was established by William Penn and 'led by Quaker merchants',
to demonstrate how deeply Quaker colonists were involved in the
slave system:

Those traders had extensive contacts through much of the Atlantic world, from London, Bristol, and Cork to Rhode Island, the mid-Atlantic, and the West Indies, and the grain and flour produced by Quaker farmers quickly began to find their way into the expanding Caribbean market. There it served to feed the growing slave population on the sugar plantation.[200]

Of course, not all Quaker settlers participated in the trade that served the slave market or were aware of the wide-ranging implications of the Atlantic slave system.[201] The same is true for other settlers in the Americas. Yet, enslaved labour is part of Quaker Atlantic history and informed the system of overseas colonisation, just as it informed Scottish drama of the seventeenth century, with which this chapter began. References to slavery and the Black Atlantic in the primary sources indicate as much. Although British settlers know how to work, '*it cannot be expected, that they know how to improve these Islands, for* Suggar, Cotton, Indigo, *&c*', as one colonist puts it.[202] The solution is, in the eyes of the colonist, '*to settle in a place where the* Nigro Slaves could do more service, and *be far more usefull than the most laborious and judicuous of our* Countrey People'.[203] Many settlers, including some Scottish settlers, accepted the fact that they participated in the oppression of others in order to win their own freedom abroad.[204] Scottish settlers wanted to escape their life of drudgery, which some compared to the fate of enslaved workers. George Lockhart writes, in a letter to Robert Barclay, that '*many others of your Countrey-men*' continue to live in '*perpetual Slavery*' by staying in Scotland rather than choosing '*the hight of good Living*' by going to the colonies.[205] Similarly, a letter by Charles Gordon to '*Mr. Andrew Irvine* Merchant [. . .] in *Edinburgh*, in *Scotland*' uses a slave metaphor to encourage migration to East New Jersey.[206] The author relates the story of a 'Scots Laird' who lived the life of '*a slave from* Dumbar' in Scotland, whereas he now lives a better life in East New Jersey.[207] Here, as elsewhere, the message is clear: Scots could free themselves by migrating to the colonies. In the process, they would turn others into slaves. Doyle's argument about the racialisation of liberty also applies to Scottish authors: 'Ironically, the idea of freedom has itself enabled the growth of modern forms of oppression.'[208] The acceptance of enslaved labour is part of the process of achieving the kind of happiness and self-improvement colonists envisioned in the Atlantic, but it is especially striking in texts in which some settlers compare themselves to slaves.

While some settlers accepted slavery as the backbone of the Atlantic economy, others felt increasingly uncomfortable with their position in the Atlantic slave trade and called for the liberation of enforced labourers. Although it would gain fuller force only in the eighteenth century, the abolitionist movement grew in the second half of the seventeenth century. Some Scottish authors were actively involved in it. The debate was international and involved abolitionists from the Netherlands, Germany, England, Ireland, Wales and Scotland. Of course, it also included, first and foremost, Africans and African Americans who 'were also thinkers and political actors, and [. . .] at certain moments they transformed and expanded the meaning of democracy'.[209] Lacking written records from enslaved labourers in 1680s New Jersey, the following discussion concentrates on writings of settlers who fought against slavery in the Middle Colonies. One familiar figure in this discussion is George Keith, whose role in the slavery debate is equally as fiery as his role in religious debates of the time. In 1693, one year before Keith returned to Great Britain, he helped to publish *An Exhortation & Caution to Friends Concerning Buying or Keeping of Negroes*. In recent years, Keith's single authorship of the text has been questioned because it seems as if it was formulated by 'a group of people and that it should be understood as a communal effort, rather than an individual one'.[210] According to Fry, 'Keit[h] wrote [. . .] the first protest against slavery to be published in America,'[211] though there was apparently an earlier, unpublished, tract called the 'Germantown Protest' that preceded *An Exhortation* and may well have served as a source for it.[212] William Bradford was the printer of *An Exhortation*. He was based in Philadelphia and was 'the city's only printer, who helped to publicise Keith's cause'.[213] Whatever Keith's exact role in the authoring and publishing process may have been, his collaboration with Dutch, German, English, Irish, Scottish and Welsh authors on *An Exhortation* indicates the transnational nature of the abolitionist movement in the second half of the seventeenth century. Moreover, it helps to shed light on the religious element in abolitionist writing because his collaborators appear to have been Quakers.[214]

An Exhortation sets out a religion-based argument against slavery. In line with other abolitionist texts of the late seventeenth century, it condemns slavery as an immoral practice and explains this immorality with the 'Golden Rule', cited above, which is '*To do to others what we would have others do to us*'.[215] The principle of Christian equality is said to forbid a system of slavery based on inequity. If

Jesus came into the world to liberate people, then Christians, too, should go into the world

> not to destroy mens Lives, but to save them, nor to bring any part of Mankind into outward Bondage, Slavery or Misery, nor yet to detain them, or hold them therein, but to ease and deliver the Oppressed and Distressed, and bring into Liberty both inward and outward.[216]

The authors write that 'our Lord Jesus Christ hath tasted Death for every Man', including '*Negroes, Blacks* and *Taunies* [who; K. S.] are a real part of Mankind, for whom Christ hath shed his precious Blood, and are capable of Salvation, as well as *White Men*'.[217] Such a line of argumentation prefigures David Hume's later comments on the question of slavery in the mid-eighteenth century, which causes Hume to lament the 'cruel and oppressive' practice of 'slavery' and to blame slave-holders for having 'little humanity'.[218] Several decades earlier, *An Exhortation* makes a similar case against slavery and calls on the Quaker congregation to stop participating in the system of racialised oppression. It asks readers 'Not to buy any Negroes, unless it were on purpose to set them *free*'.[219] Those who already own slaves should equally set them free 'after some reasonable time of moderate Service'.[220] Any slave children born in Christian households should be freed 'after a reasonable time of service [. . .], and during the time they have them, to teach them to read, and give them a Christian Education'.[221] Early on in the text, the authors give an incisive account of the Atlantic slave trade, thereby indicating that the conditions of the trade were familiar to North American settlers, or at least could have been familiar to them if they were concerned about slavery. It is worth citing a longer passage from the text in order to illustrate how sharply the paradox of freedom was already discussed in literature of the late seventeenth century:

> But what greater Oppression can there be inflicted upon our Fellow Creatures, than is inflicted on the poor Negroes! they being brought from their own Country against their Wills, some of them being stollen, others taken for payment of Debt owing by their Parents, and others taken Captive in War, and sold to Merchants, who bring them to the *American* Plantations, and sell them for Bond-Slaves to them that will give most for them; the Husband from the Wife, and the Children from the Parents; and many that buy them do exceedingly afflict them and oppress them, not only by continual hard Labour, but by cruel Whippings; and other cruel Punishments, and by short allowance of Food, some Planters in *Barbadoes* and *Jamaica*, 'tis

said, keeping one hundred of them, and some more, and some less, and giving them hardly any thing more than they raise on a little piece of Ground appointed them, on which they work for themselves the seventh dayes of the Week in the after-noon, and on the first days, to raise their own Provisions, to wit, Corn and Potatoes, and other Roots, &c. the remainder of their time being spent in their Masters service; which doubtless is far worse usage than is practiced by the *Turks* and *Moors* upon their Slaves.[222]

The description of the geographical details of the Atlantic slave trade – from 'their own Country' to North American colonies to Barbados and Jamaica – together with the phrase ''tis said' suggest that no special insider knowledge was needed in order to be aware of the violence inflicted upon slaves in the Atlantic.[223] The passage relates that there are 'cruel Whippings; and other cruel Punishments', and that enslaved labourers are not only subdued 'by short allowance of Food' but also by the separation of 'the Husband from the Wife, and the Children from the Parents'. The inhumaneness of the Atlantic slave trade comes out in the family image, as well as in the detailed depiction of bodily pain and food shortages. The authors of *An Exhortation* declare these malpractices to be contrary to Christian ideals, thereby pointing to the bigotry of the official discourses of equality, liberty and peacefulness in the Middle Colonies. They offer an early comment on the race myth of Atlantic liberty and criticise the paradoxes underlying it.

Yet, if *An Exhortation* contributes to the antislavery debate of the late seventeenth century, it also indicates the prevalence of slavery in the Atlantic at the time. Philippe Rosenberg reminds us that *An Exhortation* attests to the prevalence of slavery in the Middle Colonies because it is authored as 'a reactive process' to the widespread 'cruelty and the ethical conditions under which servants labored' in the colonies.[224] Following this argument, *An Exhortation* could only become such an outspoken document against slavery because the idea of slavery was part of colonial life and also of Quaker life. Otherwise, the text would not be addressed '*to Friends*': that is, to members of the Society of Friends, as the full title *An Exhortation & Caution to Friends Concerning Buying or Keeping of Negroes* states. Rosenberg's argument aligns with the ideas of reader-response criticism,[225] especially with Wolfgang Iser's concept of the implied reader.[226] According to Iser, every text must be read in relation to the implied reader, who influences not only the reception but the very act of writing the text. Because an author writes a work with a certain readership in mind, the implied reader determines the text from its very beginning. Reading *An Exhortation* in this light, it is possible to interpret it as evidence of the prevalence of enslaved labour among Quakers in the Middle Colonies. Accordingly, the call to end slavery in *An Exhortation* depends on the implied readers: in this case, the Quakers to which the text is addressed. If no Quakers participated in slavery, *An Exhortation* would not need to address them specifically in its title. The colonists' awareness of, and/or participation in, the Atlantic slave trade emphasises once more the fundamental paradoxes of the colonial imaginary. On the one hand, Scottish settlers praise East New Jersey for its narrative of liberty and the freedom from physical drudgery and oppression. On the other hand, some settlers seem to have participated in a system that took away the liberty, physical well-being and often the lives of slaves and other enforced labourers. Landsman notes that there is 'a considerable irony in that situation',[227] which *An Exhortation* sets out to expose. Coming back to Mannheim's *Ideology and Utopia* (1936) and Ricœur's *Lectures on Ideology and Utopia*, it is possible to offer a structural reading of this irony. Narratives of the Scottish Atlantic are shaped by the dichotomous relationship between possession and dispossession, which is one of the central paradoxes of the colonial utopian tradition. Like other utopias, colonial utopias try to replace one power structure with another. By trying to break out of oppressive systems at home, settlers frequently participated more or less forcefully in the creation of new oppressive systems abroad. Atlantic colonialism is no exception to this rule. Slavery, indigenous exploitation, the creation of spatial borders and the struggle over religious authority are part and parcel of the hierarchical relationships established in the 1680s Atlantic. Colonial utopias did not deinstitutionalise social hierarchies. Rather, they added categories of race, culture, material possessions, religion and land acquisition to the power struggles that have shaped the Atlantic ever since.

Notes

1. Kumar, *Utopianism* 5.
2. Bunyan, *The Pilgrim's Progress* 17.
3. Linebaugh and Rediker, *The Many-Headed Hydra* 97–8.
4. Appelbaum, *Literature and Utopian Politics* 78.
5. Winthrop, 'A Model' 33.
6. Dobson, *Scottish Emigration* 5, 55; Graham, *Colonists from Scotland* 11.
7. Gilroy, *Black Atlantic* 41–71.

8. Gilroy, *Black Atlantic* 48–9.
9. For example, Devine, *Recovering Scotland's Slavery Past*; Morris, *Scotland and the Caribbean*; Whyte, *Scotland and the Abolition of Black Slavery*; Whyte, *Send Back the Money!*
10. The play is now commonly dated to 1691, but the published source from 1766 dates it to 1692.
11. Wells, '"A New Toot"' 57.
12. Wells, '"A New Toot"' 57.
13. For example, Cameron, 'Theatre in Scotland' 191–205; Wells, '"A New Toot"' 57–69.
14. Wells, '"A New Toot"' 58.
15. Nussbaum, 'The Theatre of Empire' 71.
16. Findlay, 'Performances and Plays' 260.
17. Wormald, 'Confidence and Perplexity' 147.
18. MacQueen, *The Phanaticks* xxix.
19. Sydserf, *Tarugo's Wiles* 11.
20. Sydserf, *Tarugo's Wiles* 11; italics in original.
21. Sydserf, *Tarugo's Wiles* 11–12; italics in original.
22. Neville, *The Isle of Pines* 187–212.
23. Sydserf, *Tarugo's Wiles* 22–3; italics in original.
24. Sydserf, *Tarugo's Wiles* 31–2.
25. Wells, '"A New Toot"' 65.
26. Ellis, *Eighteenth-Century Coffee-House Culture*. Vol. 1.
27. Ellis, *Eighteenth-Century Coffee-House Culture*. Vol. 1 xi.
28. Ellis, *Eighteenth-Century Coffee-House Culture*. Vol. 3.
29. Daunton and Halpern, 'Introduction' 1.
30. Jackson, *Restoration Scotland* 32.
31. Linebaugh and Rediker, *The Many-Headed Hydra* 110.
32. Linebaugh and Rediker, *The Many-Headed Hydra* 125; 158.
33. Sydserf, *Tarugo's Wiles* 14; italics in original.
34. Sydserf, *Tarugo's Wiles* 41; italics in original.
35. Gilroy, *Black Atlantic* 42.
36. *OED* Online. Available at: <https://www.oed.com/> (last accessed 3 August 2020).
37. Sydserf, *Tarugo's Wiles* 14; italics in original.
38. Spurr, *The Rhetoric of Empire* 22.
39. Nussbaum, 'The Theatre of Empire' 88.
40. Gilroy, *Black Atlantic* 16.
41. Wells, '"A New Toot"' 57–69.
42. MacQueen, *The Phanaticks* xiii–xiv.
43. Cameron, 'Theatre in Scotland' 194.
44. Wells, '"A New Toot"' 66.
45. MacQueen, *The Phanaticks* xii–xiii.
46. Cameron, 'Theatre in Scotland' 194.
47. Pitcairne, *The Assembly* 1.

48. Pitcairne, *The Assembly* 2.
49. MacQueen, *The Phanaticks* 93, note 17.
50. Pitcairne, *The Assembly* 1.
51. Pitcairne, *The Assembly* 33.
52. Pitcairne, *The Assembly* 33.
53. Withers, 'Emergent Nation' 146.
54. Glass, *The Scottish Nation* 22.
55. Devine and Roessner, 'Scots in the Atlantic Economy' 36–8; Macinnes, *Union and Empire* 164–5.
56. Macinnes, *Union and Empire* 164–5.
57. Worthington, *Scots in the Habsburg Service.*
58. Stevenson, *Union, Revolution and Religion.*
59. Macinnes, *Union and Empire*, 165–7.
60. Darwin, *Unfinished Empire* 99.
61. Darwin, *Unfinished Empire* 99.
62. Most sources are collected in Leaming and Spicer, *The Grants, Concessions, and Original Constitutions of the Province of New-Jersey.* Other sources are included in Scot, *The Model of the Government of the Province of East-New-Jersey.*
63. Davis, *Utopia* 9.
64. More, *Utopia* 50.
65. Greenblatt, *Renaissance Self-Fashioning* 40.
66. Winstanley, *The Law of Freedom* 80–9.
67. Leaming and Spicer, *The Grants* 252–62.
68. Leaming and Spicer, *The Grants* 252–62.
69. Davis, *Utopia* 9.
70. Leaming and Spicer, *The Grants* 162–5.
71. Veracini, *Settler Colonialism* 1–15.
72. Veracini, *Settler Colonialism* 4.
73. Gould, 'The Aesthetic Terrain' 48–65.
74. Gould, 'The Aesthetic Terrain' 53.
75. Gould, 'The Aesthetic Terrain' 53.
76. Drummond, *An Advertisement* 5.
77. Drummond, *An Advertisement* 5.
78. Drummond, *An Advertisement* 7; italics in original.
79. Drummond, *An Advertisement* 7; italics in original.
80. Scot, *The Model of the Government* 244; italics in original.
81. Drummond, *An Advertisement* 20; italics in original.
82. Drummond, *An Advertisement* 20; italics in original.
83. Drummond, *An Advertisement* 21; italics in original.
84. Drummond, *An Advertisement* 21; italics in original.
85. Drummond, *An Advertisement* 19.
86. Drummond, *An Advertisement* 19–20.
87. Frohock, *Heroes of Empire* 137.
88. Scot, *The Model of the Government* 205; italics in original.

89. Scot, *The Model of the Government* 206; italics in original.
90. Macinnes, *Union and Empire* 165.
91. Leaming and Spicer, *The Grants* 73; 141.
92. Veracini, *Settler Colonialism* 3.
93. Mignolo, *Local Histories* 51.
94. Hill, 'Introduction' 21.
95. Houston, *The Renaissance Utopia* 161; Kumar, *Utopianism* 65; Manuel and Manuel, *Utopian Thought* 336–66; Moylan, *Demand the Impossible* 5.
96. Winstanley, *The Law of Freedom* 17; italics in original.
97. Leaming and Spicer, *The Grants* 181.
98. Leaming and Spicer, *The Grants* 181–4.
99. Ashcroft, 'Critical Utopias' 413.
100. Scot, *The Model of the Government* 155; italics in original.
101. Scot, *The Model of the Government* 155; italics in original.
102. Scot, *The Model of the Government* 155–6; italics in original.
103. Scot, *The Model of the Government* 155–6; italics in original.
104. Scot, *The Model of the Government* 72; italics in original.
105. Landsman, *Crossroads* 42–51.
106. Thomas, *An Historical and Geographical Account* 1–55.
107. Landsman, *Crossroads* 42.
108. For example, Connell, 'Modes of Marginality' 41–53; Craig, *Out of History*; Gardiner, 'Interdisciplinarity After Davie' 24–38; Hechter, *Internal Colonialism*; Riach, *Representing Scotland*; Stroh, *(Post)Colonial Scotland?*.
109. Craig, *Out of History* 11.
110. Connell, 'Modes of Marginality' 47.
111. Dobson, *Scottish Emigration* 55; Macinnes, *Union and Empire* 152–3.
112. Macinnes, *Union and Empire* 152–4.
113. Linebaugh and Rediker, *The Many-Headed Hydra* 120.
114. Doyle, *Freedom's Empire* 21; Macinnes, *Union and Empire* 152–64.
115. Graham, *Colonists from Scotland* 13–14; Macinnes, *Union and Empire* 160–4.
116. Thomas, *An Historical and Geographical Account* no page.
117. Scot, *The Model of the Government* 43–4; italics in original.
118. Insh, *Scottish Colonial Schemes* 162.
119. Insh, *Scottish Colonial Schemes* 165.
120. Anderson, *Imagined Communities* 159; italics in original.
121. Landsman, *Crossroads* 46.
122. Landsman, *Scotland* 120.
123. Landsman, *Crossroads* 53.
124. Landsman, *Crossroads* 136.
125. Scot, *The Model of the Government* 251–4; italics in original.
126. Scot, *The Model of the Government* 252; italics in original.
127. Scot, *The Model of the Government* 252; italics in original.

128. Insh, *Scottish Colonial Schemes* 171–5.
129. Insh, *Scottish Colonial Schemes* 171–5.
130. Linebaugh and Rediker, *The Many-Headed Hydra* 158.
131. Linebaugh and Rediker, *The Many-Headed Hydra* 58–9.
132. Linebaugh and Rediker, *The Many-Headed Hydra* 332.
133. Linebaugh and Rediker, *The Many-Headed Hydra* 332; italics in original.
134. Drummond, *An Advertisement* 21.
135. Drummond, *An Advertisement* 21; italics in original.
136. Thomas, *An Historical and Geographical Account* 7; Leaming and Spicer, *The Grants* 400–1.
137. Leaming and Spicer, *The Grants* 103–38.
138. Leaming and Spicer, *The Grants* 258–9.
139. Drummond, *An Advertisement* 5; italics in original.
140. Leaming and Spicer, *The Grants* 95.
141. Scot, *The Model of the Government* 187.
142. Armitage, 'John Locke' 602–27.
143. Ashcraft, *Locke's Two Treatises* 22.
144. Frohock, *Heroes of Empire* 107–37.
145. Locke, *Second Treatise of Government* Chapter 5, Article 41.
146. Gilroy, *Darker than Blue* 57–8.
147. Frohock, *Heroes of Empire* 107.
148. Wolfe, *Settler Colonialism* 2.
149. Scot, *The Model of the Government* 21; italics in original.
150. Kidd, *British Identities* 9–72.
151. Wolfe, *Settler Colonialism* 35.
152. Thomas, *An Historical and Geographical Account* 2; italics in original.
153. Scot, *The Model of the Government* 12.
154. Hale, *The Primitive Origination* 182–5.
155. Scot, *The Model of the Government* 12; italics in original.
156. Scot, *The Model of the Government* 12; italics in original.
157. Scot, *The Model of the Government* 15–16; italics in original.
158. Scot, *The Model of the Government* 13–14; italics in original.
159. Scot, *The Model of the Government* 13; italics in original.
160. Scot, *The Model of the Government* 13; italics in original.
161. Kidd, *The Forging of Races* 121–202.
162. More, *Utopia* 86.
163. Bacon, *New Atlantis* 164.
164. Boesky, *Founding Fictions* 142–60.
165. Doyle, *Freedom's Empire* 3.
166. Scot, *A Brief Advertisement* no page; italics in original.
167. Scot, *A Brief Advertisement* no page; italics in original.
168. Leaming and Spicer, *The Grants* 162.
169. Leaming and Spicer, *The Grants* 162; italics in original.
170. Greenblatt, *The Swerve* 231–2.

171. Scot, *The Model of the Government* 103–4; italics in original; Also see the law concerning religion in Leaming and Spicer, *The Grants* 162.
172. Matthew 7: 12.
173. Landsman, *Crossroads* 37.
174. For an overview of the history of the Society of Friends, see Landsman, *Crossroads* 57–9.
175. Pomfret, *The Province* 120.
176. Dobson, *Scottish Emigration* 5, 55; Graham, *Colonists from Scotland* 11.
177. Insh, *Scottish Colonial Schemes* 147.
178. Scot, *The Model of the Government* 207.
179. Insh, *Scottish Colonial Schemes* 152.
180. Insh, *Scottish Colonial Schemes* 147–8.
181. Scot, *The Model of the Government* 77; italics in original.
182. Barclay, *A Catechism*.
183. Barclay, *An Apology*.
184. Pomfret, *The Province* 242.
185. Keith, *Help in Time of Need*.
186. Keith, *The Christian Faith*.
187. Keith, *An Account*.
188. Keith, *An Account* 15; italics in original.
189. Houston, *The Renaissance Utopia* 123.
190. Eliade, 'Paradise and Utopia' 262–3.
191. Linebaugh and Rediker, *The Many-Headed Hydra* 77.
192. See Chapter 3, pp. 81–91.
193. Dubois and Scott, 'Introduction' 1–6.
194. Gilroy, *Black Atlantic* 15.
195. Gilroy, *Black Atlantic* 49.
196. Scot, *The Model of the Government* 230; italics in original.
197. Scot, *The Model of the Government* 230; italics in original.
198. Scot, *The Model of the Government* 265; italics in original.
199. Scot, *The Model of the Government* 230; 265; italics in original.
200. Landsman, *Crossroads* 91–2.
201. Landsman, *Crossroads* 92.
202. Scot, *The Model of the Government* 216; italics in original.
203. Scot, *The Model of the Government* 216–17; italics in original.
204. Daunton and Halpern, 'Introduction' 5.
205. Lockhart, *A Further Account* 1; italics in original.
206. Scot, *The Model of the Government* 223–9; italics in original.
207. Scot, *The Model of the Government* 224; italics in original.
208. Doyle, *Freedom's Empire* 445.
209. Dubois and Scott, 'Introduction' 1.
210. Gerbner, 'Antislavery in Print' 565.
211. Fry, *The Scottish Empire* 25.
212. Gerbner, 'Antislavery in Print' 560–5.
213. Landsman, *Crossroads* 70.

214. Gerbner, 'Antislavery in Print' 560–5.
215. Keith et al., *An Exhortation* 2; italics in original. Cf. Matthew 7: 12.
216. Keith et al., *An Exhortation* 1.
217. Keith et al., *An Exhortation* 1; italics in original.
218. Hume, 'Of the Populousness of Ancient Nations' 385.
219. Keith et al., *An Exhortation* 2; italics in original.
220. Keith et al., *An Exhortation* 3.
221. Keith et al., *An Exhortation* 3.
222. Keith et al., *An Exhortation* 5; italics in original.
223. Keith et al., *An Exhortation* 5.
224. Rosenberg, 'Thomas Tryon' 640.
225. Iser, *The Act of Reading*.
226. Iser, *The Act of Reading*.
227. Landsman, *Crossroads* 92.

Chapter 4

Darien, the Golden Dream

John Keats's (1795–1821) 'On First Looking into Chapman's Homer' (1816) is perhaps the most celebrated rendering of Darien in Anglophone literature.[1] The final lines of the poem imagine the moment when Hernan Cortés (1485–1547), the Spanish explorer from the first phase of Spanish colonisation of the Americas, sees a summit at the Isthmus of Panama and realises that he and his people have discovered a world previously unknown to Europeans. Darien, in the literary universe of the poem, symbolises the moment of wonder, novelty and surprise that the Spanish explorers are said to have experienced when sighting land after months of travelling across the Atlantic. The lyrical I uses this moment of wonder to compare it with its own intellectual discovery of George Chapman's English rendering of Homer. The latter is said to be equally breath-taking, equally opening up new worlds to the lyrical I, as the first glimpse of the Americas was to Cortés:

> Much have I travelled in the realms of gold,
> And many goodly states and kingdoms seen;
> Round many western islands have I been
> Which bards in fealty to Apollo hold.
> Oft of one wide expanse had I been told
> That deep-browed Homer ruled as his demesne;
> Yet did I never breathe its pure serene
> Till I heard Chapman speak out loud and bold:
> Then felt I like some watcher of the skies
> When a new planet swims into his ken;
> Or like stout Cortez when with eagle eyes
> He stared at the Pacific—and all his men
> Looked at each other with a wild surmise—
> Silent, upon a peak in Darien.[2]

Keats's poem has a special relevance for the following chapter because it links narratives of knowledge and innovation to the time when Spain started its settlement at Santa María la Antigua del Darién at the Isthmus of Panama. With its iambic pentameter and vivid body imagery, the sonnet potently associates narratives of European expansion with material possessions, scientific explorations and intellectual discoveries. Although the poem may not directly refer to Scotland's Darien venture – though perhaps indirectly through the word 'ken', the Scottish word for 'to know' or 'discover by sight' – the golden imagery of Darien in Keats's poem is highly indicative of the idealistic vision of European empire-building, of which Darien is representative here. Scottish authors from the late seventeenth century significantly helped to foster this vision of Darien as a profitable and progressive space, and as a site that is customarily associated with images of gold.

Scottish ships entered the Gulf of Darien in 1698 and 1699 with the intention of creating a permanent Scottish settlement there. Literature from this period indicates how intent some Scottish individuals were on creating a trading hub at this strategically important place in order to set up a global Scottish empire. A robust body of historical scholarship exists on Scotland's colonial undertaking at Darien.[3] Literary approaches to the colonial undertaking, though, are uncommon. Leith Davis's work on Darien as a *topos* in literature relating to the Union of Parliaments remains one of the few analyses of the rhetorical functioning of the undertaking and its effects on larger literary developments in Great Britain.[4] What the following pages hope to add to research on Darien is a focus on the intertwinement of ideological and aesthetic practices in literature written about the Darien scheme from the seventeenth century to the present. As in previous chapters, there is a dichotomy between narratives of possession versus dispossession that structures Scottish texts about Darien. The emphasis on material desires produces an entire mythology of 'Golden Darien', just as the emphasis on Scotland's dispossession at home produces an entire mythology around Scotland's allegedly benign role in the Atlantic struggle for power. By the end of the seventeenth century, these two intersecting narratives have turned into fully-fledged myths of Scottish colonial literature.

Darien's literary archive includes poems, songs, satires, life writing, political writing and, in later centuries, dramas and novels. There is a rich tradition of Anglophone writing about Darien, which provides a means for investigating both past and present understandings of Scotland's position in the Atlantic. Not everyone in the 1690s was involved in the Darien scheme, of course. Similar to the arguments made earlier, it is useful to keep in mind Karin Bowie's contention that what scholars today sometimes perceive as 'public opinion' in Scotland around 1700 is mainly the product of 'those Scots with access to print, manuscript and oral information flowing from Edinburgh to the localities; and it was not necessarily homogenous'.[5] The views of those who were not part of these networks frequently, if not habitually, remain unrecorded. The following discussion is conscious of the fact that literature about Darien was written by an educated, affluent elite that had access to print. Some ballads may reflect more popular opinions about Darien but, on the whole, Darien's literary tradition of the late seventeenth and early eighteenth centuries was forged by the wealthier, educated classes.

A timeline of the Darien scheme helps to give a chronological overview of the undertaking and serves as reference point for the following discussion (Table 4.1).

Table 4.1 The Darien Scheme and the Union of Parliaments

- to present	Indigenous peoples inhabit Central America and the Isthmus of Panama, including the Tule – also called Kuna or Cuna – with whom Scottish settlers are likely to have made contact
c. 1510	Spain claims Isthmus of Panama for Spanish empire New Cartagena
1695	Lionel Wafer's *A New Voyage and Description of the Isthmus of America* published
1695	Company of Scotland Trading to Africa and the Indies founded by Act of the Parliament of Scotland; idea of a Scottish colony at the Isthmus of Panama propagated by Scottish businessman William Paterson
16 Dec. 1695	William III expresses dissatisfaction with plan to found Scottish colony at Darien despite supporting it earlier
March 1696	William Paterson starts raising money for Darien venture
1698	Lionel Wafer hired as advisor for the Company of Scotland
July 1698	First Scottish expedition sails to Darien, consisting of five ships named *Saint Andrew, Caledonia, Unicorn, Dolphin* and *Endeavour*; approx. 1,200 people are on board, including Paterson and his wife
2 Nov. 1698	First expedition arrives at Darien, which is renamed Caledonia; Scots build settlement of New Edinburgh and Fort St Andrew
March 1699	Spanish viceroy condemns Scottish settlers at Darien
May 1699	William III puts embargo on trade with Scots at Darien
July 1699	Colony abandoned by members of first expedition

Aug. 1699	Relief ships *Olive Branch* and *Hopeful Beginning* arrive at Darien with 300 settlers and provisions; they find a deserted colony
Aug. 1699	Second expedition leaves for Darien with approx. 1,000 people, not knowing that first expedition and relief ship settlers had left the colony
Sept. 1699	Thomas Drummond returns to Darien and tries to re-erect settlement
30 Nov. 1699	Second expedition arrives at Darien, consisting of four ships named *Rising Sun, Hope of Bo'ness, Hope* and *Duke of Hamilton*; settlers find abandoned colony and many leave
February 1700	Battle at Tubuganti, where Scottish settlers defeat Spanish
March 1700	Spanish forces close in on Fort St Andrew
March 1700	Peace negotiations with Spain; Scots surrender and sign peace treaty
1701–1707	Company of Scotland continues with minor enterprises around globe
1701–1702	Paterson proposes union of England and Scotland to William III
1705	Talks between England and Scotland concerning union
1706	English Parliament passes the Act of Union
16 Jan. 1707	Scottish Parliament passes the Act of Union; Article 15 grants £398,085 to Scotland, partly to reimburse investors of Darien scheme; money becomes known as Equivalent
1 May 1707	Union of Parliaments
5 Aug. 1707	Equivalent arrives in Scotland, causing unrest

Literary Darien, 1701–2010

More than any other Scottish colonial venture of the seventeenth century, the Darien scheme has become a prevalent trope in British literature. A large body of poetry, ballads, speeches, songs and life writing, as well as drama and prose fiction, has been written about Scotland's attempt to establish a colony at the Isthmus of Panama. A number of these texts take the colonial undertaking as their main theme, and an even larger number of works comment on it as part of another narrative. The growing influence of the print publication market in the late seventeenth and early eighteenth centuries helped to turn Darien into the most widely received, and most hotly debated, colonial undertaking of the Scots before 1707. The 'exponential growth' of print publications, as well as the increasing 'marketplace for print', not only led to a much larger readership for writings about Darien and the Union of Parliaments, but, for the first time, authors wrote with an 'awareness of the power of print'[6] and frequently used this to pursue their own or other people's goals. The following chapter develops the argument that Darien was, more often than not, put into the service of larger political developments in the early eighteenth century and also in later centuries. It does so by offering a chronological overview of the literary history of Darien in the Anglophone context and a close reading of the larger narratives in which works about Darien participate. The starting point of the overview in this subchapter is after the venture officially ended in 1701. Texts written before and during the settlement period are the subject of the following subchapters.

Before coming to the texts, a genre-oriented approach helps to identify some of the larger tendencies in how Darien has been represented in literature since the early eighteenth century. In the eighteenth century, ballads frequently adopted an idealistic mode of representation. Those that featured Darien portrayed it as a largely benevolent undertaking where Scotsmen and women took up the role of noble and peaceful settlers. Satires of the same period emphasised the distinctly non-utopian outcome of Scotland's Darien venture and depicted it as an example of Scotland's general lack of progress or success. The nineteenth century saw the rise of the historical romance and, with it, the rise of romantic outlooks on Darien as a noble but eventually doomed undertaking. Twentieth- and twenty-first-century literary texts followed a larger trend towards revisionist approaches to history and focused on – sometimes fictional, sometimes non-fictional – participants of the Darien scheme in order to stress the multifaceted stories that are part of the larger collective history. Significantly, the split between utopian and dystopian narratives of Darien remained a core feature of most literary texts, and it may, indeed, be one of the reasons why the history of Darien still speaks to contemporary authors and audiences. A closer reading of Darien's literary history will help to make this point more fully and show the continuing vitality of Scotland's colonial history in Anglophone literature.

Around the time of the Union of Parliaments, politically active authors used Darien to advance their own partisan views.[7] This is particularly true of Scottish authors. Whereas pro-unionists around the turn of the eighteenth century advocated a parliamentary union, anti-unionists foresaw the loss of Scotland's independence and, with it, its power as an independent kingdom. Darien figures prominently in Jacobite texts of the eighteenth century. Murray Pittock has shown how, in the course of the eighteenth century, 'anti-Union discourse' helped to give rise to a growing tradition of Jacobite literature in eighteenth-century Scotland.[8] As the following examples illustrate, Darien turns into a literary trope that reinforces ideas of Scottish heroism, independence and nobility. In this way, it buttresses the political ideology underlying the Jacobite tradition. The anonymous song *The True Scots Mens Lament for the Loss of the Rights of their Ancient Kingdom* (1718), published in Edinburgh by John Reid, is a case in point. It refers to Darien as one incident in a long history of English aggression against Scotland. The lyrical I asks the audience to

> look back
> to ruin'd Darien:
> I'm hopeful then you will remorse,
> on former Ill that's done.[9]

Other references in the poem are to 'Edward Lang-shank's Reign', as well as, more positively, to William Wallace and Robert the Bruce. All of these figures, together with allusions to Darien, help to strengthen the poem's point that Scotland lost its liberty in 1707 and that the English are to blame for this. Darien is one of several historical tropes that function as emotionalising strategies in so far as they are linked to anti-English sentiments.[10] Scots, so the poem suggests, should never forget the story of 'Comtempt [sic] of Faith, Falshood, Deceit, / and Villany withal' that characterises English–Scottish relations.[11] The following excerpt from another anonymous song equally uses Darien as a sounding-board for an outlook on Anglo-Scottish relations that turns Scottish people into victims of English hostility:

> 'On Darien think, on dowie Glenco,
> 'On Murray, traitor! coward!
> 'On Cumberland's blood-blushing hands,
> 'And think on Charlie Stuart.[12]

Darien is lined up with people and events that symbolise treachery in general and English hostility in particular. The Massacre of Glencoe is among the events construed as an act of betrayal, together with the figure of John Murray of Broughton, who was originally a Jacobite but later turned King's evidence and subsequently became an embodiment of treason among Scottish Jacobites. Likewise, Darien stands for England's disloyal conduct towards Scotland and, in this way, shapes discourses of Scottish decency. With the help of the anaphora 'On', Darien becomes the verse's cornerstone for a distinctly Jacobite version of Anglo-Scottish history, in which the idea of English hostility forms the governing theme. As Pittock has demonstrated, this theme is often transhistorical. In works linked to Jacobitism, 'history as recurrence, myth, archetype and image is often the history sought by the defeated, whose linearity and incrementality have been exiled into colonialism or absorbed in a greater identity (as "British" history so often absorbs its peripheries)'.[13] The lines above cast Darien in the role of another timeless yet emotionally disturbing event. The dramatic language of the poem – exclamation marks mingle with imperatives and the alliteration 'blood-blushing hands' reinforces the poem's gory nature – bears out the political message behind the lines: Scotland's greatness rests, at least partially, on its passionate response towards English hostility. This is what makes Scotland superior. As a literary motif in Jacobite literature, Darien serves to preserve the ideal of the noble Scot at a time when Scotland was no longer an independent kingdom. It becomes one of a host of literary tropes symbolising English hostility versus Scottish goodness.

As generic counterparts to ballads, satires sprang up in the eighteenth century. Some satires caricatured the ideological parameters of Jacobitism and gestured towards the impossibility of simple explanations for the outcome of Darien and the Union of Parliaments. Robert Burns's (1759–96) poem 'Such a Parcel of Rogues in a Nation' opens up the complicated issue of responsibility for Scotland's loss of independence and suggests that blame lies with the Scottish, rather than the English. The poem reverses the theme of treachery and suggests that Scotland was betrayed by its own politicians, who sold the country's independence to England in order to be reimbursed for their losses at Darien. Each of the three stanzas ends with the lament 'Such a parcel of rogues in a nation', which refers not to English but to Scottish politicians.[14] The final lines introduce the image of 'English gold' as a metaphor for the Equivalent, which was assured to Scotland as part of the Acts of Union in order to reimburse Scots for their losses at Darien:

> O would, ere I had seen the day
> That Treason thus could sell us,
> My auld grey head had lien in clay,
> Wi' Bruce and loyal Wallace!
> But pith and power, till my last hour,
> I'll mak this declaration;
> We're bought and sold for English gold-
> Such a parcel of rogues in a nation![15]

Burns's poem alludes to Robert the Bruce and William Wallace as affirmative antitheses to eighteenth-century Scottish politicians. For

Burns, the Union of Parliaments may well constitute a turning point in Scotland's history, moving the country from a heroic past to a distinctly unheroic future. The difference between 'Such a Parcel of Rogues in a Nation' and Jacobite literature is that the causes for this unheroic future lie with Scottish politicians, not English officials. 'Such a Parcel of Rogues in a Nation' brings out the socio-political divides involved in the Union of Parliaments and takes side with all those who did not benefit from the Equivalent. It is notable that Burns's poem is one of the few texts in the corpus of Scottish colonial literature that fuses Scots with English. It adds a rare sense of linguistic variety to the archive of Scottish Atlantic writing. The use of dialect may outwardly emphasise the dichotomy of Scottish versus English perspectives on Darien. At a second glance, though, Burns's use of Scots seems to criticise his own countrymen and women because it emphasises the internal divisions among Scotland's population with regard to the Union of Parliaments. 'Such a Parcel of Rogues in a Nation' shatters the idea of a homogenous Scottish nation that is united against English hostility. It shows how elite networks run across regional or cultural lines in early eighteenth-century Scotland and Great Britain.

English authors of the eighteenth century, too, satirise the Darien scheme. William Burnaby's 1701 comedy *The Ladies Visiting-Day. A Comedy. As it Was Acted at the Theatre in Lincolns-Inn-Fields, by His Majesties Servants. With the Addition of a New Scene. By the Author of The Reformed Wife* includes a reference to Darien that shows how the venture had become a laughing stock in early eighteenth-century England. The play was first performed in London at Lincoln's Inn Fields and probably aimed at a largely English audience. In one scene, *The Ladies Visiting-Day* ridicules Darien as an undertaking that was meant to turn Scotland into a modern country but failed to do so. The reference is included in an exchange between the characters Lady Lovetoy and Sir Testy, who teases Lady Lovetoy about her preference for foreign fashion and food. Sir Testy asks her 'why, Madam, would not right *English*, or right *Scotch* do as well?', to which Lady Lovetoy replies: 'Ha, ha, ha! Nay, as to the *Scotch*, I don't know how they may be improv'd since they liv'd at *Darien*: But before that *I* wou'd no more ha' Traded with their Country, than ha' Travail'd thither.'[16] The passage mocks the idea of Scotland as a progressive and profitable country. It uses fashion as a symbol of modernity, as well as economic power, to make its point. The laughter of Lady Lovetoy shows that Scotland's position in inner British and global politics has become a matter of ridicule in early eighteenth-century England. The Darien scheme appears to have been known well enough in England around

1701 for the author to be able to capitalise on it and turn it into a source of satire.

Moving from the eighteenth to the nineteenth century, literary representations of Darien become scarcer, but not extinct. As Ian Watt notes, Sir Walter Scott mentions Scotland's Darien scheme in his *Tales of a Grandfather*, where Scott refers to 'the disastrous history of the Darien colony' and uses it to criticise the 'tendency to daring speculation, which rests at the bottom of the coldness and caution of the Scottish character'.[17] The comment links Scottish colonialism to a certain kind of idealism that is non-pragmatic, irrational and, according to Scott, typically Scottish. A more positive nineteenth-century image of the Darien venture can be found in Eliot Warburton's trilogy *Darien; Or, The Merchant Prince. A Historical Romance* (1852). The novels are powerful examples of how historical romance claims Darien as part of Scotland's noble, if unfortunate, history. The three volumes tell the story of the Spanish merchant Alvarez and William Paterson, also known as Tinwald, whose fates intertwine in the course of the novels. In this way, the novel emphasises the interconnectedness of the seventeenth-century Atlantic world, with the Scottish banker and businessman Paterson at its centre. Some background on the historical figure of William Paterson helps to pave the way for a reading of Warburton's trilogy as a romantic take on the Scottish past that fits into the larger Scottish revival in the Victorian period.

William Paterson (1658–1719) was a banker and financier; he was a leading figure in the 1694 founding of the Bank of England and, in 1695, in the founding of the Bank of Scotland. He is one of the central figures who invented the narrative of Darien's riches and propagated the idea that Darien could propel Scotland into an age of modernity. Paterson was born in Tinwald, in what nowadays comes under the council of Dumfries and Galloway, in April 1658. He spent some time travelling, probably to the West Indies and other Atlantic locations,[18] though the fact that the Company of Scotland later hired Wafer to gain first-hand information about the Isthmus of Panama makes it unlikely that Paterson had extensive knowledge of Darien itself. Before returning to Scotland, Paterson repeatedly tried to convince political leaders elsewhere to create a colony at the Isthmus of Panama. Paterson first approached James VII and II about establishing a trading post at Darien and, after James declined, went to the Elector of the German state of Brandenburg, while also being in contact with the Prince of Orange on the question of overseas colonisation.[19] Such attempts to enter into alliances with other European powers are nothing unusual in the history of the Atlantic.

Gilroy's *The Black Atlantic* makes a powerful case against purely nationalistic understandings of European colonialism when arguing that the emergence of the 'black Atlantic' was, by and large, an 'intercultural and transnational formation'.[20] Scotland was not at the centre of colonial networks in the seventeenth century, but some Scottish individuals, including Paterson, did try to enter the power circles of Atlantic trade. Other Scottish migrants worked and lived in the Dutch Republic, where they were 'involved in social networks in Holland which covered trade, seamanship, medicine and religious life, and which maintained powerful links with Scotland'.[21] That such international networks and trade co-operation established by Scottish migrants living in continental Europe did not lead to a more systematic approach to the colonisation of Darien in the late seventeenth century is 'surprising' to some scholars today.[22] Elspeth Jajdelska argues that a 'utilitarian' approach towards knowledge among Scots in the Netherlands may have prevented them from sharing important information with fellow Scotsmen and women at home that would have been useful for colonists in the long run, such as the kinds of provision to take or the trade items that were in high demand at the time.[23] As will be seen later, seventeenth- and eighteenth-century works about Darien frequently pick up on this question of poor planning and cast Paterson as a figure who personifies the split between the desires and the realities of Scottish colonialism in the late seventeenth century.

After Paterson returned to Scotland in 1695, his idea of a trading site at Darien found supporters among the board members of the Company of Scotland. *Darien; Or, The Merchant Prince* draws on this story of Paterson and turns it into a historical romance. As to be expected with a nineteenth-century romance, a number of love stories are woven into the fabric of the text, which abounds with cultural and gender stereotypes that give the romance the characteristic flavour of passion, exoticism, adventure and European supremacy. For the purposes of this chapter, Warburton's trilogy is particularly interesting for its representation of Darien as a founding moment of post-1707 Scotland. Through its emphasis on the figure of Paterson, *Darien; Or, The Merchant Prince* turns the story of the undertaking into a myth of heroism and moral superiority but also into a story of a noble failure. As such, the trilogy resonates strongly with Scotland's role in Victorian Britain as an idealised, yet marginalised, part of the UK. To construe Darien as a founding myth of Scotland after the Union of Parliaments is possible in Warburton's trilogy because the novels do not formulate any desire to change the status quo.

Instead, the novels reinforce Scotland's professed nobility, as well as its purported marginality after the Union of Parliaments. The argument comes out most clearly when taking a look at the novels' depiction of how Darien ended.

Volume III of *Darien; Or, The Merchant Prince* turns the premature end of the Darien scheme into a foundational moment of post-Union Scotland. The language is pervasively nostalgic, with tropes of nobility, passionate love and moral superiority staking out the literal and symbolic parameters of romance as a popular genre. Darien may have been an unsuccessful enterprise in the eyes of most seventeenth- and eighteenth-century commentators, but in a genre characterised by happy endings, it is a necessity to give the undertaking's termination a positive twist. Warburton's solution is to link the story of Darien to a new kind of Scottish creation myth, one that is based on suffering and sorrow. The novel stresses the traumatic impact of the undertaking on the larger Scottish population and embellishes the moment with emotional urgency: 'The fatal truth concerning Darien soon spread throughout Scotland. The nation reeled under the blow. Every family suffered in the great calamity.'[24] Darien constitutes a collective trauma for Scotland's population in Warburton's novels, which rhetorically fuse physical suffering with emotional grief. The reason for the suffering turns into a founding moment of the survivors' identity. After Darien, Scotland is more united than before because all survivors share in the agony of its outcome, or so is the message of Warburton's trilogy. The idea of suffering is part of the romance narrative, and the Scottish people become collectively associated with victimhood. King William's embargo is part of the explanation for the end of the colonial venture, though the novel is careful not to enter serious political debates by focusing on individual woes and romantic reminiscences rather than on Anglo-Scottish relations.[25] The narrator laments that once 'Darien was abandoned, [. . .] the noblest scheme of colonization that was ever planned' came to an end.[26] Rhetorical idealisation functions as a strategy to reduce the potential of an actual revolt. It is possible to romanticise Darien in the nineteenth century because Scottish colonial endeavours were no longer of any danger to those in power. Instead, they became a matter of myth. *Darien; Or, The Merchant Prince* turns the colony's end into a foundation myth for post-1707 Scotland, a rhetorical strategy on which a later section of this chapter further elaborates. In Warburton's novel, Darien's end serves as an emblem for the inauguration of Scotland's new role in the larger UK, which is portrayed as one of nobility, loss and victimisation. Such an image fits the larger cultural conception of Scotland in nineteenth-century Britain. While Queen Victoria contributed to a rehabilitation of Scotland's inner British political status after the Jacobite movement,[27] Warburton's depiction of the Darien scheme contributes to the fashioning of Scotland's cultural identity as a romantic, as well as a nostalgic, space. Scottish colonists may be noble but, essentially, they were less successful than the English in their Atlantic pursuits. After the Union of Parliaments, Scotland became a powerful part of the British Empire and Scottish individuals and groups became involved in all kinds of colonial activities around the globe.[28] Such comparisons between pre-1707 and post-1707 colonial undertakings by Scottish settlers and colonists are not made explicit in Warburton's novel. Yet, they are implicit in their depiction of a noble yet ultimately doomed Scottish colony at Darien, which can be celebrated precisely because it was no threat to established power constellations in Victorian Britain. The British Empire was still at its height at the time of the trilogy's publication in 1852. A romantic image of empire-building is indicative of the period's prevalently optimistic colonial ideology, just as the depiction of Scottish settlers at Darien as brave but ineffective colonisers prior to 1707 is indicative of the inner British power dynamics of the mid-nineteenth century.

Almost a century and a half passed between Warburton's *Darien* trilogy from the 1850s and the revival of Darien as a literary theme around 2000. In that year, Douglas Galbraith (born 1965) published his novel *The Rising Sun* (2000), followed by David Nicol's *The Fundamentals of New Caledonia* (2003) and Alistair Beaton's (born 1947) drama *Caledonia* (2010). All three texts offer a revisionist approach to the Darien scheme, which both speaks to and participates in the movement towards critical re-examinations of historical events in the early 2000s. By focusing on stories of individual people, all three texts try to capture the individual dreams and desires that spurred Scotland's colonial undertaking in the 1690s, while simultaneously siting the domestic situation in transnational networks of the seventeenth-century Atlantic. Darien is not a linear design with a clear ideological, political or economic outcome in Galbraith's, Nicol's or Beaton's texts. Instead, it is an enterprise driven by the hopes and fears of the Scottish people, some of whom were wealthy and educated while others were not. This emphasis on the hopes and fears of the people resonates potently with the utopian dimension of Darien, which emerges both in the original sources and in twenty-first-century literary works about Darien.

The Rising Sun by Galbraith uses the name of one of the vessels that left Scotland in 1699 to sketch the story of Scotland's high ambitions and equally high losses at Darien. It narrates the story through the eyes of Roderick Mackenzie, a young Scot who is hired to supervise the ship's cargo and to manage, together with a figure named William Paterson, the expedition's provisions. Similar to the figure of Paterson, Mackenzie's name harkens back to a histori- cal figure: Roderick Mackenzie, the Secretary of the Company of Scotland.[29] In *The Rising Sun*, Mackenzie tells his story in the form of a journal that spans the phases prior to, during and after the settlement of Darien. In this way, Galbraith's novel captures the changing moods of optimism and pessimism that characterise nar- ratives about Darien. It begins with the phase of initial excitement, which portrays Atlantic colonialism as a solution to the suffocating forces of poverty, harvest failures, disease and unemployment in late seventeenth-century Scotland. The novel offers readers insight into what has been called the 'Ill Years' of the 1690s: 'Beginning at a national level following the deficient harvest of 1695, the country experienced multiple harvest failures, high grain prices, a reduc- tion in pastoral flocks and herds, increased mortality, economic difficulties and social dislocation.'[30] *The Rising Sun*'s protagonist, Mackenzie, is one of those suffering from these conditions. He joins the expedition after he finds no other work in 1690s Scotland. Mackenzie writes in his journal how 'the Company had become the whole hope and faith of the nation'.[31] Galbraith's novel cap- tures the utopian nature of the Darien venture in passages like this, where domestic hardships lead people to believe in finding the solu- tion to their problems by going abroad. In another scene, the novel narrates how people stand in long rows to buy shares in the under- taking. Idealism is the governing mood in the beginning stages of the Darien scheme and an attribute of its utopian quality.

One of the most powerful passages in which *The Rising Sun* ren- ders the initial idealism about Darien is when the ships that were manufactured for the second expedition arrive in the Firth of Forth. People from all over Scotland have come to look at them. The follow- ing scene describes the moment when the flagship of the expedition, *The Rising Sun*, appears on the horizon. Just as the metaphorical name of the flagship expresses the vision of newness and light, so the jubilation of the people signifies their hope that Darien will propel Scotland into a new era of glory:

> I don't believe I shall ever live to see a more glorious sight. I swear she was proud: she swaggered over the sea to us, knowing her own magnificence. [. . .] I cried out when I saw her: 'Yes!' I shouted. 'Yes! There she is! There!'[32]

Here, as elsewhere in the text, the ship with its symbolic name serves as the material embodiment of Scotland's desire for change. In the course of the novel, such images of hope are juxtaposed with images of death and despair, which offer a counterpoint to the idealism of the initial undertaking. To show how this structural contrast works, it is useful to compare the scene above with a passage that describes the situation of the settlers a few months after their arrival at Darien. Scottish settlers have built a settlement called New Edinburgh but their life in the colony turns out to be much more difficult than imagined. Neither the narrator nor anybody else in the novel continues to be enthusiastic about the colony. The characters' only hope is for survival in the tropical climate:

> The heat has become more intense, but it is easier to find shade than it ever was to avoid the endless dousing we have had since last November. Vapour rises from every part of New Edinburgh's sodden and miserable plot, returning a small part of this watery bombardment to where it came from. As it goes, the universal mud thickens and crusts. [. . .] The air is thick with the smell of canvas and mould.[33]

The smell of 'mould' highlights in olfactory terms how the settlers come to experience the colony as foul.[34] Such imagery serves as an antithesis to the earlier trope of hope and idealism that informs the novel's representation of the venture's beginning. *The Rising Sun* brings out the discrepancy between the initial idealism of the colonists and the later despair of the settlers.

The Rising Sun ends with a scene that connects Darien's end with the Union of Parliaments. Mackenzie is one of those who survive the venture and, after physically recovering from a tropical disease he caught during the expedition, witnesses how Scottish politicians agree to enter the Union of Parliaments with England in exchange for money. Mackenzie talks to a friend about Scotland's agreement to the Treaty of Union in a narrated dialogue that brings out the different perspectives:

> I tried to keep silent as long as I could, listening to how everyone involved in the Company had been a fool, how its failure had been predictable to the very last detail, how the country had played the Prodigal Son and now, having thrown its money in the sea, was whining all the more for being welcomed back, for having all its losses restored by its kindly southern uncle. This was too much and I told him angrily that the only place Scotland was being welcomed into was the house of a thief, permanently indentured to earning back

what had been taken from her. He laughed at this, called it poetry and asked me if I really believed it. Because I didn't, I shouted at him, 'I've lost my country!'[35]

The debate with the friend works as a means of showing how divided Scotland was over the Union of Parliaments. Stylistically, the immediate revocation of Mackenzie's final assertion suggests that it was difficult for individuals to know what to think about Scotland's loss of independence. Through the interplay of different viewpoints, *The Rising Sun* offers a historiographical perspective on Darien that is supported through the use of reported speech, dialogic narration and historical names and records. On a literary level, such narrative construction aligns with the emphasis in critical empire studies on re-examining linear or monolithic theories of European expansion. According to Darwin,

> Empires were not made by faceless committees making grand calculations, nor by the 'irresistible' pressures of economics or ideology. They had to be made by men (and women) whose actions were shaped by motives and morals no less confused and demanding than those that govern us now.[36]

Galbraith's version of Darien is about such individual hopes and dreams but also about the losses that follow the dreams. It offers a version of Scotland's history that complicates any straightforward rendering of the colonial scheme. The multiple perspectives in the novel remind readers of the heterogenous nature of empire-building and emphasise the changing roles that Scotland inhabited in the Atlantic.

Nicol's *The Fundamentals of New Caledonia* (2003) similarly partakes in a revisionist rendering of Darien, which it mainly achieves through its temporal and linguistic design. The author's decision to write the novel in historical Scots reinforces the particularly Scottish nature of the Darien scheme, which is narrated in the rhythm, syntax and idiom of early modern Scots. The linguistic choice creates a distancing effect that makes readers aware of their own temporal and cultural remoteness from the historical events. The novel uses a dual time scheme to narrate both a twenty-first-century perspective on Darien and a seventeenth-century one. It begins with a fictional preface that narrates how an earlier text about Darien is 'discovered during renovations of a certain building in Edinburgh's Royal Mile'.[37] The fusion of contemporary and historical perspectives continues through the novel's time-travelling episode. A young man walks into a job centre in Edinburgh in 1992 and is recruited for the Darien scheme by two historical figures from the seventeenth century, Doctor McKenzie and Herries.[38] The protagonist, Billy Budd, is time-warped into 1690s Scotland. He is hired as assistant to the surgeon McKenzie, the same figure who was the protagonist in Galbraith's novel. Together with McKenzie, Billy Budd accompanies the first expedition to Darien in 1698 on board the *Unicorn*. Similar to Galbraith's *The Rising Sun*, *The Fundamentals* alludes to the job scarcity in late seventeenth-century Scotland and the allure that the prospect of an overseas settlement must have held for young Scotsmen like Billy. At the same time, Billy's first-person narrative shows how the colonial undertaking turns from a utopian ideal into a synonym for death, disease and disappointment. Billy tells about the colonists' experiences at the Isthmus of Panama, especially their difficulties of coping with the tropical climate. While he himself is allowed to stay on board because he is responsible for medical supplies, he pities those who have to live on the mainland:

> The planters hae noght but palmetto thack tae protect thaim fra the warst effects o this climate. It is especially horrid att this season. The sun is unbearably hott, the air blustery and damp. The lift is rarely cloudless, but perpetually full o thunder and lightning. Heiven seems tae gush like a waterfall ilka day, making a mire o the grund aneath our feet. This torrent never lats up, sauf in the forenight. Whairu-pon the air becomes sae fetid and humid, and thick wi insects and poysonous vapours, that nae relief can be gotten ava. The planters are droukit and flee blawn als beasts in a field. It seems they maun bide in purgatory, als far fra the paradise they war led tae expect in this wretched land, as they are twined fra their ain countrie.[39]

The final sentence uses the metaphorical opposition between paradise and purgatory to emphasise the contrast between the settlers' expectations and the realities on site. Similar to Galbraith's *The Rising Sun*, *The Fundamentals* stresses the physical realities of settler life. Nicol's novel opens up a socio-economic perspective on the undertaking by showing how different groups of settlers are subject to different living standards and how this leads to internal conflict. The rest of the narrative borrows from the genre of historical romance – though without the nostalgia – by featuring a love affair between Billy and his shipmate Henri, who is really Henrietta. Although *The Fundamentals* ends almost paradoxically on the hopeful note of a baby born in the colony, the novel is noteworthy for its depiction of the dystopian sides of settler life and its revisionist take on rank, as well as on the physical realities of Scottish Atlantic colonialism in the 1690s.

Beaton's play *Caledonia* (2010) is the most recent work to narrate the story of Darien for contemporary audiences. The play had its premiere at the Edinburgh International Festival in 2010 and has since been published by Methuen Drama. Beaton's preface to the text makes it clear why the author considers the historical event to be of ongoing relevance for audiences today. It also indicates the kind of narrative the drama tries to tell: '*Caledonia* is a story of greed, folly and mass delusion. In that respect it is a very modern tale. But it is also a darkly tragic and fitfully heroic tale of its time.'[40] Similar to Galbraith's and Nicol's novels, *Caledonia* captures the changing moods in different phases of the undertaking: from euphoria and desire to disappointment and frustration. It does so by focusing on the figure of William Paterson, who serves as focaliser of the play and through whose story the dreams, hopes and expectations of the colonists are conveyed. The dialogic structure of the drama enables Beaton to bring in a variety of viewpoints, some of which challenge and contradict Paterson's perspective. In this way, *Caledonia* interacts with historiographical approaches that emphasise the need for multiple, contrasting viewpoints on historical events. From a utopian perspective, it is particularly interesting to note how Paterson is represented as an idealist who views Atlantic colonialism as a large-scale restoration programme for Scotland:

> **Paterson** Yes, and when the sands of history are shifting, that's when a man of the world can make a fortune. And at the same time, benefit his native land. Wealth for one. Wealth for all, that's what I'm offering. We are entering a new age. Men will trade not only in goods but in company shares. Buying and selling. Selling and buying. Making money out of money. Trade will increase trade. Money will beget money. This is the simple idea that is going to transform the world. What I offer you, gentlemen, is nothing less than wealth without end.[41]

While the generally positive tone of the passage points towards the utopianism of the Darien scheme, the concept of gentlemanly capitalism offers a useful background for a reading of the more nuanced comments the passage makes on the prospects of Scottish colonialism in the final decade of the seventeenth century.

A new financial sector developed in Britain in the 1690s, largely based on the establishment of financial institutions such as the Bank of England, tax rises, the introduction of government bonds and the eventual development of the stock market. This new financial sector also resulted in the rise of a group of bankers and financial agents who were interested in developing both the British finance system and their own private funds. Paterson was one of these bankers, who saw both the domestic and the Atlantic markets as a possibility for personal and national advancement. These developments had a profound influence on British imperialism, as London businessmen and merchants became first among global investors of the time.[42] In Scotland, Darien was the first Atlantic scheme to promote a similar strategy of buying shares in overseas trading schemes so as to increase one's personal and the nation's financial gains. The next section of this chapter discusses how Scottish investors sought to participate in the new Atlantic trade sector by investing thousands and thousands of Scots pounds in the Darien venture. In Beaton's play, this financial hype around Darien is personified and partially caricatured in the figure of Paterson. The character enthuses about 'Making money out of money'[43] and thereby embodies the commercial enthusiasm of the financial market in which he was involved. *Caledonia* captures the financial interests of gentlemanly capitalists such as Paterson while also reflecting their underlying greed. The monarchy supported the advent of 'Atlantic capitalism',[44] primarily because it looked forward to the additional tax income, despite the social struggles that also came with the emergence of this new class of gentlemen and women. *Caledonia* seizes the idealism of Paterson while at the same time mocking the impossibility of realising the Atlantic utopia through its hyperbolic language. Paterson envisions trade at Darien as 'the pursuit of paradise on earth' and adds: 'All men need to believe in paradise. Some believe it's for the life hereafter. I believe it can also be here on earth.'[45] In such instances, Beaton's play identifies the utopian impulses behind the Scottish undertaking. It invites twenty-first-century audiences to try to understand why Atlantic colonialism offered such grand narratives of utopianism for Scottish people and for businesspeople like Paterson at the same time as it emphasises its critique of such ideas through hyperbole and irony.

Like previous works by Galbraith and Nicol, *Caledonia* juxtaposes the initial optimism of the colonists with their later experiences of hunger, death and disease. The drama's focus on Paterson serves to convey the harshness of settler life at the isthmus because Paterson, after having fallen out with the company directors, lived with the settlers on the mainland rather than with the other councillors on board the ships. Once again, socio-economic issues move into the foreground of the text and prevent a generalising perspective on Scottish settler colonialism. There is a scene in which Paterson writes a letter back home to people in Scotland and refuses to put down any negative experiences. When one of the sailors asks him to tell the people in Scotland 'the truth of our situation', meaning the experiences of death and disease, Paterson replies:

> If [. . .] you wish to tell them about the swamps, and the fevers, and the depredations, and the hunger, then by all means, tell them. Tell them that we bury a dozen men a day. Tell them that New Edinburgh is but a row of straw huts. Tell that Fort St Andrew is but a half-built palisade placed upon a stinking marsh. Let tales of death and disaster circulate in Scotland. Let them think that we are half-drowned rats not worth saving. Let all of Scotland know that the Spaniard is more powerful than we thought and may soon attack us in overwhelming numbers. And when because of your wretched accounts of our great endeavour they decide to build no more ships and our needful supplies are not sent and we succumb to hunger and despair, come to me and say you are proud of what you wrote.[46]

The quotation is at once a reference to the misfortunes of the colonists and a meta-textual comment on the unreliability of literary documents written in a colonial context. All documents have a target audience, or what reader-response criticism refers to as implied readers.[47] This target audience informs not only the reception of a text but its very conception by the author(s), whether consciously or not. In colonial contexts, the target audience is often a group of supporters that either awaits good news or is given good news in order to offer further assistance. *Caledonia* illustrates how this process of writing a colonial text with the implied readers in mind works even under dire circumstances. In a setting such as Darien, where the experiences on site differ so vastly from what the settlers had expected, readers must be careful not to equate the written word with reality. The quotation from Beaton's play allegorically summarises one of the main arguments of this book, which is that colonial writing is always fictional writing to some extent. Beaton's scene echoes contemporary theoretical approaches towards colonial literature in so far as it stresses the unreliability of all sources produced in the context of Atlantic expansion. In so doing, *Caledonia* draws attention to its status as historical fiction and alerts readers to the inherently unstable relationship between writing and reality. Beaton's play is a meta-textual comment not only on contemporary approaches to Darien but also on historical writings from the seventeenth and early eighteenth centuries. As such, it serves as a useful reminder of the intertwinement of ideological and artistic practices in early modern colonial writing about Darien, which is also the focus of the following two subchapters.

'Golden' Darien

Images of gold are among the most pronounced textual strategies of early modern Atlantic writing. They carry many connotations, most noticeably, perhaps, the promise of material riches and a 'golden' age of glory. The Spanish conquest of Peru with its legendary amounts of gold was a paramount model for European colonisers in the sixteenth and seventeenth centuries. Many explorers and colonial companies were hoping to find similar riches of gold in the Americas. Walter Raleigh's *The Discoverie of the Large, Rich, and Bewtiful Empyre of Guiana* (1596) makes a famous case for the existence of gold in the Americas. Even if the description of Guiana as a place that 'hath more abundance of Golde then any part of Peru'[48] turned out to be spectacularly exaggerated, the search for gold constitutes a leitmotif of early modern colonial writing. This leitmotif helped some writers, including Raleigh, to secure financial and royal support for their Atlantic explorations and colonial efforts. As Keats's poem at the beginning of this chapter indicated, narratives of Darien have equally developed an aesthetic that is closely associated with images of gold. The following discussion suggests that this link between Darien and its alleged 'realms of gold'[49] was significantly developed by Scottish authors in the late seventeenth century as part of their colonial utopian aesthetic.

Throughout the sources relating to Darien, images of gold function as leitmotif of the colonial imagination. One report of the Company of Scotland declares that the company would 'reserve to themselves, the 1/20th part of all Gold-dust, Mines of Gold, Silver, or other Metalls or Minerals, to be delivered above ground free of all Charges'.[50] If the sum of 1/20th does not seem very high, then this is a sign that the company directors expected the colonists to find significant amounts of gold, of which even a small percentage would benefit the company considerably. From the report of Captain Long, a member of the first expedition to Darien from 1698, readers equally learn that he and his crew were instructed 'to discover gold or other treasures' at Darien, and that the promise of 'rich gold mines' induced many colonists to travel overseas.[51] Likewise, *The History of Caledonia: Or, The Scots Colony in Darien in the West-Indies. With an Account of the Manners of the Inhabitants, and Riches of the Countrey. By a Gentleman lately Arriv'd*, published anonymously in 1699, celebrates Darien as a site that 'tho it be Rich and Fruitful on the surface, is yet far Richer in its Bowels, there being great Mines of Gold'.[52] The personification of the land's 'Bowels' is a poignant metaphor for the subterranean natural resources that early modern colonists were hoping to discover in Central America.[53] Perhaps the choice of body language appeals to a sense of humour or perhaps it expresses a certain sense of physical greed when it comes to the consumption of natural resources. What is certain is that this description goes back to one of the main sources of Darien's gold imagery: namely, Lionel Wafer's *A New Voyage* (1695). Wafer's travelogue offered an extensive first-person account of the Isthmus of Panama. It constitutes, together with William Dampier's *A New Voyage Round the World* (1697), one of the main sources for Scottish authors writing about Darien in the 1690s.

As shown in the discussion of Nova Scotia literature, Scottish Atlantic writing frequently relies on other people's travel narratives for its conception of the colonial spaces abroad. Although research suggests that those who were interested in Darien may well have had the opportunity to read up broadly on international experiences of Atlantic trade and travels – for instance, those by Dutch travellers to the West Indies whose works were translated into English – such books do not seem to have been in high demand among Scottish colonists of the 1690s.[54] Instead, most Scottish authors writing about Darien derived their information from Wafer's and Dampier's accounts, and they used these to paint an image of the isthmus as a quasi-perfect settlement site. The Company of Scotland Trading to Africa and the Indies hired Wafer to advise them on the undertaking and to share with them his knowledge of the region. *A New Voyage* renders Wafer's journey to Central America and his time among the Tule people between 1680 and 1684. Upon its publication, *A New Voyage* became popular not only in Great Britain but also across continental Europe. For the Scottish undertaking at Darien, Wafer's travelogue is important because it serves as a source of information for many of the colonial authors. While Wafer's general influence on the Darien scheme is well established, a comparative reading of texts suggests that the information provided by Wafer was handled strategically by the Scottish authors so as to portray the colonial scheme in the most positive of lights. This also pertains to the portrayal of the region's gold resources.

Wafer's *A New Voyage* relates how the Tule sieve gold dust out of rivers and then process the dust to turn it into solid gold. According to Wafer, 'if they meet with good Success and a favourable Time, they carry with them [. . .] 18 or 20 thousand Pound weight of Gold'.[55] Scottish colonial authors later use Wafer's depiction of this mining process to praise the riches of Darien and to make readers believe in the abundance of gold there.⁵⁶ The company directors partly reproduce Wafer's account and supplement it with the suggestion that enhanced mining techniques would yield even more gold than the Tule people are said to be able to mine. Where the latter use 'little Wooden Dishes which they dip into the water and take it up half full of sand, and at every dipping they find some Gold mixed with the sand',⁵⁷ Scottish authors suggest that more gold could be extracted from the soil if the hand-sieving method were developed into something more efficient by European settlers: 'It's easy to guess from this what vast Mines may in time be discovered, when Art and Industry are joined together.'⁵⁸ 'Art and Industry' are keywords here that shift the focus from the natural resources to the technological improvement of the mining processes. This shift is crucial because it implies that Scottish colonists bring the craft, technology and industriousness with them that would make gold mining more efficient in the region. Gold imagery thus turns into a mode of persuasion in Scottish colonial texts. It serves to idealise both the colonial territory and the Scottish settlers' envisaged roles in developing this territory into a source of prosperity.

There is a map of Darien from the late 1690s that visualises how golden imagery became a fixed feature of colonial narratives. It was published in Edinburgh in 1699 as *A New Map of the Isthmus of Darien in America, The Bay of Panama, The Gulph of Vallona or St. Michael, with its Islands and Countries Adjacent. A Letter Giving A Description of the Isthmus of Darian*. In the map's highly aesthetic visualisation of Darien, 'The Gold R. and Mines' graphically reproduce what literary narratives promise rhetorically: the abundance of gold and, with it, the promise of riches in the colonial territory. Whereas, in East New Jersey, land was the primary trope of possession, Darien is closely linked to the trope of gold and other subterranean treasures that would make the settlers not only materially comfortable in the colony but profoundly rich. Cartographically, 'The Gold R. and Mines' are located near the mountain range towards the bottom of the map (Figs 4.1 and 4.2).

Another text, Isaac Blackwell's *A Description of the Province and Bay of Darian: Giving an Full Account of All It's Situation, Inhabitants, Way and Manner of Living and Religion, Solemnities, Ceremonies and Product, Being Vastly Rich with Gold and Silver, and Various Other Commodities, by I. B., a Well-Wisher to the Company who Lived there Seventeen Years* (1699), equally stresses the riches of the colonial site. Its subtitle combines the promise of gold with a claim towards the account's authenticity. Scholars have been unable

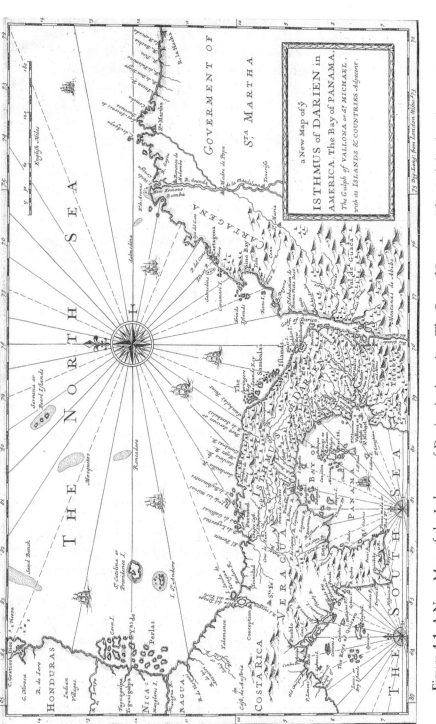

Figure 4.1 A New Map of the Isthmus of Darien in America, The Bay of Panama, The Gulph of Vallona or St. Michael, with its Islands and Countries Adjacent. Source: A Letter Giving a Description of the Isthmus of Darian. Edinburgh: Printed for John Mackie, 1699. Spencer e2. Reproduced with permission of the University of Glasgow Library, Archives & Special Collections.

Figure 4.2 Enlargement. A New Map of the Isthmus of Darien
in America, The Bay of Panama, The Gulph of Vallona or
St. Michael, with its Islands and Countries Adjacent. Source:
A Letter Giving a Description of the Isthmus of Darian.
Edinburgh: Printed for John Mackie, 1699. Spencer e2.
Reproduced with permission of the University of Glasgow
Library, Archives & Special Collections.

so far to trace the author, Isaac Blackwell, and to determine the truth
value of his autobiographical statement in the subtitle. Jajdelska calls
Isaac Blackwell an 'untraceable unknown [. . .] who had written an
account which now seems rather dubious of Darien'.[59] Stylistically, it
is notable how the truth claims of Blackwell's subtitle are supported
by authenticating devices in the text. Blackwell offers place names,
detailed descriptions of the surrounding landscape and the narration
of personal encounters with people on site that seem to strengthen his
position as a first-person traveller. In the light of these authenticating

devices, his comment on the existence of gold at Darien may likewise serve as a way to prove his reliability as an author:

> There is likewayes found in these Rivers, viz. *Darian* & *Sancta-Maria* Rivers great plenty of Gold-dust, which the *Indians* drains [sic] through small Vessels with holes in the bottome of them, in the time of these great Rains. The Gold is washed from the Mines of *Sagra* and the Mountains of *Carabana* & *Guattimala*: Hills in short, it's a Rich Countrey with Gold; for I have been told by very Antient Natives of the Place, that they have laughed at their *Southern* Neighbours *Peruvians* who have boasted of their having Houses full of Gold;[60]

The passage is reminiscent of the rhetorical devices that Raleigh uses in his description of Peru. This pertains above all to the promise that there will be plenty of gold in the colony, which is substantiated with the claim that indigenous inhabitants not only know all about the country's rich resources but are willing to talk about them with European travellers. The reported speech in the passage – 'for I have been told by very Antient Natives of the Place, that they have laughed at their *Southern* Neighbours *Peruvians* who have boasted of their having Houses full of Gold'[61] – fulfils a dual function. It assures readers of the alleged truthfulness of Blackwell's account and, in addition, induces them to become personally involved in the narrative by sharing in the laughter and merriment of the narrator. Despite the alleged humour of the text, there is no comedy in Blackwell's account. Viewed from a rhetorical perspective, the laughter is full of desire for other people's material riches. It renders the trope of possession as part of a moment of comic relief and thereby illustrates how colonial utopian narratives use an entire repertoire of emotionalising and aestheticising devices to persuade readers of their claims.

Golden imagery interacts with other materialist narratives that structure Scotland's Darien literature. To take one example, Paterson's 'A Proposal to Plant a Colony in Darien; To Protect the Indians Against Spain; And to Open the Trade of South America to All Nations' (1701) abounds with images of prosperity and capitalist gains. Paterson's main rhetorical tactic to promote the Darien venture is the reduction of complex information to simple, popular messages, many of which revolve around the satisfaction of material desires. He writes that a colony at Darien would be 'opening this door of commerce' for Scotland by offering 'more easy access unto, and correspondence with, the ends of the earth'.[62] Wafer's *A New Voyage* is an immediate source text for Paterson, even if the latter mainly takes affirmative examples from Wafer's original and reduces them to straightforward promises. Where Wafer balances a description of the 'excellent Soil within Land'[63] with a report about soil so 'swampy' in other parts of Darien that walking there is impossible,[64] Paterson praises the mountainous landscape, the harbours, the routes leading through the inland regions and the river near which the Scottish planters are settled.[65] When mentioning the potential difficulties of walking in the countryside, Paterson waves potential worries away by stating that the land might 'at present [be; K. S.] troublesome enough; but that two leagues might likewise easily be made good and passable by an industrious hand'.[66] An 'industrious hand' can be read as synonymous for Scottish settlers, who are, in Paterson's view, the ideal settlers for Darien. The careful selection of information and the cutting or condensation of less favourable material are ways of turning Darien into a utopian space in the Scottish colonial imagination.

It is likely that most Scottish writers of the time had never been to Panama and simply synthesised Wafer's work for their own purposes. The anonymously published *A Short Account from, and Description of the Isthmus of Darien, Where the Scots Collony Are Settled. With a Particular MAP of the Isthmus and Enterance to the River of Darien. According to Our Late News, and Mr. Dampier, and Mr. Wafer* (1699) likewise condenses Wafer's detailed depiction of the rainy season to a mere one-liner: 'The *Weather* is Warm, and has a Season of Rain.'[67] For readers without knowledge about Darien's tropical climate, such a one-liner could easily translate into the idea of quickly growing crops, possibly with more than one harvest per year. That this narrative proved popular, at least with parts of the Scottish population, shows in ballads of the day, in which a gilded image of colonialism echoes the generally idealistic mood of Darien investors.

The anonymously published 'The Golden Island, or the Darien Song, in Commendation of All Concerned in that noble Enterprise of the Valiant Scots' (1699) is one of the numerous literary texts that survive from the time of the Darien scheme. The subtitle states that it was written 'by a Lady of Honour', but otherwise the author's identity remains obscure. In the song's title, the adjective 'Golden' has both literal and figurative connotations. On the literal level, it alludes to the possibility that there is gold on the island, thus echoing the promises made by Wafer and the company directors. On a metaphorical level, the idea of a 'golden island' suggests an unflawed dwelling place for Scottish colonists, not unlike Ovid's description of the Golden Age in Book One of the *Metamorphoses*.[68] Ovid praises the simplicity, effortlessness and affluence of the Golden Age, just as

'The Golden Island' celebrates the idyll of the Atlantic and construes it as a site of desire. Here are two verses of the song, which are representative of its heroic language and religious connotations:

> 'The Golden Island, or the Darien Song, in Commendation of All Concerned in that Noble Enterprise of the Valiant Scots, by a Lady of Honour'
>
> When we were on the Darien main,
> And viewed the noble land.
> The trees joined hands and bowed low
> For honour of Scotland.
>
> And still we bless the Lord of Hosts.
> And all our benefactors,
> And drink a health to Albany,
> For all our bravo directors.[69]

The poem's threefold stress on nobility – in the author's self-description, in the Scottish settlers and in the Darien landscape – invents a narrative for Darien based on themes of honour and national pride. Nature imagery contributes to this celebration of Scotland's nobility, with the trees symbolically bowing down before the newly arrived settlers.[70] Ecocritical approaches might point out how nature serves as a mirror for the poem's anthropocentrism, while postcolonial approaches might stress how the subdual of the environment goes hand in hand with a subdual of the colonised land and its people. In the ballad mode of 'The Golden Island', nature and colonialism work together to create an ideal settlement story. Human kindness meets nature's kindness, and all of it is sanctioned by the 'Lord of Hosts'.[71] Given the longstanding tradition of associating colonialism with religious predestination, which earlier chapters have commented on, the nobility of the undertaking and its divine nature add to the golden imagery that suffuses Scottish visions of Darien in the late seventeenth century.

Topographically, 'The Golden Island' refers to a place distinct from the Scottish settlement site at Darien. Wafer describes a place called Golden Island in *A New Voyage*, but makes it clear that the island only serves as a reference point for travellers and that it is unsuitable for colonisation.[72] Still, maps such as the one in Figure 4.3 show how prominently the Golden Island features in the Darien imaginary. The map was originally included in *The Scots Settlement in America called New Caledonia A.D. 1699* and was later reprinted in Herman Moll's

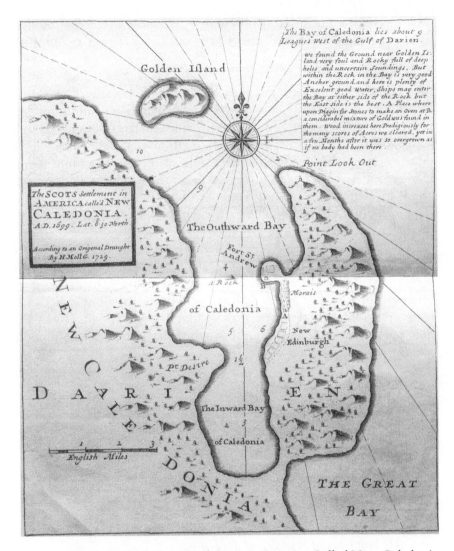

Golden Island

The Bay of Caledonia *lies about* 9 *Leagues west of the Gulf of Darien*.

we found the Ground near Golden Is:
land very foul and Rocky full of deep
holes and uncertain Soundings, But
within the Rock in the Bay is very good
Anchor ground. and here is plenty of
Excellent good Water, Ships may enter
the Bay at either side of the Rock but
the East side is the best. A Place where
upon Diggin for Stones to make an Oven at B.
a considerabel mixture of Gold was found in
them. Wood increases here Prodigiously for
the many scores of Acres we cleared, yet in
a few Months after it was so overgrown as
if no body had been there.

The SCOTS *Settlement in* AMERICA *call'd* NEW CALEDONIA. A.D. 1699. Lat. 8 30 North.

According to an Original Draught By H. Moll G. 1729.

Point Look Out

The Outhward Bay

Fort St Andrew

a Rock

of Caledonia

Morais

New Edinburgh

pt Desire

The Inward Bay

of Caledonia

English Miles

THE GREAT BAY

Figure 4.3 The Scots Settlement in America Called New Caledonia A.D. 1699, According to an Original Draught by H. Moll. Published in Herman Moll's *Atlas Minor*, 1736. Spencer f18. Reproduced with permission of the University of Glasgow Library, Archives & Special Collections.

Atlas Minor (1736), which makes it likely that Moll (c. 1654–1732) was the map's artist. Moll was a Dutch cartographer and the possibility that he drew a map of the Scottish settlement at Darien attests to the international popularity of the scheme.

It has been argued that Moll's map is based on 'sketches provided by the colonists themselves', as it provides details of the region that only settlers on site were likely to know.[73] Examples are the watchtower on the summit near Point Look Out, as well as the exact location of New Edinburgh and Fort St Andrews. The short narrative in the upper corner of the map states that travellers found gold at Darien when 'digging for stones'. Miraculous narratives such as this support the golden trajectory of the Darien venture, which has a quasi-religious dimension to it. Where Jesus turned water into wine, Darien settlers turn stone into gold, or so the narrative on the map seems to suggest.

A combination of religious and worldly imagery also features in the ballad *Trade's Release: Or, Courage to the Scotch-Indian-Company. Being an Excellent New Ballad; To the Tune of, The Turks are all Confounded* (1699–1700). The ballad consists of twenty-two verses that draw on images of gold and religious sanctification in order to turn Darien into a Scottish version of the Promised Land. Here are the first two verses of the ballad, in which images of gold take on a utopian connotation through their references to Solomon and his Golden Temple:

> Come, rouse up your Heads, Come rouse up anon!
> Think of the Wisdom of old *Solomon*,
> And heartily Joyn with our own *Paterson*,
>   To fetch Home INDIAN Treasures:
> *Solomon* sent a far for Gold,
> Let us do now as he did of old,
> *Wait but three Years for a Hundred-sold*
>   *Of Riches and all Pleasures.*
>
> *His Throne with Gold was overlaid,*
> *He hundreds of Shields and Targets had*
> *Of beaten Gold, and* (as is said)
>   *Gold Vessels all for Drinking:*
> *Cedars he made as the Sycamore-Tree,*
> *Silver as Stones abounding to be,*
> And TRADE from all Incumbrance free,
>   *For Reason rul'd his thinking.*[74]

Verbal hyperbole is a defining feature of the verses. Its gilded imagery speaks to the economic idealism of the poem. Four repetitions of 'Gold' mingle with a reference to 'INDIAN Treasures' and to 'TRADE', which illustrates how golden imagery fuses with vocabulary from the late seventeenth-century trade market and with the trope of dispos-session. In allegorical terms, the mysticism of the colonial aesthetic is matched by the use of the figure of King Solomon. The latter is a well-known character in early modern travel writing, who links the colonial to the utopian tradition not only in this poem but also in other texts of the time.[75] James VI and I liked being compared to Solomon, the epitome of wisdom and peace. Legend has it that Solomon's temple was built with pure gold, transported to Jerusalem from Tharshish, a Mediterranean port mentioned in the Bible.[76] The source of Solomon's gold supply was an ongoing matter of speculation in the early modern period, and travellers such as Columbus believed they could find Solo-mon's gold mines in the Americas. One destination Columbus had in mind was near Panama.[77] The lines from *Trade's Release* do not men-tion Columbus but they, too, associate Solomon's search for gold with Central America. The poem enters a dialogue with the biblical story of Solomon and borrows from it its gilded imagery, which it develops into the Atlantic realm. In another verse, there is talk of 'Cargoes of *Ore*', which are supposed to 'enrich this Nation', meaning in this case not Israel but Scotland.[78] Such an allegory of Scotland as another select nation is a prime specimen demonstrating the intersections of religious and economic language in late seventeenth-century Scottish Atlantic writing.

The Darien venture was one of a number of attempts to improve Scotland's economic situation in the 1690s and to make the kingdom internationally competitive.[79] William Ferguson notes that it was 'part of a programme designed to free Scotland from the economic restrictions imposed on her by English policy'.[80] Specifically, he men-tions the English Navigation Acts from 1688 that excluded Scot-land from tax-free trade with England and its overseas dominions. When the Company of Scotland hired William Paterson in 1695 to advise them in matters of international trade, they did so with the purpose of strengthening 'the growth of trade and the progress of the industry of this kingdom'.[81] According to Paterson, the chief aim of Darien should be 'employing and relieving the poor', which Scotland could achieve through the regulation of trade in grain and corn, as well as minerals, salt, fish and manufacturing goods.[82] A pat-tern emerges here, well known from earlier Scottish colonial writing, where authors present Atlantic settlements as a potential solution to Scotland's domestic problems. In some estimates, Scotland's popula-tion declined by between 5 and 15 per cent in the 1690s, with some areas in 'the Highlands and upland areas with losses in excess of 20 per cent'.[83] Narratives of Darien can be read as a response to this national crisis, where the emphasis on gold and national enrichment via Atlantic colonialism offers a solution to the poverty, unemployment and scarcity at home. Although, economically, the relief of the poor and the discovery of gold are only partially related, the material imagery in accounts of Darien functions as an implicit answer to the economic conditions shaping Scotland. They turn the Atlantic into a space of wealth and satisfaction. Paterson strengthened such links by insisting on the economic value of the overseas settlement and by depicting it as an essential step towards remodelling Scotland's financial and commercial sector.

Linebaugh and Rediker have shown how, in the context of Atlantic colonialism, '[t]he emphasis in modern labor history on the white, male, skilled, waged, nationalist, propertied artisan/citizen or industrial worker has hidden the history of the Atlantic proletariat of the seventeenth, eighteen and nineteenth centuries'.[84] Even in this book, which seeks to diversify narratives of Atlantic colonialism through its focus on Scotland, the prioritisation of the elite is inevitable because it is from here that most literary sources come. The networks of colonial supporters were predominantly shaped by rank and metropolitan connections, whereas 'peripheral peoples and places were, by definition, less well integrated into Europe's core news and information networks'.[85] Scotland is no exception to this rule. A look at the subscription books that were opened for the Darien venture in 1696 indicates these imbalances. A significant number of names are from the aristocracy or established elite. Among the several hundred subscribers are a large group of noblemen and women. 'Anne Dutches of Hamilton and Chastlerault, &c.', 'Margarett Countesse of Rothesse', 'Lady Margarett Hope of Hopetoun', 'Sir Robert Cheislie, Lord Provist of Edinburgh', 'Sir William Hope of Kirklistone', 'Sir James Hall of Dunglass' and 'Sir Robert Dickson of Sornbeg' are among the first of several hundred subscribers.[86] Numerous other members of the aristocracy and economic elite are also listed in the subscription book, which counts thirty-eight pages for Edinburgh and another seven for Glasgow.[87] Other shareholders included surgeons, physicians and lawyers, as well as widows, soldiers, ministers and craftsmen. There was a first peak in capital raising between March 1696 and March 1697, which can be considered a material manifestation of the gold imagery used in Darien literature. In the first year, investors provided the company with approximately £600,000.[88] Two-thirds of this sum, approximately £400,000, came from Scottish investors.[89] The sum 'represented a vast financial commitment by the Scots and was at least four times the annual revenue of the government'.[90] Some estimates say that the money amounted to 'half of the liquid capital in Scotland', others that it amounted to 'a quarter' of it.[91] Either way, the sum was enormous. If ever there was a financial colonial utopia, Darien was perhaps it.

It is worth pausing over the appearance of women's names on the list of Darien investors. For most other Scottish colonial schemes, it is impossible to identify female participants or to speculate about a gendered perspective on the Atlantic. In the case of Darien, this is different. Anne, Duchess of Hamilton, is the first subscriber on the Edinburgh list, which attests to her position as 'the head of one of the most powerful of the Scottish noble houses'.[92] Like other women from the educated aristocracy at the time, Anne Hamilton had a strong position in Scottish political circles. 'Informal social realms combined with elite women's ability to engage in written correspondence enabled these women to participate in parliamentary politics.'[93] It apparently also enabled them to engage in colonial schemes and to invest considerable sums of money into them. The Duchess of Hamilton pledged £3,000 to the Company of Scotland – an amount that only three other people pledged in Edinburgh and two others in Glasgow, out of several hundred subscribers. Anne Hamilton is followed by two other female investors: Margaret, Countess of Rothes, and Lady Margaret Hope of Hopetoun.[94] Both of them subscribed the still large sum of £1,000 for themselves and additional sums for their sons: another £1,000 for Margaret Rothes's son, and another £2,000 for Lady Margaret Hope of Hopetoun's son.[95] Together, these three women invested £8,000 in the Company of Scotland. Such investments by women in imperial endeavours are not altogether unusual in the late seventeenth century, as Margaret Hunt shows in her analysis of female fiscal investments in sailors and overseas ventures at the time.[96] Within a Scottish context, the list of subscribers is still remarkable because it offers one of the few pieces of evidence we have of the active, albeit probably still peripheral, role that women played in the Scottish Atlantic between 1603 and 1707. Needless to say, women were not on the board of directors of the Company of Scotland.[97] Yet, their presence on the list of investors suggests that an elite circle of women participated in Scottish colonialism before 1707. Perhaps future research will reveal a connection between one of the female investors – Anne Hamilton, Margaret, Countess of Rothes and Lady Margaret Hope of Hopetoun – and the 'Lady of Honour' who authored 'The Golden Island'. Certainly, the gender diversity of Scottish colonialism becomes more pronounced in the late seventeenth century and yields insight into the range of Atlantic desires.

Poems and songs are powerful platforms for the popularisation of Scotland's Atlantic imagery in the 1690s. Even though it is impossible to trace most of the ballads to specific authors or individuals, it is possible to read them in the context of the Scottish ballad tradition with its persuasive rhetorical and frequently political design.[98] Ballads were originally part of the oral tradition. From the late seventeenth century onwards, they were increasingly written down and recorded, although at first unsystematically, for a wider public. Many ballads take as their theme some folk event or story. Others take larger political or societal events as springboards from which to explore larger currents in Scottish society. What most ballads have in common is that they are active commentaries rather than neutral observations of the stories they tell: 'ballads are always active, self-contained dramas rather than comments upon past action'.[99] As part of the growing print publication market, this commenting function of ballads becomes part of public opinion-making in late seventeenth-century Scotland. Even if no argument can be made about ballads as evidence for a public sphere, simply because the transmission processes are too patchy and the geographical range of recorded ballads too narrow in the late seventeenth century, ballads may be closer to Scottish folk traditions than some of the other sources cited in this book. 'A Poem Upon the Undertaking of the Royal Company of Scotland Trading to Africa and the Indies' (1697) is an example of how ballads use their aesthetic repertoire to forge opinions actively on public events. In this particular case, the text promotes a utopian vision of Scotland's Atlantic trade by portraying Paterson as the prophet who will lead Scotland into an age of prosperity, liberty and progress. It ends with a long list of advantages that Darien will bring to Scotland. The closing lines are worth quoting in full, because they illustrate not only how much Scotland's relief through overseas colonisation is idealised but also how it is bound up with the Atlantic slave trade:

> On some such Shoar from all Preluctancy,
> *This Company designs a Colony.*
> To which all Mankind freely may resort,
> And find quick Justice in an open Port.
> To that the weary Labourer may go,
> And gain an easie Wealth in doing so.
> Small Use of tiresome Labour will be there,
> That Clyme richly rewards a little Care,
> There every Man may choose a plesant Seat,
> Which *poor Men* will make Rich, & *Rich Men* Great
> Black Slaves like bussie Bees will plant them Canes

Have Juice more sweet then honey in their *Veins*
Which boil'd to Sugar, brings in constant gains
They'l raise them *Cotton*, *Ginger*, *Indigo*.
Luselons, *Potatoes*, and the rich *Coco*.
Ships thence encrease to fetch these Goods away,
For which the Stock will ready Money pay.
By Manufactures here the Poor will live,
So they that do and they that stay will thrive.
Then *Caledonia* by her Lovers won,
Will now Light *Shining Nuptial* Robes put on,
Sea Gods, and *Nymphs* will dance, & *Tritons* play
And yearly Celebrate her Wedding Day.
            F I N I S.[100]

The poem's iambic pentameter expresses stability while the regular rhyme scheme makes the closing scene of Scotland's Atlantic vision both catchy and constant. The promise of prosperity, expressed in the 'easie Wealth' of the '*Colony*', matches the vision of the 'quick Justice' of 'an open Port' that will bring social equality to Scotland. This equation, however, works only when others are left out of the prosperity paradigm. Similar to the paradox of freedom discussed in relation to the Middle Colonies, literature about Darien displays the racialised conception of liberty, material wealth and narratives of progress in the seventeenth-century Atlantic. To compare 'Black slaves' to 'bussie Bees' who will 'plant them Canes' and, in so doing, 'brin[g] constant gains' to Scottish settlers is a telling metaphor for Scotland's vision of Atlantic colonialism. The economic improvement of Scots is possible only through the dispossession and enslavement of others. The poem's list of goods that is meant to increase Scotland's trade supports this reading of the text. It names '*Cotton*, *Ginger*, *Indigo*. / *Luselons*, *Potatoes*, and the rich *Coco*' as commodities of the Atlantic trade. It does not hide the fact that 'Black Slaves' will be the ones to 'raise' these crops. On the contrary, it seems to be part of the ballad's emphasis on comfort to refer to enslaved workers as part of the colony's social system. To employ an animal metaphor for 'Black Slaves' shows how seventeenth-century literature participates in the emergent discourses of racialisation that cut across European literatures of expansion from the early modern period onwards.[101] This is also true for the representation of the indigenous populations of the Americas in Scottish colonial writing.

The poem 'An Ode Made on the Welcome News of the Safe Arrival and Kind Reception of the Scottish Colony at Darien in America' (1699) shows how the idealisation of Scotland's economic gains at Darien goes hand in hand with the rhetorical dispossession of the Tule People. As in earlier examples, images of gold serve to strengthen the division by depicting Scotsmen and women as the new possessors of the indigenous peoples' gold:

> The *Countrey* now will be at ease,
> the tender *Mothers* will no more
> their Sons *Uncertain* Fate deplore;
> And *Indian Gold* shall soon release
> The Nation from Its *Tempral Poverty Grand Disease*.[102]

If gold is the ultimate image of abundance, then the poem's mother figure is a gendered allegory of Scotland's paucity. It serves to legitimate the dispossession of the Tule people. The mother's task, so the poem seems to say, is to feed Scotland's children, which is a means of naturalising colonial desires through kin imagery. In other parts of the poem, an antithetical construction emerges that juxtaposes phrases related to economic scarcity – '*Beggars*', *Vagabounds*', 'frugal *Countrey*' – with phrases associated with abundance – 'increase', 'our *Store*', '*Treasures*', '*Common Interest*', '*Wealth*'.[103] The antithetical imagery repeats the by now familiar message of the Darien venture, and of Scottish colonial undertakings in the seventeenth century more generally: Scotland can free itself from poverty by accessing the treasures of the Americas. In this way, 'An Ode' shapes a narrative that associates seventeenth-century Scotland with economic scarceness while portraying Atlantic colonialism as a solution to Scotland's domestic problems, even if this implies the dispossession of the indigenous peoples.

To conclude this discussion of Darien's gold imagery, it is worth pointing out that many Scots who actually went to Darien on one of the expeditions expressed frustration with the lack of gold in the colony. James Byres, one of the settlers, writes in *A Letter to a Friend at Edinburgh from Roterdam* from 1702: 'That which was called gold dust, is indeed very thick here, particulary at our watering place, in and about the water, but it proves really nothing at all but slymie stuffe verifying the Proverbe, 'TIS NOT ALL GOLD THAT GLITTERS.'[104] There is perhaps no better phrasing for the radical reversal of the gold imagery in Darien literature than in Byres's letter. Other settlers confirm that they could not find gold at the isthmus, neither during the first nor during the second expedition.[105] The earlier promises of gold, as well as the idealistic rendering of the undertaking, seem to have been one reason for the collective disappointment felt by the settlers. As one letter-writer puts it: 'Now, to conclude this long melancholy letter, in caice we have ommitted ought, the best way to understand that, is to read o're what was formerly written, and judge ye truth to lye on the other side.'[106] The propaganda texts had said little about possible difficulties, diseases and the tropical climate. Instead, they said much about gold that was never found at Darien.

Colonial Myths

Several myths pervade Scotland's colonial literature from the early to the late seventeenth century. These myths call into question conventional understandings of what power looks like in the colonial sphere because they complicate common categories of supremacy, victimhood and resistance in the early modern Atlantic. The following section suggests that mythical renderings of Scotland's colonial activities at Darien participated in the legitimisation and naturalisation of Scottish expansion projects before 1707, not only but specifically at the Isthmus of Panama. If, in Scotland, 'the seventeenth century became the breeding ground for myth',[107] then Atlantic mythologies are among the understudied narratives of this period. Myths about Darien commonly cast Scottish settlers in the role of kind, benevolent and freedom-loving colonists who are crushed by the hostile English. This myth revolves around William III's embargo on Scottish settlers at Darien, which some people in Scotland construed as the main reason for the premature ending of the undertaking. Many texts also cast Scottish settlers as liberators of the Tule people, who allegedly suffer at the hands of the Spanish and welcome Scottish settlers as saviours. These interlinked myths – the one of Scottish nobility, the other of 'English hostility'[108] and the third of the Tule as grateful to Scottish settlers for their intervention at Darien – further develop the narratives of possession and dispossession known from earlier decades of Scottish Atlantic writing. More precisely, they channel these narratives to make them intersect with another dichotomy in the Scottish literary and cultural tradition: the juxtaposition of the 'righteous Scots' with the 'barbarous Englishmen'.[109] John Barbour's *The Bruce* (1375) is a well-known example in which a similar narrative of English hostility versus Scottish nobility is rehearsed,[110] and so is William Dunbar's and Walter Kennedy's *The Flyting of Dumbar and Kennedie* (c. 1500). What is particular about Atlantic myths is that the formula of representing Scots as righteous people partly justifies the dispossession of the indigenous populations

at Darien and the practices of Atlantic slavery. In this way, mytho-
logical renderings of Scottish settlers as benign colonisers do not concern only Anglo-Scottish power relations. They extend to third parties
whose role in the colonial sphere becomes part of a larger struggle for
dominance in the seventeenth-century Atlantic.

My use of the term myth follows Northrop Frye's definition of
myths as founding stories of a nation or a culture.[111] In Frye's view,
myths interlink with utopianism in so far as they imagine a culture or
nation or society in its original or ideal form. Frye observes that utopias are a special kind of myth because they are primarily focused on
what is to come. Change is always located in the future. He uses the
term '*speculative* myth' for a utopia that directs attention towards
the future, towards '*telos* or end at which social life aims'.[112] Renderings of Darien frequently align with such an idea of speculative myth
by envisaging a new kind of Scotland that will arise out of the colonial settlement site. Paterson, for one, writes that the colonisation of
Darien is a means for Scotland of 'opening this door of commerce,
and of more easy access unto, and correspondence with, the ends of
the earth'.[113] He also writes that the Scottish will be 'more and better
fitted and qualified persons for the leading and directing of this or
the like undertaking than in all the rest of Europe' because there is 'a
more solid union among ourselves' than among other colonising cultures.[114] Frye's idea that utopias are myths that are directed towards
the future helps to explain such rhetoric, in which Scottish settlers
feature as future heroes of empire whose move into the world will go
hand in hand with the transformation of the entire Scottish kingdom.
And yet, although the temporal logic of Frye's theory is persuasive,
there is something to be said for a critical reconsideration of utopian
myths because the '*telos*'[115] imagined in the colonial utopian tradition is limited to certain parts of the population.

Looking at Scotland's tradition of seventeenth-century colonial
writing, it is clear that the temporal dimension of utopianism applies
only to a select group. As the previous chapters have show, most
sources – literary, visual and other – come from a group of Scots
that can be considered part of the elite. This elite was mostly aristocratic, or otherwise well educated, financially powerful and, often,
politically active. Nobles, courtiers, politicians, religious leaders and,
in the late seventeenth century, a new class of emerging businessmen and women are among the principal agents of Scottish colonialism prior to the Union of Parliaments. Members from these groups
can be considered as being inside Frye's 'myth oriented towards the
future', whereas other groups are excluded from the future-driven

temporality of utopian myths. Chapter 2 discussed how a 'new' Atlantic-oriented Scotland figures as progressive in elite circles. The golden images of Darien, together with the financial investment culture sustaining the colonial venture, show that a similar narrative of future-oriented success shaped 1690s Scottish colonial literature. Socio-economic hierarchies in the colonial utopian tradition intersect with normative narratives of temporality. Those who are part of the colonial elite are seen as future-oriented and those who are excluded from the colonial elite are associated with the past. The same is true for narratives of colonial competitors, which are figuratively rendered as remnants of a past while Scottish settlers at Darien are cast as future heroes of empire.

The Spanish frequently serve as a foil for the future-oriented myth of Scotland's progressiveness. Paterson contrasts the imagined community of Scottish settlers with the Spanish colonisers at Darien, whom he portrays as lazy, pretentious and unable to govern the region successfully:

> Thus, as in some sort of distempered bodies, where the nourishment feeds not the patient, but the disease, and where the stronger and more cordial is still the more dangerous, so this immense wealth of the Indies, which otherwise might have given strong and wholesome nourishment to the body politic of Spain, by misapplication has proved only oil to the flame of their more than inhuman inquisition.[116]

Protestant–Catholic rivalry plays a role in this passage, as it does in earlier depictions of Scotland's colonial superiority.[117] This rivalry adds to the founding myth of a future Scottish Atlantic, which is implicitly rendered as a Protestant one. The passage personifies the Spanish Empire as an ailing body, one that no medicine can heal because it is already too weak to deal with the remedy. The body metaphors subtly imply that Scottish settlers would not even have to fight the Spanish at Darien because their death, literal or figurative, is certain. Scottish colonists are, by implication, a healthier colonial body than the Spanish. Frye's reading of speculative myth as literary structures that ascribe archetypal meaning not only to the past but also to the future helps to conceptualise Scottish writing about Darien as a strategy to endow the colonial venture with epic meaning. If all cultures begin in myth,[118] then Scotland's imagined future at Darien figures as the beginning of a 'new' Scotland, one that will no longer be poor or politically marginalised but rather superior to one of the largest imperial players in the seventeenth century: that is, Spain.

Spanish claims over the Isthmus of Panama go back to the early sixteenth century. Around 1510, Spanish explorers claimed the region as part of their empire of New Spain.[119] Scottish writers at the end of the seventeenth century spilled much ink on explaining why they should enter this strategically important site despite Spanish claims to the region and, in so doing, risk conflict with Spain. In a thirty-four-page tract titled *Scotland's Right to Caledonia (Formerly Called Darien) And the Legality of its Settlement, Asserted in Three Several Memorials Presented to His Majesty in May 1699* (1700),[120] the company directors defend their choice of Darien and deny the priority of Spanish claims to the colony on the grounds of Spain's negligence towards Scotland. The directors declare that Spain may have reached certain agreements with England concerning Atlantic settlements, but since Scotland was left out of the agreements, there is no reason for Scottish settlers to refrain from going abroad. Likewise, Robert Ferguson's 244-page treatise *A Just and Modest Vindication of the Scots Design, for the Having Established a Colony at Darien* (1699) devotes many pages to the reasons for the choice of Darien and the denial of Spanish claims to it.[121] In these texts, Scottish settlers are rhetorically invented as superior colonisers. Paterson claims that the Spanish established a 'tyranny in the Indies' and turned the natives into slaves.[122] Scottish settlers are called to free the Tule from the Spanish and to establish a more benign rule at Darien. In some ways, the Tule are given a central role in Scottish myths of benign colonisation, even if their role is restricted to that of the immobilised victims. The actual situation on site seems to have been far different.

Panama's indigenous population is rich in variation. There are at least eight different indigenous groups with different languages in Panama today. Scottish settlers in the 1690s are most likely to have encountered two of those groups, the 'Cuna and Chocó', who lived at 'the belt of country forming the south-easterly part of the Isthmus of Panama'.[123] Most contact seems to have been with the San Blas Kuna Indians, who refer to themselves as Tule.[124] Several Scottish accounts represent the Tule as oppressed by Spanish colonialism. This allows the Scottish authors to portray their own colonial endeavour as an act of liberation. Paterson contends that Scottish settlers have the duty to help the Tule to 'break and shake off the unjust and tyrannical yoke of the Spaniards'.[125] Similarly, the company directors note that the local inhabitants would be better off if Scotsmen and women were 'to make some secure settlement in Darien, and, by a fair correspondence with the natives, engage them in defence against all enemies', including the Spanish.[126] These accounts are crudely out of joint with the experiences of other European settlers in the Atlantic in the second half of the seventeenth century. Indigenous populations across the Americas were seldom interested in inner European power politics. Instead, they were trying to forge new roles for themselves in the radically changing world of the Atlantic. The Dutch in Surinam, for instance, experienced how the indigenous Surinamese entered 'alternative cooperation' with European settlers, depending on specific circumstances and changing conditions.[127] Whether Paterson, who had lived for some time in the Netherlands, was entirely unaware of such indigenous practices is impossible to say. What seems likely is that he and the Company directors used the Tule as emblematic figures in their narratives of colonial liberation, which cast both the Scottish and the indigenous populations of Panama in the role of noble people. According to Gallup-Diaz, '[t]he organizers of the Scottish Company miscalculated in planning their operations on the assumption that the Indian population of the isthmus was a single tribal entity that was uniformly hostile to the Spanish.'[128] Bearing in mind the literary strategies used to promote the Darien settlement, especially the condensation of complex information and the mythologisation of Scotland's role at Darien, such miscalculation seems to have been partly tactical. The Scottish colonial aesthetic was, by and large, intent on linking Darien to a new era of Scotland's global prominence. Both the place and its people became part of Scotland's speculative myth of Darien.

The myth of the noble Tule people partly goes back to earlier writings about Darien. Scottish authors based their depiction of Panama's indigenous population largely on Wafer's *A New Voyage*, which describes the 'Indians'[129] as a complex people with their own customs, cultures and internal hierarchies. Wafer writes about gender relations, child-rearing, polygamy, medical knowledge and societal relations. At the same time, the ideal of the noble savage looms large over the text. Wafer praises the strength of the male inhabitants, their 'clean-limb'd, big-bon'd, full-breasted, and handsomly shap'd' features as well as their physical swiftness, being 'very nimble and active, running very well'.[130] The highly aesthetic physique goes hand in hand with the emphasis on the body, as opposed to the mind, that is particular to the noble savage trope.[131] Wafer insists that the Tule are 'kind and free-hearted', and mostly hospitable towards strangers,[132] even if he also has the experience of being forcibly taken by Chief Lacenta, who only allows the traveller to leave on the promise of returning later in order to marry his eldest daughter.[133] Similarly, Scottish authors praise the hospitality of the indigenous peoples they meet at Darien. The anonymous *A Short Account from, and Description of the Isthmus of Darien, Where the Scots Collony Are Settled* describes the good relations with the Tule, who are said to have 'received us very Kindly, there not being many of them, and their Plantations but a few'.[134] The passage continues by relating how the Tule provide the Scottish settlers with '*Plantaines, Yams, Potatoes, Sugar Canes,* Cocks and Hens, and such things as the Countrey affords'.[135] Taking this idea of benevolence one step further, Borland writes about the 'poor naked people' of Darien, who are 'contented with their share, and seldom thoughtful for to morrow', and whose simplicity in life is, in the eyes of the Scottish minister, a virtue: 'they live more cheerfully, in better health, and are most lusty and strong in their old age. They have small care to please their appetites with divers and sundry dainty meats; A little sufficeth them.'[136] Once more, the focus is on the corporeality of the Tule people. In Borland's account, they are healthy, cheerful, vigorous and stout, and their ability to live on small quantities of food is a tribute to their resilience. Their nobility shows in their health, as well as in their alleged hostility towards the Spanish.

Wafer writes how the Tule men cut off their hair after victory and use this 'as a distinguishing Mark of Honour to him who has kill'd a *Spaniard*, or other Enemy'.[137] Paterson echoes Wafer when he writes in his account that the Tule have a 'wonderfull hatred and horrour for the Spainiards'.[138] Such renderings must be read with the myth of Scottish nobility in mind. Colonial texts are always a product of their context. 'Even in the cases in which the words or experiences of a [sic] Indians are recorded with curiosity, sympathy, or at considerable length, the nature of the colonial relationship under which they were recorded must always be kept in mind.'[139] The rendering of the Tule as victims of Spanish oppression constitutes one such myth that serves the Scottish purpose of mythologising their own role at Darien more than anything else. If myths have the function of establishing, explaining and developing cultural identities, then literary analyses can help to read and explain the underlying narratives of such myths. Scotland's speculative myth of Atlantic colonialism has various functions, one of them being the legitimisation and naturalisation of Scottish claims over Darien by casting Scottish settlers in the role of benevolent, morally superior colonists. The Tule are part of this narrative of Scottish nobility in Darien literature. They feature as noble colonised who await the arrival of the Scottish settlers in order to free them from Spanish tyranny.

How difficult it is to escape renderings of the Tule as benign victims of European colonialism, even more than three hundred years after Scotland's involvement with the Isthmus of Darien, is discussed by Nat Edwards in his 2007 book, *Caledonia's Last Stand*. Edwards relates how he travelled to the Isthmus of Panama with the goal of revisiting the site of Scotland's Atlantic undertaking, and how he found some of the old colonial structures still in place. This pertains to place names such as 'Bahia Caledonia, Punta Escoces, Puerta Escoces (Nuevo Edimburgo on some maps), Isla Caledonia, San Andreas Reef and the Caledonia Mountains'.[140] It also pertains, at least partly, to the structural differences that exist between the twenty-first-century indigenous populations and the descendants of the European settler populations. Most of these populations are not from Scottish descent but from Spanish. Yet, the structural inequalities and the long-term effects of European colonialism are evident, and they underline Wolfe's argument about the prolonged existence of settler colonial structures long after the period of colonialism has officially ended.[141] Edwards relates how '[t]he majority of the servants I saw in Panama were either indigenous peoples or dark-skinned mestizo country people,' and how 'a gulf remains between the rural poor and the wealth of Panama City that is most in evidence in the country's domestic service culture'.[142] The long-term effects of European settler colonialism are still evident in the economic, social and geographical discrepancies in Panama today. Scottish authors and settlers may not be the originators of European colonialism in Central America, and they may not have been the most influential colonisers there to date. Yet, the ongoing legacy of the Scottish presence at Darien brings to mind one of the central tenets of critical empire studies, which is that an analysis of settler colonial experiences from European perspectives alone is not enough. What is needed is dialogue, critical dismantling of ongoing power relationships and greater interest in the perspectives of those who were traditionally left voiceless in the colonial scenarios. Julie Orr's *Scotland, Darien, and the Atlantic World, 1698–1700* (2018) offers an entry into the possibilities of such dialogue among colonial agents that includes not only the indigenous populations but also Spanish voices and a focus on slavery. *Scottish Colonial Literature* does not claim that it will change the social or political structures in the Americas. Perhaps, though, it offers a way of rereading not only past but also contemporary representations of Scottish colonialism.

Narratives of the Scottish as superior colonisers are remarkable for their longevity. John M. Mackenzie and T. M. Devine remark, in their introduction to *Scotland and the British Empire* (2011), how recent scholarship on Scotland's colonial activities has given rise to 'a new myth, that of Scottish "exceptionalism"'.[143] The authors mention Fry's *The Scottish Empire* (2001) as one of the works that 'imply that Scots migration constituted a diaspora of both major proportions and a uniquely gifted people'.[144] Focusing on the depiction of Scottish colonialism prior to 1707, another myth can be added to that of exceptionalism: namely, that of Scottish benevolence. Fry forges a link between Scottish colonists and the Tule people by suggesting that Scottish 'Highlanders often thought in their encounter with Indians to find soulmates, springing like them from a tribal society founded on military prowess and oral culture'.[145] Similarly, Bridget McPhail argues in an article on Darien that '[f]or many of the Scottish settlers, to meet the Indians was to meet a more golden, less hairy, and considerably cleaner version of themselves.'[146] Some decades earlier, Prebble's *The Darien Disaster* (1968) rehearses the myth of Scottish victimhood by explaining Darien's end with the statement that 'Scotland's noble colony on the Isthmus of Panama [. . .] had been destroyed by the English.'[147] Such narratives of heroism, victimisation and nobility participate in the ongoing mythologisation of Darien as a superior, yet ultimately doomed, colonial undertaking. Chapter 5 investigates more closely how narratives of failure have shaped ideas of Scottish colonialism prior to 1707 and argues that such narratives are linked to normative conceptions of European colonialism. For now, it is useful to turn to the myth of English hostility, which equally enforces the idea that Scots are superior, if ultimately luckless, agents in the Atlantic sphere and, in so doing, reinforces narratives of dispossession in the Scottish Atlantic.

In relation to Darien, the myth of English hostility is closely linked to William III's decision to put an embargo on trade with the Scottish settlers at Darien. William III had earlier expressed his suspicion of the Darien venture, so his lack of support may not have come as a total surprise to insiders within his administration.[148] Reasons for his disapproval probably lay in Spain's involvement with the Isthmus of Panama, as well as with England's own economic interests. English merchants and businessmen feared that the Company of Scotland could become a rival to the East India Company, which might lose its monopoly status if Scotland's international trade increased. Prior to the embargo, members of the English Parliament had written a letter to the King, asking him to withdraw his support for the Company of Scotland.[149]

Whatever the King's motivation for prohibiting trade with Darien settlers may have been, Scottish reactions to the embargo were highly emotional and quickly turned into a myth of English hostility. Ferguson's *A Just and Modest Vindication* (1699) notes the disappointment of Scottish settlers when they heard that William's embargo on '*the* Scots, *in their Colony at* Darien' would deny '*them any assistance with Arms, Ammunitions, Provisions or any thing else whatsoever*'.[150] In 1700, George Ridpath (d. 1726), a supporter of the Whig party whose pamphlet was burned in London,[151] produced *Scotland's Grievances Relating to Darien &c. Humbly Represented to the Parliament*. It was published by James Watson, the Edinburgh printer and 'editor of the first newspaper in Scotland'.[152] In Ridpath's text, the word 'Treachery' features three times in relation to William III's decision not to support the Scottish colonists at Darien.[153] Such rhetorical tools foreshadow Ridpath's later political outlook on Scotland as suffering under English dominance ever since the Union of Crowns.[154] The end of Darien provided one more cause for Ridpath to circulate and expand the myth of English hostility, this time with William III at the centre of the myth. For Ridpath, it is clear that those who helped to make William III decide in favour of the embargo are either 'Traytors' or 'Enemies to the Kingdom of *Scotland*'.[155] Ridpath averts any blame from Scotland and uses a simple rhetorical dichotomy to portray supporters of the scheme as good and non-supporters as bad. Even some contemporary commentaries still rely on such rhetorical binaries. Tom Nairn, for one, describes the Union as 'the loss of 1707' that gave rise to a 'dismembered nation', characterised, above all, by 'the Scots' most famous and unshakable drinking companion: "lack of self-confidence"'.[156] Ultimately, such myths of English hostility versus Scottish benevolence help to reduce the responsibility of Scotland's involvement in the Atlantic sphere and to formulate an image of Scottish settlers as noble, if ultimately doomed, colonists.

It is impossible to say whether or not Scotland would have been able to establish a permanent colony at Darien if William III had supported the settlers on site. Other circumstances, including the tropical climate, disease and, arguably, a lack of proper provisions, also contributed to the rapid departure of most Scottish settlers from New Edinburgh and Fort St Andrew. What is notable is that the myth of English hostility continued to feature in debates about inner British power dynamics in the early years of the eighteenth century, when the Jacobite movement was on the rise and the prospect of the Union of Parliaments intensified political tensions between England and Scotland. Lord Belhaven's *A Speech in Parliament on the 10th day of January 1701, [. . .] On the Affair of the Indian and African Company, and its Colony of Caledonia* (1701) shows how an idealistic interpretation of Scotland's colonial endeavours at Darien operates to spur anti-English sentiments. Belhaven was himself an investor in the Darien venture and a member of the Company of Scotland's board of directors,[157] which might explain his nostalgic view of the undertaking. The myths of Scottish nobility and English hostility feature strongly in some excerpts from his speech, including the following:

> *My Lord*, I must say, never any Nation in *Europe* provided a larger Stock for such an Undertaking at their first up-setting, never was any Project of Trade managed by Persons of greater Quality or Integrity, without any Charge to the Common Stock. Never was there a better Equipage of Ships and Men, with all things necessary for such a Design, and yet, by the Malice of our Enemies, all our Endeavours have proved unsuccessful and Abortive.[158]

The mythologisation of Darien as part of Scotland's 'victim' history is part of a rhetorical strategy that diverts blame from Scotland and directs it towards England. The threefold repetition of 'never' emphasises how the colony was supposed to become a foundation stone of Scotland's Atlantic empire, and how the English are to be blamed for having confounded this plan. The accusation that the 'Malice of our Enemies' has 'give[n] us the deadly Blow at one Stroke' is directed against those English businessmen and politicians who induced William III to issue the embargo on the Scottish settlers. In a different context, Wormald notes that the use of myth in seventeenth-century Scotland was frequently a means 'to conceal failure'.[159] Even if the subsequent chapter will trouble the use of 'failure' as a concept in colonial and postcolonial studies, Wormald's argument helps readers to interrogate the anti-English ethos underlying Belhaven's rendering of Darien.

As Davis has shown, myth and nation-building interact in Belhaven's speech. The author uses 'myth and history in his representation of the Scottish nation'.[160] Specifically, he uses references to Roman history, as well as a 'mythic image of the nation', to construe the idea of a homogenous Scottish nation.[161] The mythologisation of the Darien scheme adds to such a construction of the mythical Scottish nation as a people of superior, if unfortunate, heroes. Daniel Defoe famously responded to Belhaven's anti-Union rhetoric in a series of publications that sought to invalidate the anti-English charges by calling Belhaven a storyteller and deceiver.[162] Because Belhaven was 'one of the few members of Parliament who made a point of publishing his speeches for popular distribution',[163] his mythical renderings of Darien gained a relatively wide audience and helped to spread the myth of Darien as a betrayal by the English. Pittock remarks that his speeches were especially widely received on 'the streets' of Scotland,[164] which shows how the ongoing change in media cultures at the time – from oral towards printed narratives – interacted with the construction of national identities in the early eighteenth century.[165] Written documents about Darien helped to shape narratives that were based on a binary opposition of the English versus the Scottish people around the time of the Union of Parliaments.[166] Scotland's Atlantic undertaking is part of this rhetorical construction of Scotland as opposed to England. Although only a few people participated in debates about Darien, those few construed accounts of an allegedly united Scotland that stands uniformly opposed to England and feels betrayed by its southern neighbour. In their works, Darien becomes a symbol of victimhood and betrayal.

In the anonymously written *The People of Scotland's Groans and Lamentable Complaints, Pour'd out Before the High Court of Parliament* (1700), the myths of Scottish nobility and English hostility are similarly endorsed through various rhetorical strategies. At one time, Scotland is compared to a child 'depriv'd of the Kindness and Protection of One of their Parents'.[167] The opening paragraphs make it clear that the deserting parent is William III, whereas the lone caring parent is the Scottish Parliament, to whom the text is addressed:

> We have no other Remedy left Us then, most Noble Representatives, but to prostrate Our Selves at Your Feet, and to throw Our Selves into your Arms, as those of Our Other Parent, humbly imploring, nay Conjuring You by all that is Sacred, and by the Honour of the SCOTTISH Name, that You would not suffer this Ancient and Gallant Nation to be so much Contemn'd and Injur'd. We beg of You to consider, how Our Soveraignty and Freedom is Violated, Our Laws trampled upon, and our Trade interrupted; how Our Brethren have been Starved and made Slaves, Our Colony deserted, and Our Ships burnt and lost Abroad; whilst Our Petitions have been rejected, Our Company baffled, Our People Famish'd, Our Metropolis burnt, and flames of Division kindled amongst Us at Home.[168]

The passage uses a host of images reinforcing the idea that Scotland was deceived by England. The personification of the 'Feet' and 'Arms' of the parliament is reminiscent of religious symbolism, in which Christ's disciples wash his feet while he opens his arms to welcome the castaways and exiles. A similar religious connotation is evident in the use of the word 'Brethren', which suggests that Scotsmen and women are like a religious congregation seeking salvation from evil. Here, as elsewhere in seventeenth-century Scottish literature, '[t]he heavy pall of sin, the presumptuous dispensing of God's law, and the devil stalking the land hangs over much of the religious and legal language.'[169] Scots are not simply victims but 'Slaves',[170] which shows once more how the myth of English hostility serves to diffuse the power relations in Scotland's Atlantic imaginary. It portrays the Scottish people as victims of colonial mechanisms rather than participants in them. Doyle's concept of the 'liberty plot', according to which 'a myth in which the capacity for liberty places the ruling "races" above others',[171] features in this passage, which blames the English for not allowing Scotland to become part of the liberty ideal of the Atlantic. The passage uses the parent–child allegory to suggest that interfamily disloyalty prevents Scotland from becoming, in Doyle's framework, part of the 'ruling races' of the Atlantic. The choice of words suggests that the hierarchical system of masters and slaves was accepted as part of the power imbalances in the Atlantic, which is reminiscent of Ricœur's argument that utopias are about changes in the hierarchical structures of a given society but not about the dissolution of social hierarchies.

Of course, there were also critics of the myth of English hostility. The Introduction discussed how the question of culpability led to harsh political and public debates, including two book burnings in Edinburgh and in London. In addition, there were other writers whose works were part of the debate. James Byres, a participant in the Darien expedition, writes in *A Letter to a Friend at Edinburgh from Roterdam* (1702) that it was not the English but the directors of the Company of Scotland who were to blame for the premature ending of the venture. He accuses them of idealising the colonial undertaking when they knew, or should have known, that the settlement plans had been fraught from the beginning. Byres criticises the company directors, who 'warmly threw the blame on the *English Government* or some or other that was out of the way',[172] but failed to endow the settlers with the required knowledge and material resources for the settlement.[173] Another leading critic of the myth of English hostility is the settler Walter Harris, sometimes also spelled Herries, whose writings were among those burned at the Edinburgh Cross.[174] Harris was a surgeon on one of the ships that sailed to Darien and returned home after the settlers abandoned the colony. In *A Defence of the Scots Abdicating Darien: Including an Answer to the Defence of the Scots Settlement there* (1700), Harris casts Scottish settlers in the roles of offenders, who are responsible for Darien's premature ending. He claims that a cargo '*of* Scotch *Cloth, Slippers, Periwigs and Bibles*' was an ill-planned basis for entering the Atlantic market and that this poor planning led to the death of hundreds of migrants.[175] The result, according to Harris, was the loss of '1050 Men' who were sent 'by the *Scotch* Company on a blind Project, of getting Riches for them with five or six months Allowance at most, no Credit, and a ridiculous Cargo'.[176] Harris uses an animal comparison to point out the subhuman conditions on board: 'our Men fell down and died like rotten Sheep'.[177] Statistical evidence of the number of deaths on board exists in Roderick Mackenzie's list of people who perished on the voyage to Darien in the first two months of the settlement. The list was printed in 1699 in Edinburgh (Fig. 4.4).

Following Mackenzie's list, most settlers died of fever or flux, which at the time were terms for all sorts of illness, including 'smallpox, plague, cholera, dysentery, typhoid, and the mosquito borne yellow fever and malaria'.[178] As John R. McNeill argues, the 'disease environment of the Caribbean was a cultural artifact' because many of the diseases, especially 'yellow fever and malaria' came to the Americas with the Atlantic slave trade.[179] The Scottish settlers were, in all likelihood, unaware of these biomedical links, but they did know that the death toll on their voyage was significant and that their settlement experience was far removed from the utopian quality of pre-settlement literature. Although Mackenzie's narrative at the bottom of the page maintains that the number of deaths is actually lower than to be expected during such a voyage – he claims that '*so few are dead*' and that more people '*might have died by this time*' if they had stayed in Scotland[180] – the mortality rates grew with the second expedition, when 'near 300 men' were buried in the course of four months.[181] By 1699, the total number of deaths had risen up to '460 (35 per cent) of the 1,300 who left the Clyde in August'.[182] McNeill explains that the 'ecological conditions' of the Caribbean led to particularly high death rates among European settlers, including Scottish settlers, who were, according to McNeill, ill prepared to face the viruses, tropical diseases and general living conditions at the Isthmus of Panama.[183]

To come back to the myths of Scottish nobility versus English hostility, it is possible to connect Harris's criticism to this chapter's larger argument that the organisers of the Darien scheme preferred idealistic narratives of a Scottish settlement at Darien over more realistic ones. Recent research into the role of Scottish merchants

An Exact LIST *of all the Men, Women, and Boys that Died on Board the* Indian *and* African Company's *Fleet, during their Voyage from* Scotland *to* America, *and since their Landing in* Caledonia, *Together with a particular account of their qualities, the several Days of their Deaths, and the respective Distempers or Accidents of which they Died.*

Nota.   *By Volunteers are meant such Young Gentlemen as went in no particular station, but only in hopes of preferment as opportunity should offer.*

July 23.	A	Alexander Fiery, a Planter	Fever
Auguſt 8.		Daniel Martin, a Sailer	Flux
22.		Robert Donaldſon, a Planter	Flux
30.		George Menzies, a Planter	Flux
Septem. 11.		John Forreſter, a Planter	Flux
16.		James Dunnie, a Planter	Flux
19.		Robert Hardy, Volunteer	Fever
21.		John Stewart, Volunteer	Fever
		Robert Baillie, a Planter	Fever
23		John Smith, Sailer	Fever
25.		Alexander Elder, Sailer	Fever
27.		Jeromy Spence, Sailer	Fever
28.		Andrew Baird, Sailer	Flux
29.		Walter Johnſtoun, Chirurgeon's Mate	Fever
October. 1.		John Duffus, Sailer	Fever
5.		Thomas Dalrymple, Planter	Fever
7.		James Paterſon, Volunteer	Flux
10.		Charles Hamilton, Mid-ſhipman	Flux
11.		Jacob Yorkland, Volunteer	Flux
15.		James Davidſon, Planter	Flux
16.		Henry Charters, Volunteer	Flux
19.		Lieutenant John Hay's Wife	Flux
20.		Adam Hill, a Planter	Flux
		Walter Eliot, a Midſhip-man	Fever
21.		Adam Cunningham, a Midſhipman	Fever
		Adam Bennet, a Midſhipman	Fever
23.		Mr. Thomas James Miniſter	Fever
		Peter Mackintoſh, Sailer.	Fever
24.		John Daniel, Planter	Flux
25.		David Henderſon, a Sailer	Flux
		James Graham, Volunteer	Flux
26.		William Miller, Volunteer	Fever
27.		John Chiefly, Volunteer	Flux
28.		Mr. John Malbon Merchant	Fever
		Alexander Tailor, Sailer	Fever
		Robert Gaudie, Planter	Flux
		John Aird, a Planter	Decay
		Lievetenant Hugh Hay	Fever
		Peter Paterſon, a Sailer	Flux
		James Montgomery	Flux
31.		John Luckiſon, Volunteer	Flux
Novem. 1.		David Hay, Volunteer	Flux
2.		Thomas Fenner, Clerk to Mr. Paterſon	Fever
3.		Lieutenant James Inglis	

After Landing.

Novem. 5.	Hugh Barclay, Sailer	Fever
	Henry Grapes, Trumpeter	Fever
6.	Archibald Wright, Volunteer	Flux
7.	James Clark, Volunteer	Flux
9.	James Weems Volunteer	Flux
11.	John Fletcher, a Planter	Flux
14.	Mr. Paterſons Wife,	Fever
15.	Archibald Mofman, Volunteer	Flux
16.	John Cannie, Sailer	Flux
	John Sim Sailer,	Flux
20.	Mr. Adam Scot, Miniſter	Flux
22.	Roger Munckland, Volunteer	Flux
	Andrew Hamilton, a mid ſhipman	Fever
23.	William Baird, Sailer	Flux
27.	James Young, Sailer	Fever
29.	James Montgomery, a Planter	Flux
Decem.	John Burrol, a Sailer	Flux
3	James Borthwick, a Sailer	Fever
6.	David Miller, Planter	Flux
	Enſign William Hallyburton.	Flux
7.	William Erskin, Planter	Flux
8.	Robert Biſhop Chirurgeons Mate	Flux
10.	Recompence Standburgh, one of the Mates on Board the St Andrew }	Fever
11.	Robert Pendreick, William Tenter, William Aſackellau a Boy }	Drown'd
	David White, a Planter	Fever
17.	William Barron, a Planter	Flux
24	Alexander Wraite, a Planter	Flux
	Andrew Brown, a Boy on board the French Ship	Drown'd
	Peter Telfer, a Planter	Flux
25.	Captain Thomas Fullarton, commander of the Dolphin after warm walking	died ſuddenly

This is a true LIST compared by Me *ROD. MACKENZIE Secy.* to the ſaid Company.

*N*O doubt, every one will juſtly Regret the loſs of his own neareſt Freind, but it's a great and General Mercy that, of ſo many as went Crowded in Five Ships, upon ſo long and tedious a Voyage as they had, ſo few are dead; Eſpecially conſidering, that on their way they had the misfortune of taking in bad Water, upon an Uninhabited Iſland, in the beginning of the Rainy Seaſon, which occaſioned general Sickneſs among them; tho' ſoon after their Landing in Caledonia (thanks be to GOD) they Recovered their Health ſo much (even beyond expectations) that, when the Expreſs came away, there were but Five of all our Men who were not at Work in Building of Forts and Houſes. And as even a greater Number of ſo many as went, might have died by this time, had they all remain'd at Home; ſo it may be ſome Satisfaction to the neareſt Friends of the deceaſed that their Names ſhall ſtand upon Record as being amongſt the firſt Brave Adventurers that went upon the moſt Noble, moſt Honourable, and moſt Promiſing Undertaking that Scotland ever took in Hand.

EDINBURGH, Printed by George Moſman, in the Year 1699.

5. Δ. 277 (5)

Figure 4.4 Roderick Mackenzie, *An Exact List of all the Men, Women, and Boys that Died on Board the Indian and African Company's Fleet, during their Voyage from Scotland to America, and since their Landing in Caledonia, Together with a Particular Account of their Qualities, the Several Days of their Deaths, and the Respective Distempers or Accidents of which they Died.* Edinburgh: George Mosman, 1699. The Bodleian Libraries, The University of Oxford. 5 DELTA 277 (5), recto. Reproduced with permission of the Bodleian Libraries, The University of Oxford.

in the seventeenth-century Atlantic and the circulation of knowledge among these merchants and the Darien plotters supports this argument. According to Jajdelska, the directors of the Company of Scotland could have had access to the trading and cargo experiences of the Scottish merchant Andrew Russell, who was based in Rotterdam. Russell was in regular 'correspondence' with John Borland, the brother of the Darien settler Francis Borland.[184] Jajdelska surmises that no such communication took place, neither between Russell and the Company directors nor between the Darien planners and any other Scottish merchants in the Netherlands, many of whom had valuable knowledge about Atlantic trade. Instead, the directors based their preparations on Wafer and Dampier, and on what Jajdelska calls the 'dubious' account of Isaac Blackwell, whose reliability as a source is uncertain even today, as the previous section showed.[185] Harris does not name Blackwell specifically. He does, however, accuse the Company directors for their faulty planning and notes that their reliance on myth, rather than methodical information, was part of Darien's problem:

> *if you had not misapply'd the Money intrusted to your Management (the Want whereof is so much felt at Home by the great Number of needy Persons, who expected their Dividends before now.) And if you had listen'd to the wholesome Advice of Mr.* Douglas, *an eminent and experience'd Man in* India, *who offer'd himself for your Pilot, and his Substance for your Security, which was more than the Three best Shares in your Capital Stock; and had not been bewitch'd to the Golden Dreams of* Paterson *the Pedlar, Tub-preacher, and at last Whimsical Projector; you might e'er now have been possest of a good Colony in* India, *where no Body could disturb you: And not have run on an Airy Project, which (altho' you should have met with an Opposition from the* Spaniard) *four times your Capital Stock could not have brought to any reasonable Pitch of Answering the End.*[186]

Harris's critique of the company directors, and of Paterson, endorses the argument that myth-making was a powerful tool in the development of the Darien undertaking. Idealised images of the future colony helped to raise '*Capital Stock*' but, in the end, the entire settlement design turned out to be '*an Airy Project*'.[187] According to Harris, it lacked practical information and useful supplies. The metaphorical blindness of the directors in the excerpt emblematically points to the utopian or dreamy quality of the undertaking. Harris rhetorically enforces his argument through the antithetical construction of William Paterson, who personifies the myth-making tradition, and

Mr Douglas in India, who represents a more methodical approach to colonial trade and European expansion. As in earlier examples of Darien literature, Harris uses golden imagery to link Darien to utopian ideals, only in this case the utopian ideals have turned out to be unrealisable.

Of course, Harris's text was also written with a certain purpose in mind and cannot be taken at face value. It has been speculated whether Harris may have been paid to write his anti-Darien pamphlet by the English Secretary of State, James Vernon.[188] Whether or not such theories are true is impossible to say. What is certain, from a rhetorical viewpoint, is that the imagery and language Harris uses yield insights into the author's own toolbox of turning history into a source of myth. To call Paterson a 'Pedlar, Tub-preacher, and at last Whimsical Projector'[189] invents an alternative myth, one that is based on single responsibility rather than collective answerability. The English, for Harris, are more rational in their planning and decision-making. He defends the English for not supporting Scottish settlers at Darien by pointing to the diplomatic environment in which this decision was made: '*this Nation* [England; K. S.], *who had heard of no War with* Spain, *and who had no great Reason to suffer their own Subjects to desert their Plantations*', did not have any cause 'to *advance the* Scotch *Colony in their own Wrong*'.[190] Harris's account offers the opposite of the utopian images of Darien literature. Its tone is satirical, but at its heart it paints a deeply dystopian image of the undertaking and of those who bought into its design. From a literary perspective, it illustrates how myth is a prevailing form of claiming power in the Atlantic. Even if not all speculative or future myths become true, they occupy a central space in the narratives of Darien that have existed from the late seventeenth century to the present.

Notes

1. I would like to thank Christoph Bode and Karly Kehoe for fruitful conversations on Keats's poem with me.
2. Keats, 'On First Looking' 1396–7.
3. For example, Claridge, 'The Darién Scheme' 59–84; Edwards, *Caledonia's Last Stand*; Gallup-Diaz, *The Door of the Seas*; Hart, *The Disaster of Darien*; Insh, *The Darien Scheme*; Jajdelska, 'Unknown Unknowns' 393–414; McNeill, *Mosquito Empires* 105–23; McPhail, 'Through a Glass, Darkly' 129–47; Prebble, *The Darien Disaster*; Watt, *The Price of Scotland*.

4. Davis, *Acts of Union* 26–30; Davis, 'The Aftermath of Union' 56–70.
5. Bowie, 'Public Opinion' 227.
6. Davis, 'The Aftermath of Union' 57.
7. Bowie, 'Public Opinion' 231.
8. Pittock, *Scottish Nationality* 61.
9. Anon., *The True Scots Mens Lament*.
10. Anon., *The True Scots Mens Lament*.
11. Anon., *The True Scots Mens Lament*.
12. Qtd in Pittock, *Poetry and Jacobite Politics* 176.
13. Pittock, *Poetry and Jacobite Politics* 9–10.
14. Burns, *Canongate Burns*.
15. Burns, *Canongate Burns*.
16. Burnaby, *The Ladies Visiting-Day* 26; italics in original.
17. Scott, *Tales of a Grandfather* 390; also qtd in Watt, *The Price of Scotland* 79.
18. Bannister, 'Biographical Introduction' xiv.
19. Bannister, 'Biographical Introduction' xxvi and cxvii.
20. Gilroy, *The Black Atlantic* ix.
21. Jajdelska, 'Unknown Unknowns' 394.
22. Jajdelska, 'Unknown Unknowns' 394.
23. Jajdelska, 'Unknown Unknowns' 394.
24. Warburton, *Darien; Or, The Merchant Prince* Vol. III, 194.
25. Warburton *Darien; Or, The Merchant Prince,* Vol. III, 165–79.
26. Warburton, *Darien; Or, The Merchant Prince* Vol. III, 200.
27. Pittock, *The Invention of Scotland* 99–128.
28. MacKenzie and Devine, *Scotland and the British Empire*.
29. See Chapter 4, pp. 177–8.
30. Cullen, *Famine in Scotland* 1.
31. Galbraith, *The Rising Sun* 196.
32. Galbraith, *The Rising Sun* 203–4.
33. Galbraith, *The Rising Sun* 381.
34. Galbraith, *The Rising Sun* 381.
35. Galbraith, *The Rising Sun* 516.
36. Darwin, *Unfinished Empire* xi.
37. Nicol, *The Fundamentals* 1.
38. For a discussion of Walter Harris, or Herries, see Chapter 4, pp. 176–80. For a discussion of Roderick Mackenzie, see Chapter 4, pp. 177–8.
39. Nicol, *The Fundamentals* 131–2.
40. Beaton, *Caledonia* vii.
41. Beaton, *Caledonia* 13.
42. Cain and Hopkins, 'Gentlemanly Capitalism' 525.
43. Beaton, *Caledonia* 13.
44. Linebaugh and Rediker, *The Many-Headed Hydra* 145.
45. Beaton, *Caledonia* 50.
46. Beaton, *Caledonia* 96–7.

47. Iser, *The Act of Reading*.
48. Raleigh, *The Discoverie* 136.
49. Keats, 'On First Looking' 1396.
50. Burton, *The Darien Papers* 51.
51. Burton, *The Darien Papers* 81–2.
52. Anon., *The History of Caledonia* 18.
53. Anon., *The History of Caledonia* 18.
54. Jajdelska, 'Unknown Unknowns' 398.
55. Wafer, *A New Voyage* 21.
56. Anon., *The History of Caledonia* 19.
57. Anon., *The History of Caledonia* 19.
58. Anon., *The History of Caledonia* 19–20.
59. Jajdelska, 'Unknown Unknowns' 400.
60. Blackwell, *A Description* 4; italics in original.
61. Blackwell, *A Description* 4; italics in original.
62. Paterson, 'A Proposal' 117.
63. Paterson, 'A Proposal' 37–9.
64. Paterson, 'A Proposal' 35–9.
65. Paterson, 'A Proposal' 140–4.
66. Paterson, 'A Proposal' 142.
67. Anon., *A Short Account* 5; italics in original.
68. Ovid, *Ovid's Metamorphoses* Book I, lines 89–112.
69. Qtd in Bannister, *The Writings* Vol. 3, 280.
70. Qtd in Bannister, *The Writings* Vol. 3, 280.
71. Qtd in Bannister, *The Writings* Vol. 3, 280.
72. Wafer, *A New Voyage* 34.
73. Edwards, *Caledonia's Last Stand* 171–2.
74. Anon., *Trade's Release* 1–16; italics in original.
75. Claeys, *Searching* 76.
76. Genesis 10; 1 Kings 10: 22.
77. Claeys, *Searching* 76.
78. Anon., *Trade's Release* 23–4; italics in original.
79. Kidd, *Subverting* 33.
80. Ferguson, *Scotland's Relations* 177.
81. Paterson, 'Proposals and Reasons' 19.
82. Paterson, 'Proposals and Reasons' 28.
83. Cullen, *Famine in Scotland* 2; see also Kidd, *Subverting* 33.
84. Linebaugh and Rediker, *The Many-Headed Hydra* 332.
85. Stewart, 'Introduction' 715.
86. Burton, *The Darien Papers* 371–2.
87. Burton, *The Darien Papers* 371–417.
88. Burton, *The Darien Papers* 371–417.
89. McNeill, *Mosquito Empires* 108.
90. Watt, *The Price of Scotland* 63.
91. McNeill, *Mosquito Empires* 108.

92. Carr, 'Women' 48.
93. Carr, 'Women' 48.
94. Watt, *The Price of Scotland* 51.
95. Watt, *The Price of Scotland* 51.
96. Hunt, 'Women and the Fiscal-imperial State' 29–47.
97. Watt, *The Price of Scotland* 58.
98. Lindsay, *History of Scottish Literature* 143–52.
99. Lindsay, *History of Scottish Literature* 147.
100. Anon., 'A Poem' 13; italics in original.
101. Doyle, *Freedom's Empire* 3.
102. Anon., 'An Ode' 41–5; italics in original.
103. Anon., 'An Ode' 32–45; italics in original.
104. Byres, *A Letter to a Friend* 26–7; emphasis in original.
105. Borland, *The History of Darien* 16.
106. Qtd in Burton, *The Darien Papers* 217.
107. Wormald, 'Confidence and Perplexity' 123–49.
108. Wormald, 'Confidence and Perplexity' 143.
109. Carruthers and McIlvanney, 'Introduction' 3.
110. Carruthers and McIlvanney, 'Introduction' 3.
111. Frye, 'Varieties' 25–49.
112. Frye, 'Varieties' 25.
113. Paterson, 'A Proposal' 117.
114. Paterson, 'A Proposal' 157.
115. Frye, 'Varieties' 25.
116. Paterson, 'A Proposal' 130.
117. See Chapter 2, pp. 51–2.
118. Frye, *Anatomy of Criticism*.
119. Elliott, *Spain, Europe & the Wider World*.
120. Company of Scotland, *Scotland's Right to Caledonia*.
121. Ferguson, *A Just and Modest Vindication* 1–42.
122. Paterson, 'A Proposal' 148.
123. Joyce, 'Introduction' 166.
124. Gallup-Diaz, *The Door of the Seas* 'Introduction' note 3.
125. Paterson, 'A Proposal' 153.
126. Bridgewater et al., 'Proceedings' 260.
127. Jajdelska, 'Unknown Unknowns' 401.
128. Gallup-Diaz, *The Door of the Seas* Chapter 4.
129. Wafer, *A New Voyage* 78–111.
130. Wafer, *A New Voyage* 78.
131. See Chapter 2, p. 67.
132. Wafer, *A New Voyage* 7.
133. Wafer, *A New Voyage* 22–3.
134. Anon., *A Short Account*, no page.
135. Anon., *A Short Account* no page; italics in original.
136. Borland, *The History of Darien* 11.

137. Wafer, *A New Voyage* 79; italics in original.
138. Burton, *The Darien Papers* 184.
139. Gallup-Diaz, *The Door of the Seas* Introduction.
140. Edwards, *Caledonia's Last Stand* 207.
141. Wolfe, *Settler Colonialism*.
142. Edwards, *Caledonia's Last Stand* 111.
143. Mackenzie and Devine, 'Introduction' 9.
144. Mackenzie and Devine, 'Introduction' 9.
145. Fry, *The Scottish Empire* 65.
146. McPhail, 'Through a Glass, Darkly' 141.
147. Prebble, *The Darien Disaster* 4.
148. Fry, *The Scottish Empire* 25–6.
149. Fry, *The Scottish Empire* 29.
150. Ferguson, *A Just and Modest Vindication* 42; italics in original.
151. See Introduction.
152. Davis, 'The Aftermath of Union' 57.
153. Ridpath, *Scotland's Grievances* 3–9.
154. Kidd, *Subverting* 34.
155. Ridpath, *Scotland's Grievances* 3.
156. Nairn, *After Britain* 154; 101.
157. Davis, *Acts of Union* 20; 33.
158. Belhaven, *A Speech* 8; italics in original.
159. Wormald, 'Confidence and Perplexity' 123–49.
160. Davis, *Acts of Union* 31.
161. Davis, *Acts of Union* 31.
162. Davis, *Acts of Union* 34–5; see Defoe, *The Works of Daniel Defoe, Vol. 7* and Defoe, *The Works of Daniel Defoe, Vol. 8*.
163. Davis, *Acts of Union* 37.
164. Pittock, *Poetry and Jacobite Politics* 153.
165. Anderson, *Imagined Communities*.
166. Davis, *Acts of Union* 26–30.
167. Anon., *The People of Scotland's Groans* 1.
168. Anon., *The People of Scotland's Groans* 1.
169. Wormald, 'Confidence and Perplexity' 145.
170. Anon., *The People of Scotland's Groans* 1.
171. Doyle, *Freedom's Empire* 16; 12–13.
172. Byres, *A Letter* 142; italics in original.
173. Byres, *A Letter* 142.
174. See Introduction.
175. Byres, *A Letter* 142.
176. Harris, *A Defence* 150; italics in original.
177. Harris, *A Defence* 51.
178. Watt, *The Price of Scotland* 150.
179. McNeill, *Mosquito Empires* 6.
180. Mackenzie, *An Exact List*.

181. Borland, *The History of Darien* 73.
182. Watt, *The Price of Scotland* 190.
183. McNeill, *Mosquito Empires* 122.
184. Jajdelska, 'Unknown Unknowns' 400.
185. Jajdelska, 'Unknown Unknowns' 400.
186. Harris, *A Defence*, Epistle Dedicatory no page; italics in original.
187. Harris, *A Defence* Epistle Dedicatory no page; italics in original.
188. Bowie, *Scottish Public Opinion* 30.
189. Harris, *A Defence* Epistle Dedicatory no page; italics in original.
190. Harris, *A Defence* Epistle Dedicatory no page; italics in original.

Chapter 5

Conclusion: Failure and Scottish Colonialism

The concept of failure looms large over studies of Scotland's colonial history in the seventeenth century. Looking at past and present publications in the field, there is a common narrative that interprets Scottish overseas activities before the Union of Parliaments in 1707 as failures. This is particularly true of accounts of Nova Scotia and the Darien scheme. Some scholars write that 'the few official attempts at Scottish colonization in the Americas, at Nova Scotia in the 1620s and Cape Breton Island later the same decade, ended in failure'.[1] Others call the settlement of Nova Scotia and Cape Breton 'an example of European failure in America'.[2] Yet others admit that the concept of failure is linked to normative conceptions of colonialism, but they still reproduce the idea that William Alexander's initial attempts to settle Nova Scotia 'can at best be judged a qualified failure'.[3] Scotland's short-lived attempt to colonise South Carolina has equally been described as 'a failure',[4] despite the fact that little is still known about this settlement scheme and its people on site. I should like to linger for a while on the concept of failure in studies of Scottish colonialism because it brings together a set of conversations that have shaped this book. These include the conceptual links between colonialism and progress, and Scotland's position in the fields of colonial and postcolonial studies, as well as our understanding of Scottishness in the long seventeenth century.

For Darien, the paradigm of failure has become almost a master narrative in both past and present publications. Fry describes Darien as the 'greatest but most disastrous of the colonial undertakings by the Scots while still an independent nation'.[5] Likewise, the two most comprehensive accounts of the Darien scheme mark their subjects as instances of failure. Francis Russell Hart's *The Disaster of Darien:*

*The Story of the Scots Settlement and the Causes of its Failure 1699–
1701* (c. 1930) and John Prebble's *The Darien Disaster* (1968) both
use the alliteration 'Darien disaster' or 'Disaster of Darien' to coin
a sticky label for an undertaking that did not end in a permanent
colony for Scotland. Others refer to Darien as an 'utter failure' and
state that 'Scotland [has] not one single successful colonial enterprise
on its record.'[6] Darien even gets an entry in *The Mammoth Book
of Losers* (2014), where it is discussed, as the only colonial scheme
of a European or non-European power, under the heading 'Worst
Attempt to Found a Colonial Empire'.[7] My inquiry into the literary
nature of the Darien scheme, and Scotland's Atlantic history more
generally, in the previous chapters reveals a different story. Suggesting that Scotland's undertakings at Darien or Nova Scotia were failures because they did not result in long-term colonies for Scotland
misses the mark. Most interpretations of Darien that resort to the
paradigm of failure use language that seems unconsciously to link
long-term colonial settlements by European powers to success and
the lack thereof to backwardness.

To be sure, both Prebble's and Hart's books originate from a
time when postcolonial criticism was not yet a standard of academic
thought. It is unreasonable to judge them for not adhering to critical
standards that came after their time. Still, I am struck by the possibility that similar patterns of thinking may be one of the reasons why
Scotland's Atlantic activities prior to 1707 continue to be narrated in
terms of failure, and why relatively little scholarship exists on Scotland's seventeenth-century colonial schemes that does not try to market them, at one time or another, in terms of Scotland's misfortunes.
Equally, I am struck by the possibility that there might be an overall
scarcity of literary scholarship on Scotland's colonial schemes before
the Union of Parliaments because of an underlying, if unspoken,
assumption that only those colonial undertakings are worth study-
ing that were, in conventional terms, 'successful'. Although important research has been done lately on the role that Scotland played in
the emergence and development of the British Empire,[8] many studies
focus on the period after the Union of Parliaments, when Scotland
was no longer an independent kingdom. This poses questions about
the perception of Scottish colonialism in the seventeenth century.
By focusing on colonial schemes that are frequently excluded from
anthologies and collections of British and European empire-building,
Scottish Colonial Literature wishes to intervene in a critical debate
on the concepts of failure and success in the intellectual history of
European empire-building. Literature and culture from the early

stages of Scottish colonialism illustrate how deeply the concepts of progress and modernity are ingrained in Western epistemologies of the Atlantic. By unfolding some of these narratives and discussing their aesthetic forms and effects, *Scottish Colonial Literature* hopes to open up further ground for discussions of the conceptions of failure and success in the Atlantic sphere.

In one of her articles on subaltern histories and historiography, Gayatri Chakravorty Spivak lays out how the concepts of 'failure or success' are part of 'an implicitly evolutionist or progressivist set of presuppositions'.[9] Spivak situates the paradigm of failure within Western narratives of progress and suggests that European colonialism has conventionally been viewed as a sign of modernity. Colonial 'success' is linked to progress and 'failure' to the lack thereof. As others have shown, the idea of progress is a core concept of Western thought, and colonial expansion is habitually seen as part of Western modernity. Writing about the nineteenth century, Dipesh Chakrabarty notes that 'the ideology of progress or "development"' helped to 'enabl[e] European domination of the world in the nineteenth century' through the principles of historicism, which promoted a '"first in Europe, then elsewhere" structure'.[10] For all the differences between early modern and nineteenth-century narratives of progress, there are some parallels at which seventeenth-century trajectories of colonial utopianism intersect with later conceptions of progress.

There is a strong mode of utopianism in Scotland's colonial literature prior to 1707. In some ways, this utopian tradition seems to be continued in narratives that equate Atlantic colonialism with modernity and the lack of colonies with backwardness. *Scottish Colonial Literature* has suggested that narratives of progress were unleashed in a context where considerable parts of the population felt underprivileged in Scotland. Although colonial writing was mostly a product of the elite, this elite suggested that great parts of the Scottish population needed to participate in Atlantic colonialism in order to make the kingdom as a whole more progressive. Numerous authors framed these narratives of progress in utopian aesthetics that allowed them to rehearse overlapping tropes such as economic and material improvement, upward social mobility, liberty, nation-building, religious improvement or the desire for political order. The dispossession of others was part and parcel of this utopian aesthetic. It justified the subjugation and deprivation of non-European cultures by emphasising Scotland's own material and structural deficits. Scotland's colonial literature from the seventeenth century is not alone in developing such ideas. Yet, the material studied in this book affords a pertinent illustration of how enduring the equation of colonialism with progress, and the concomitant acceptance of dispossessing others in advancing one's own status, still are. The formula of Scotland's alleged failures in pre-1707 colonial activities is one of the narratives in which the cultural logic of Western colonialism is still being continued today.

There are other colonial schemes in the early years of British empire-building that are commonly marked as failures. Raleigh's Roanoke, Fort Caroline and Sable Island have all been filed under the label 'Failed Colonies'.[11] The term makes the coupling between narratives of colonialism and narratives of progress explicit because it marks 'failure' as an exception to the rule. By turning to these histories of supposedly unsuccessful colonisation, it is possible to see how the concepts of failure and success are still deeply entangled with underlying norms of progress in colonial history. Failure and success are normative categories that, in the colonial context, mark those colonial undertakings as successes that resulted in long-term colonies and those as failures that did not. Perhaps Scotland's colonial ventures prior to 1707 ran contrary to Western ideas of profitability, progress and modernity. To mark them as failures, however, means to adhere to these standards even at a time when the long-term effects of colonialism on global relations and international hierarchies are at the centre of much research. *Scottish Colonial Literature* has traced how literary works participated in the patterns of idealising and aestheticising the Atlantic in a way that contributed to the naturalisation and popularisation of colonial thought in early modernity. By way of conclusion, it is necessary to ask how far similar tools endow contemporary narratives of Scotland's alleged failures in colonial history with normative ideas about European expansion.

Like Spivak, other critics have tackled the question of how to delink colonialism from concepts of Western modernity. More than twenty-five years ago, Homi Bhabha expressed the hope that postcolonial criticism might help to 'transfor[m] [. . .] our understanding of the narrative of modernity and the "values" of progress' that have equated colonialism with improvement.[12] Bhabha challenged the global cultural hierarchy of modern versus backward cultures, and he foresaw a pivotal role for postcolonial studies in delinking such binary conceptions. More cautious criticism is less optimistic about the transformative power of postcolonial studies. In his book *In Theory: Classes, Nations, Literatures* (1992), Aijaz Ahmad argues that postcolonial criticism still clings to overarching concepts of modernity and progressiveness that go back to colonial thinking. One example is the use of binary concepts such as East and West or coloniser and colonised, which not only oversimplify global relations for Ahmad but implicitly associate the one with progress and the other with backwardness.[13] Ahmad warns readers not to believe in a

> seamless and unified history of European identity and thought [that] runs from Ancient Greece up to the end of the nineteenth century and well into the twentieth, through a specific set of beliefs and values which remain essentially the same, only becoming more dense.[14]

According to Ahmad, the acknowledgement of internal differences is one step towards delinking colonialism from ideas of progress. Another is to recognise how binary conceptions of failure versus success continue to shape understandings of colonialism and turn them into monolithic narratives of Western modernity.

Scottish Colonial Literature has tried to destabilise categories of colonial versus colonised cultures in early modern Europe by emphasising the internal contradictions in Scottish colonial literature. It has shown that a select group of people promoted overseas colonialism as a reform strategy for the Scottish people, but that their own power struggles were frequently at the heart of their writings. Authors of colonial literature commonly presented these power struggles as pertaining to the entire Scottish nation. This book has suggested, though, that references to the nation have to be read as rhetorical devices that serve a particular means, usually that of gaining support for the colonial undertaking and promoting it as a wholesome reform strategy for Scotland. The diversity of responses – from enthusiastic support to furious book burnings, from significant financial investments to complete unawareness of the colonial schemes – illustrates how Scotland's Atlantic schemes in the long seventeenth century can best be thought of as fragments. They do not narrate a unified history of a Scottish nation.

The concept of the nation is a frequently used one in Scottish studies. Titles such as *The Scottish Nation* or *Scottish Nationality* recur in past and present publications.[15] Most scholars adopt a nuanced approach to the field and emphasise the internal diversity and historical transformations of the Scottish nation or, more appropriately, Scottish nationhoods over time. Nicola Royan and Dauvit Broun argue that different 'Versions of Scottish Nationhood' existed between 850 and 1707,[16] and a similar argument can be made for subsequent centuries. They emphasise temporal change as a decisive category for understanding different forms of nationhood in Scotland. The editors of *The Edinburgh History of Scottish Literature* take a similarly multilayered approach when arguing that all conceptions of Scottishness must be accompanied by the question of '*Whose* history?' we are talking about. Scotland has always been defined by linguistic, regional, cultural and social diversity. Societal patterns of change are key to coming to terms with conceptions of Scottishness.[17] In addition to these parameters of temporal change and societal diversity, I would like to add another component to the methodological complexities of Scottishness in the long seventeenth century: that of transnational spaces.

The Atlantic was one geopolitical sphere in which debates of Scottish nationhood were being forged in the long seventeenth century. Although only a small group of people was involved in colonial activities in Scotland before 1707, the repeated and resolute references to nationhood in Scottish colonial literature are striking. The 'Sorry Poor Nation' from *Caledonia, or the Pedlar Turn'd Merchant*, the 'Ancient and Gallant Nation' from *The People of Scotland's Groans and Lamentable Complaints, Pour'd out Before the High Court of Parliament*, the promise that '*Indian Gold* shall soon release / The Nation from Its *Tempral Poverty Grand Disease*'[18] in 'An Ode Made on the Welcome News of the Safe Arrival and Kind Reception of the Scottish Colony at Darien in America' (1699) or Gordon's rhetorical question in the 1620s as to whether Scotland is 'so farre inferiour to other Nations'[19] not to have a colony of its own: all of these are examples of how prominently the nation is constructed as a discursive reality in writings about the Atlantic. None of this means that the nation was really united in supporting Scotland's colonial enterprises. As the previous chapters have shown, there is little reason to assume that large parts of the Scottish population were involved in Atlantic activities in the seventeenth century. There is no unified story about Scotland's colonial history prior to 1707. Neither before nor after the Union of Parliaments did colonialism act as a unifying force in Scotland. As Colley has shown, it was mostly 'the Welsh, Scottish and Anglo-Irish landed élites' who forged a more common British identity after 1750, partly by means of 'reinvigorating the power structure of the British Empire and forging a unified and genuinely British ruling class that endured until the twentieth century'.[20] In the years before the Union of Parliaments, similar societal divisions characterised attitudes towards the Atlantic. They led to diverging ideas about Scotland's role in overseas settlements. Perhaps this diversity is one reason why discourses of nationhood enter colonial writings of the seventeenth century so vehemently: to construct unity discursively where heterogeneity was the norm.

The concept of the nation works as a stabilising rhetorical device in writings about the Scottish Atlantic. While Michael Gardiner is surely right in stating that 'Scotland has never been a colonising *nation-state*,'[21] the discourses of nationhood nevertheless function as influential tools in Scottish colonial writing. Frequently, they are put into the service of idealising both the Atlantic space and Scotland's role in it. Following Cooper's argument that '[t]he Spanish Empire wasn't entirely Spanish and certainly not national,'[22] it is possible to think about Scottish colonialism in the seventeenth century as 'not entirely Scottish' in the sense that only a minority of people was involved in it. Nevertheless, or because of this, discourses of nationhood interacted with narratives of Scottish colonialism. This coupling of colonial with national narratives can even be seen in accounts that imagine what would have happened had Scotland's colonial activities ended differently.

S. G. E. Lythe notes with regard to Nova Scotia that 'if it had been developed and held, [it] would at one stroke have elevated Scotland to the top rank of colonial powers'.[23] Others write about Darien that '[h]ad the Scots made the attempt in another decade, some of the adverse circumstances would not have obtained, and their chances of success might have been better.'[24] Consciously or not, colonialism seems to be implicitly associated with success in such comments. From a postcolonial perspective, such historical subjunctives are problematic. *Scottish Colonial Literature* has grappled with the antinomies of colonial narratives in seventeenth-century Scotland and shown that discourses of Scottish colonialism are deeply shaped by a history of geopolitical expansion, slavery, exploitation and racial oppression.[25] The idea that Scotland would have grown stronger through the dispossession of others is an anachronistic one. And yet, in another twist, it helps to illuminate why it is so difficult, on a historical and theoretical level, to come to terms with Scotland's position in the field of colonial and postcolonial studies today.

The rhetoric of dispossession works together with the rhetoric of possession in Scottish colonial literature. This antithesis helps to explain some of the complexities that surround discussions of Scotland's position in colonial and postcolonial studies. Narratives of dispossession continue to shape certain discourses of Scottishness and Scottish nationhood until this day. The use of postcolonial rhetoric in political texts issued in favour of the Scottish Independence referendum in 2014 is a case in point.[26] Likewise, conceptions of Scottish nationhood are frequently associated with anti-Union discourse and with postcolonial claims. The argument commonly goes that Scottish independence would be a form of decolonisation from the English or larger British coloniser. In their article 'Three Referenda and a By-election: The Shadow of Empire in Devolutionary Politics' (2015), Jimmi Østergaard Nielsen and Stuart Ward quote the former Scottish Prime Minister Alex Salmond with his statement in favour of Scottish independence, which he backs with the words: 'the age of empires is over'.[27] Leaving aside the moral and historical appropriateness of such comparisons, the association of Scotland with a British colony illustrates how the Union of Parliaments is frequently equated with an act of dispossession even if, in reality, some members of the Scottish elite benefited from it.

On the one hand, there were those in Scotland who saw in the Union of Parliaments the chance to continue with Atlantic expansion after 1707. Mostly, this view was adopted by figures from the elite, who promoted the Union of Parliaments as a means of reviving Scotland's imperial agenda with sustained energy. The Earl of Cromarty writes, in the early eighteenth century, that the union might bring to Scotland 'the 'Golden Fleece' of empire' that its own imperial efforts in the Atlantic had failed to produce.[28] The wording takes up the leitmotif of gold known from earlier literature about Darien and implies that Scotland could still search for gold – materially and metaphorically – after the Union of Parliaments, perhaps even more successfully than before. Cromarty's metaphor shows how, in some circles of Scottish society, the Union of Parliaments was linked to an earlier Atlantic imaginary according to which Scotland could become a global imperial player on a par with other European colonial powers of the time. Silke Stroh comments on this relocation of colonial imaginaries from a Scottish to a larger British perspective after 1707.[29] Some Scotsmen and women became eager participants in the activities of the British Empire after the Union of Parliaments.

On the other hand, there were many who opposed the Union of Parliaments and viewed it as a hostile act against Scotland and its people. There was strong opposition to the 1707 Union in large parts of the Scottish population. Many people felt that Scotland had been sold to the English. Article fifteen of *The Articles of the Union* stated that England would pay the amount of £398,085 and 10 to Scotland as part of the union treaty, and that this money was partly reserved for the compensation for those who had invested money in 'the African and Indian Company of Scotland', which the Article stated should be 'dissolved and cease' with the Union.[30] The widespread resistance against the Union reinvigorated the Jacobite cause after 1707, which culminated in the Risings of 1715 and 1745. As Pittock states:

> anti-Union discourse continued to be strong, and one of its most potent forms was that of the appeal to Scotland's history as a struggle for liberty, a battle by a small nation for its independence from a far more powerful neighbour, won only by the heroic and unparalleled quality of Scottish valour and now betrayed for gold by an indolent nobility corrupted by luxury [. . .].[31]

Clearly, the collisions of interests in such anti-Union discourse cannot be solely understood in terms of colonial or postcolonial trajectories. And yet, Scottish resistance to the Union of Parliaments has at times been read in terms of postcolonial resistance against a dominant colonising nation.[32] Andrew Hadfield counters this tendency to postcolonial readings of the Union of Parliaments with the argument that

> it is hard to read Anglo-Scottish relations simply in terms of an English desire to dominate, control and Anglicise their immediate neighbours, however potent such feelings may have been for many English writers and thinkers in the sixteenth and seventeenth centuries.[33]

The relationship between Scotland and England is too complex and too entangled to apply any straightforward model of coloniser and colonised. A shift towards the Atlantic does not ignore these issues revolving around power, possession and dispossession in Anglo-Scottish relations around 1707. On the contrary, it heightens the debate by raising the sensitive issue of Scotland's own desire for possession prior to 1707 and arguing that the struggle for power in the long seventeenth century had more than one geospatial trajectory. In addition to Scotland's long and complex relationships to England, Ireland, Wales and the European continent, the Atlantic increasingly turned into a space in which narratives of Scottishness and, with it, narratives of possession and dispossession, took shape.

Colonial history is always literary history. This book has shown that Scotland's Atlantic activities between 1603 and 1707 are known to us today primarily through literary artefacts, visualised stories or otherwise aesthetically moulded narratives. These narratives are not mere documents but active tools in the effort to exert power over the Atlantic. Several decades before social reform utopias in Great Britain attempted to solve issues such as poverty, unemployment and the lack of cultivatable land, colonial writing began to seek solutions to domestic problems in Atlantic territories. Many envisioned the foreign place as an ideal settlement site. The utopian tradition offered one generic and aesthetic framework to express the desires of European settlers and to give them more weight than the needs of other agents in the colonial context. The indigenous populations of the Americas, enslaved people from Africa and their descendants, as well as many other people, are habitually excluded from the wish-fulfilment of Scottish colonial utopias. If the outcome of this book is to complicate rather than resolve some of these debates, including the one about utopianism and colonialism, as well as that about Scotland's alleged failures in the seventeenth-century Atlantic, then *Scottish Colonial Literature* has fulfilled its purpose.

Notes

1. Devine and Roessner, 'Scots in the Atlantic Economy' 30.
2. Reid, *Acadia* 184.
3. Nicholls, *A Fleeting Empire* 62.
4. Devine and Roessner, 'Scots in the Atlantic Economy' 38.
5. Fry, *The Scottish Empire* 19.
6. Claridge, 'The Darién Scheme' 59; 66.
7. Shaw, *The Mammoth Book of Losers*.
8. For example, Armitage, *The Ideological Origins*; Glass, *The Scottish Nation*; Gardiner et al., *Scottish Literature and Postcolonial Literature*; Sassi and van Heijnsbergen, *Within and Without Empire*; Stroh, *Gaelic Scotland*.
9. Spivak, 'Subaltern Studies' 7.
10. Chakrabarty, *Provincializing Europe* 7.
11. National Humanities Center, '6. Failed Colonies'.
12. Bhabha, 'Postcolonial Criticism' 439.
13. Ahmad, *In Theory* 172.
14. Ahmad, *In Theory* 167.
15. For example, Devine, *The Scottish Nation*; Glass, *The Scottish Nation*; Pittock, *Scottish Nationality*.
16. Royan and Broun, 'Versions of Scottish Nationhood' 168–83.
17. Brown et al., 'Scottish Literature' 3–15.
18. Anon., 'An Ode' 41–5; italics in original.
19. Gordon, *Encouragements* C2v–C2r.
20. Colley, *Britons Forging* 156.
21. Gardiner, 'Interdisciplinarity After Davie', 24.
22. Cooper, *Colonialism in Question* 164.
23. Lythe, *The Economy* 72.

24. McNeill, *Mosquito Empires* 122.
25. Gilroy, *The Black Atlantic* 2.
26. Sandrock, 'Postcolonial Perspectives' 337–52.
27. Østergaard Nielsen and Ward, 'Three Referenda and a By-election' 213.
28. Qtd in Watt, *The Price of Scotland* 243.
29. Stroh, *(Post)Colonial Scotland?* 493–502.
30. *The Articles of the Union* 6–7.
31. Pittock, *Scottish Nationality* 61.
32. Nairn, *After Britain* 154; 101.
33. Hadfield, *Shakespeare, Spenser and the Matter of Britain* 6.

Works Cited

Ahmad, Aijaz. *In Theory: Classes, Nations, Literatures* (London: Verso, 1992).

Alexander, William. *An Encouragement to Colonies, By Sir William Alexander, Knight* (London: William Stansby, 1624). Early English Books Online <https://quod.lib.umich.edu/e/eebogroup/> (last accessed 23 September 2019).

—. *Doomes-day, or The Great Day of the Lords Ivdgement* [1614], in Sir William Alexander, *The Poetical Works of Sir William Alexander, Earl of Stirling: The Dramatic Works*, ed. L. E. Kastner and H. B. Charlton. 2 vols. Vol. 2 (Manchester: Manchester University Press, 1921), pp. 5–379.

Anderson, Benedict. *Imagined Communities: Reflections on the Origin and Spread of Nationalism*, rev. edn (London: Verso, 2016).

Andrews, Kenneth R. *Trade, Plunder and Settlement: Maritime Enterprise and the Genesis of the British Empire, 1480–1630* (Cambridge: Cambridge University Press, 1984).

Anon. *A New Map of the Isthmus of Darien in America, The Bay of Panama, The Gulph of Vallona or St. Michael, with its Islands and Countries Adjacent. A Letter Giving A Description of the Isthmus of Darian* (Edinburgh: Printed for John Mackie, 1699). University of Glasgow, Special Collections Department <http://special.lib.gla.ac.uk/exhibns/month/may2005.html> (last accessed 14 April 2019).

Anon. 'An Extract of The Scots Settlement in America Called New Caledonia A.D. 1699, According to an Original Draught by H. Moll. Published in Herman Moll's *Atlas Minor*, 1736'. Scottish Archives for Schools <https://www.scottisharchivesforschools.org/union1707/chapter2-1.asp> (last accessed 10 October 2019).

Anon. 'An Ode Made on the Welcome News of the Safe Arrival and Kind Reception of the Scottish Colony at Darien in America' (Edinburgh: James Watson in Craig's Close, 1699). Early English Books Online <https://quod.lib.umich.edu/e/eebogroup/> (last accessed 22 October 2019).

Anon. 'A Poem Upon the Undertaking of the Royal Company of Scotland Trading to Africa and the Indies' (Edinburgh: Printed for James Wardlaw, 1697). Early English Books Online <https://quod.lib.umich.edu/e/eebogroup/> (last accessed 4 November 2019).

Anon. *A Short Account from, and Description of the Isthmus of Darien, Where the Scots Collony Are Settled. With a Particular MAP of the Isthmus and Enterance to the River of Darien. According to Our Late News, and Mr. Dampier, and Mr. Wafer* (Edinburgh: John Vallange, 1699). Early English Books Online <https://quod.lib.umich.edu/e/eebogroup/> (last accessed 12 June 2019).

Anon. *Caledonia, or the Pedlar Turn'd Merchant. A Tragi-Comedy, as It Was Acted by His Majesty's Subjects of Scotland in the King of Spain's Province of Darien* (London, 1700). The Making of the Modern World <https://www.gale.com/intl/primary-sources/the-making-of-the-modern-world> (last accessed 19 May 2020).

Anon. 'The Golden Island, or the Darien Song, in Commendation of All Concerned in That Noble Enterprise of the Valiant Scots, by a Lady of Honour' [1699]. Early English Books Online <https://quod.lib.umich.edu/e/eebogroup/> (last accessed 17 June 2019).

Anon. *The History of Caledonia: Or, The Scots Colony in Darien in the West-Indies. With an Account of the Manners of the Inhabitants, and Riches of the Countrey. By a Gentleman lately Arriv'd* (London: John Nutt, 1699). Early English Books Online <https://quod.lib.umich.edu/e/eebogroup/> (last accessed 30 May 2019).

Anon. *The Land of Cokaygne*, in Charles W. Dunn and Edward T. Byrnes (eds), *Middle English Literature* (New York: Garland, 1990), pp. 188–92.

Anon. *The People of Scotland's Groans and Lamentable Complaints, Pour'd out Before the High Court of Parliament* (Edinburgh: c. 1700). Early English Books Online <https://quod.lib.umich.edu/e/eebogroup/> (last accessed 4 October 2019).

Anon. 'The Scots Settlement in America Called New Caledonia A.D. 1699, According to an Original Draught by H. Moll. Published in Herman Moll's *Atlas Minor*, 1736'. Spencer f18. University of Glasgow Library, Archives & Special Collections.

Anon. *The True Scots Mens Lament for the Loss of the Rights of their Ancient Kingdom* (Edinburgh: John Reid, 1718). Edinburgh: National Library of Scotland: Digital Gallery <https://digital.nls.uk/broadsides/view/?id=15827&transcript=1> (last accessed 11 September 2019).

Anon. *Trade's Release: Or, Courage to the Scotch-Indian-Company. Being an Excellent New Ballad; To the Tune of, The Turks are all Confounded* [1699–1700]. Early English Books Online <https://quod.lib.umich.edu/e/eebogroup/> (last accessed 1 November 2019).

Appelbaum, Robert. *Literature and Utopian Politics in Seventeenth-Century England* (Cambridge: Cambridge University Press, 2002).

Armitage, David. 'John Locke, Carolina, and *Two Treatises of Government*'. *Political Theory* 32.5 (2004): 602–27.

—. 'Making the Empire British: Scotland in the Atlantic World 1542–1707'. *Past & Present* 155 (1997): 34–63.

—. *The Ideological Origins of the British Empire* (Cambridge: Cambridge University Press, 2000).

Ashcraft, Richard. *Locke's Two Treatises of Government* (London: Allen & Unwin, 1987).

Ashcroft, Bill. 'Critical Utopias'. *Textual Practice* 21.3 (2007): 411–31.

Bacon, Francis. *Francis Bacon: The Essays or Counsels Civil and Moral*, ed. Brian Vickers (Oxford: Oxford University Press, 1999).

—. *New Atlantis*, in Susan Bruce (ed.), *Three Early Modern Utopias: Utopia, New Atlantis and* The Isle of Pines (Oxford: Oxford University Press, 2008), pp. 149–86.

Bannister, Saxe (ed.). 'Biographical Introduction'. *The Writings of William Paterson, of Dumfrieshire, and a Citizen of London; Founder of the Bank of England, and of the Darien Colony* [1859]. 3 vols, 2nd edn (New York: Augustus M. Kelley, 1968), pp. ix–cxliv.

—. *The Writings of William Paterson, of Dumfrieshire, and a Citizen of London; Founder of the Bank of England, and of the Darien Colony* [1859]. 3 vols, 2nd edn (New York: Augustus M. Kelley, 1968).

Barclay, Robert. *A Catechism and Confession of Faith: Approved of and Agreed Unto by the General Assembly of the Patriarchs, Prophets, and Apostles, Christ Himself Chief Speaker in and Among Them* [1673]. Early English Books Online <https://quod.lib.umich.edu/e/eebogroup/> (last accessed 21 June 2019).

—. *An Apology for the True Christian Divinity, as the Same Is Held Forth, and Preached by the People, Called in Scorn, Quakers: Being a Full Explanation and Vindication of their Principles and Doctrines, by Many Arguments, Deduced from Scriptur and Right Reason, and the Testimonys of Famous Authors, Both Antient and Modern, with a Full Answer to the Strongest Objections Usually Made Against Them, Written and Published in Latine for the Information of Strangers, by Robert Barclay; and Now Put into Our Own Language for the Benefit of His Countrey-Men* (Aberdeen: John Forbes, 1678). Early English Books Online <https://quod.lib.umich.edu/e/eebogroup/> (last accessed 21 June 2019).

Beaton, Alistair. *Caledonia* (London: Methuen Drama, 2010).

Behn, Aphra. *The History of Oroonoko, or the Royal Slave* (Doncaster: Charles Gildon, 1770).

Belhaven, Lord. *A Speech in Parliament on the 10th day of January 1701, By the Lord Belhaven, On the Affair of the Indian and African Company, and its Colony of Caledonia* (Edinburgh: 1701). Eighteenth Century Collections Online <https://www.gale.com/intl/primary-sources/eighteenth-century-collections-online> (last accessed 28 August 2019).

Bhabha, Homi. 'Postcolonial Criticism', in Stephen Greenblatt and Giles Gunn (eds), *Redrawing the Boundaries: The Transformation of English and American Literary Studies* (New York: Modern Language Association of America, 1992), pp. 437–65.

Biard, Pierre. 'Biard to the Provincial', in Alexander Brown (ed.), *The Genesis of the United States*, Vol. 2 (Cambridge: Riverside Press, 1890), pp. 533–6. Internet Archive <https://archive.org/stream/TheGenesis OfTheUnitedStatesV1/GenesisUnitedStatesNarrativeOfMovement_

Brown_v1_682pgs57407930_djvu.txt> (last accessed 12 November 2019).

Bitterli, Urs. *Cultures in Conflict: Encounters Between European and Non-European Cultures, 1492–1800*, trans. Ritchie Robertson (Stanford: Stanford University Press, 1989).

Blackwell, Isaac. *A Description of the Province and Bay of Darian: Giving an full Account of all it's Situation, Inhabitants, Way and Manner of Living and Religion, Solemnities, Ceremonies and Product, Being vastly rich with Gold and Silver, and various other Commodities, by I. B., a Well-Wisher to the Company who Lived there Seventeen Years* (Edinburgh: Andrew Anderson, 1699). Early English Books Online <https://quod.lib.umich.edu/e/eebogroup/> (last accessed 9 October 2019).

Boesky, Amy. *Founding Fictions. Utopias in Early Modern England* (Athens: University of Georgia Press, 1996).

Borland, Francis. *The History of Darien. Giving a short Description of that Country, an Account of the Attempts of the Scotch Nation to Settle a Colony in that Place, a Relation of the Many Tragical Disasters which Attended that Design; Practical Reflections upon the whole. By the Rev. Mr. Francis Borland, sometime Minister of the Gospel at Glassford; and one of the Ministers who went along with the last Colony to Darien. Written Mostly in the Year 1700, While the Author was in the American Regions. To which is added, A Letter to his Parishioners* (Glasgow: 1779). Eighteenth Century Collections Online <https://www.gale.com/intl/primary-sources/eighteenth-century-collections-online> (last accessed 20 September 2019).

Bowie, Karin. 'Public Opinion, Popular Politics and the Union of 1707'. *Scottish Historical Review* 82.2 (2003): 226–60.

—. *Scottish Public Opinion and the Anglo-Scottish Union, 1699–1707* (Suffolk: Boydell Press, 2007).

Bridgewater, J. Locke, Ar. Hill Tankerville, J. Pollexfen. 'Proceedings of the Board of Trade about the Scotch Company'. Notes to Vol. I. Saxe Bannister (ed.), *The Writings of William Paterson, Founder of the Bank of England*. 3 vols. Vol. 3 [1859], 2nd edn (New York: Augustus M. Kelley, 1968), pp. 257–60.

Brown, Ian, Thomas Owen Clancy, Susan Manning and Murray Pittock. 'Scottish Literature: Criticism and the Canon', in Thomas Owen Clancy and Murray Pittock (eds), *The Edinburgh History of Scottish Literature. Vol. One: From Columba to the Union (until 1707)* (Edinburgh: Edinburgh University Press, 2007), pp. 3–15.

Bucholz, Robert, and Newton Key. *Early Modern England, 1485–1714: A Narrative History*, 2nd edn (Malden, MA: Wiley–Blackwell, 2009).

Bunyan, John. *The Pilgrim's Progress: From This World to That Which Is to Come* [1678]. Illustr. George Cruikshank (London: Oxford University Press, 1932).

Burnaby, William. *The Ladies Visiting-Day. A Comedy. As it Was Acted at the Theatre in Lincolns-Inn-Fields, by His Majesties Servants. With the*

Addition of a New Scene. By the Author of The Reformed Wife (London: Peter Buck, 1701). Eighteenth Century Collections Online <https://www.gale.com/intl/primary-sources/eighteenth-century-collections-online> (last accessed 25 June 2019).

Burns, Robert. *The Canongate Burns: The Complete Poems and Songs of Robert Burns*, ed. Andrew Noble and Patrick Scott Hogg (Edinburgh: Canongate, 2001).

Burton, J. H. (ed.). *The Darien Papers: Being a Selection of Original Letters and Official Documents Relating to the Establishment of a Colony at Darien by the Company of Scotland Trading to Africa and the Indies. 1695–1700* (Edinburgh: Thomas Constable, 1849). Internet Archive <https://archive.org/details/darienpapersbe9000compuoft> (last accessed 28 September 2019).

Byres, James. *A Letter to a Friend at Edinburgh from Roterdam; Giving an Account of the Scots Affairs in Darien. By James Byres* [1702]. Eighteenth Century Collections Online <https://www.gale.com/intl/primary-sources/eighteenth-century-collections-online> (last accessed 7 September 2019).

Cain, P. J., and A. G. Hopkins. 'Gentlemanly Capitalism and British Expansion Overseas I. The Old Colonial System, 1688–1850'. *The Economic History Review* 39.4 (1986): 501–25.

Calloway, Colin G. *White People, Indians, and Highlanders: Tribal Peoples and Colonial Encounters in Scotland and America* (Oxford: Oxford University Press, 2008).

Cameron, Alasdair. 'Theatre in Scotland 1660–1800', in Andrew Hook (ed.), *The History of Scottish Literature. Vol. 2: 1660–1800* (Aberdeen: Aberdeen University Press, 1987), pp. 191–205.

Campanella, Tommaso. *The City of the Sun*, ed. Will Jonson (Leipzig: Amazon Distribution, 2014).

Carr, Rosalind. 'Women, Presbyterianism, Political Agency, and the Anglo-Scottish Union', in Jodi A. Campbell, Elizabeth Ewan and Heather Parker (eds), *The Shaping of Scottish Identities: Family, Nation, and the Worlds Beyond* (Guelph: Centre for Scottish Studies, 2011), pp. 43–58.

Carruthers, Gerard, and Liam McIlvanney. 'Introduction', in Gerard Carruthers and Liam McIlvanney (eds), *Cambridge Companion to Scottish Literature* (Cambridge: Cambridge University Press, 2013), pp. 1–12.

Cartier, Jacques. *A Shorte and Briefe Narration of the Two Navigations and Discoveries to the Northweast Partes Called Newe Fraunce: First translated out of French into Italian, by that famous learned man Gio: Bapt: Ramutius, and now turned into English by John Florio: Worthy the reading of all Ventures, Trauellers, and Discouerers* [1580], trans. John Florio. Internet Archive <https://archive.org/details/cihm_95136/page/n9> (last accessed 28 May 2019).

Cavendish, Margaret. *The Description of a New World, Called the Blazing World: And Other Writings*, ed. Kate Lilley (London: Pickering & Chatto, 1992).

Chakrabarty, Dipesh. *Provincializing Europe: Postcolonial Thought and Historical Difference* (Princeton: Princeton University Press, 2000).

Claeys, Gregory. *Searching for Utopia: The History of an Idea* (London: Thames and Hudson, 2011).

Claridge, Claudia. 'The Darién Scheme: Failure and Its Treatment in the Press', in Stefan Brakensiek and Claudia Claridge (eds), *Fiasko – Scheitern in der Fruehen Neuzeit. Beitraege zur Kulturgeschichte des Misserfolgs* (Bielefeld: transcript, 2015), pp. 59–84.

Coates, Ken S. *The Marshall Decision and Native Rights* (Montreal: McGill-Queen's University Press, 2000).

Colley, Linda. *Britons Forging the Nation 1707–1837* (New Haven: Yale University Press, 1992).

Company of Scotland. *Scotland's Right to Caledonia (Formerly Called Darien) And the Legality of its Settlement, Asserted in Three Several Memorials Presented to His Majesty in May 1699. The Lord President of the Session and Lord Advocate, on behalf of the Company of Scotland, Trading to Africa and the Indies* [1700]. Early English Books Online <https://quod.lib.umich.edu/e/eebogroup/> (last accessed 30 May 2019).

Connell, Liam. 'Modes of Marginality: Scottish Literature and the Uses of Postcolonial Theory'. *Comparative Studies of South Asia, Africa and the Middle East* 23.1–2 (2003): 41–53.

Cooper, Frederick. *Colonialism in Question: Theory, Knowledge, History* (Berkeley: University of California Press, 2005).

Cowan, Edward J. 'Land and Freedom: Scotland, 1314–1707', in Thomas Owen Clancy and Murray Pittock (eds), *The Edinburgh History of Scottish Literature. Vol. One: From Columba to the Union (until 1707)* (Edinburgh: Edinburgh University Press, 2007), pp. 135–43.

—. 'The Myth of Scotch Canada', in Marjory Harper and Michael E. Vance (eds), *Myth, Migration, and the Making of Memory* (Halifax: Fernwood, 1999), pp. 49–72.

Craig, Cairns. *Out of History: Narrative Paradigms in Scottish and English Culture* (Edinburgh: Polygon, 1996).

Cullen, Karen J. *Famine in Scotland: The 'Ill Years' of the 1690s* (Edinburgh: Edinburgh University Press, 2010).

—. 'The Famine of the 1690s and Its Aftermath: Survival and Recovery of the Family', in Elizabeth Ewan and Janay Nugent (eds), *Finding the Family in Medieval and Early Modern Scotland* (Aldershot: Ashgate, 2008), pp. 151–62.

Dampier, William. *A New Voyage Round the World: The Journal of an English Buccaneer* [1697], ed. Giles Milton (London: Hummingbird Press, 1998).

Dandelet, Thomas James. *The Renaissance of Empire in Early Modern Europe* (Cambridge: Cambridge University Press, 2014).

Darwin, John. *Unfinished Empire: The Global Expansion of Britain* (London: Allen Lane, 2012).

Daunton, Martin, and Rick Halpern. 'Introduction: British Identities, Indigenous Peoples, and the Empire', in Martin Daunton and Rick Halpern (eds),

Empire and Others: British Encounters with Indigenous Peoples, 1600–1850 (London: University College of London Press, 1999), pp. 1–18.

Davis, J. C. *Utopia and the Ideal Society: A Study of English Utopian Writing, 1516–1700* (Cambridge: Cambridge University Press, 1981).

Davis, Leith. *Acts of Union: Scotland and the Literary Negotiation of the British Nation, 1707–1830* (Stanford: Stanford University Press, 1998).

—. 'The Aftermath of Union', in Gerard Carruthers and Liam McIlvanney (eds), *Cambridge Companion to Scottish Literature* (Cambridge: Cambridge University Press, 2013), pp. 56–70.

Defoe, Daniel. *The Works of Daniel Defoe. Vol. 7: The History of the Union of Great Britain. Part* I, ed. D. W. Hayton (London: Pickering & Chatto, 2002).

—. *The Works of Daniel Defoe. Vol. 8: The History of the Union of Great Britain. Part II*, ed. D. W. Hayton (London: Pickering & Chatto, 2002).

Devine, Thomas M. (ed.), *Recovering Scotland's Slavery Past: The Caribbean Connection* (Edinburgh: Edinburgh University Press, 2015).

—. *Scotland's Empire, 1600–1815* (London: Allen Lane, 2003).

—. *The Scottish Nation: 1700–2007*, rev. edn (London: Penguin, 2006).

—, and Philipp R. Roessner, 'Scots in the Atlantic Economy, 1600–1800', in Thomas M. Devine and John M. Mackenzie (eds), *Scotland and the British Empire*. Oxford History of the British Empire Companion Series (Oxford: Oxford University Press, 2011), pp. 30–52.

Dobson, David. *Scottish Emigration to Colonial America, 1607–1785* (Athens: University of Georgia Press, 1994).

Doyle, Laura. *Freedom's Empire: Race and the Rise of the Novel in Atlantic Modernity, 1640–1940* (Durham, NC: Duke University Press, 2008).

Drayton, Michael. *The Works of Michael Drayton, Esq; A Celebrated Poet in the Reign of Queen Elizabeth, King James I. and Charles I* (London: J. Hughs, 1748). Eighteenth Century Collections Online <https://www.gale.com/intl/primary-sources/eighteenth-century-collections-online> (last accessed 22 October 2019).

Drummond, James. *An Advertisement Concerning the Province of East New-Jersey in America: Published for the Information of Such as Are Desirous to Be Concerned Therein, or to Transport Themselves thereto* (Edinburgh: John Reid, 1685). Early English Books Online <https://quod.lib.umich.edu/e/eebogroup/> (last accessed 6 September 2019).

Dubois, Laurent, and Julius S. Scott. 'Introduction', in Laurent Dubois and Julius S. Scott (eds), *Origins of the Black Atlantic* (New York: Routledge, 2010), pp. 1–6.

Edwards, Nat. *Caledonia's Last Stand: In Search of the Lost Scots at Darien* (Edinburgh: Luath Press, 2007).

Eliade, Mircea. 'Paradise and Utopia: Mythical Geography and Eschatology', in Frank E. Manuel (ed.), *Utopias and Utopian Thought* (Boston: Houghton Mifflin, 1966), pp. 260–80.

Elliott, John H. *Spain, Europe & the Wider World: 1500–1800* (New Haven: Yale University Press, 2009).

Ellis, Markman (ed.). *Eighteenth-Century Coffee-House Culture. Vol. 1: Restoration Satire* (London: Pickering & Chatto, 2006).

—. *Eighteenth-Century Coffee-House Culture. Vol. 3: Drama* (London: Pickering & Chatto, 2006).

Ferguson, Robert. *A Just and Modest Vindication of the Scots Design, for the Having Established a Colony at Darien. With a Brief Display, How Much It Is their Interest, to Apply Themselves to Trade, and Particularly to that which Is Foreign* [1699]. The Making of the Modern World <https://www.gale.com/intl/primary-sources/the-making-of-the-modern-world> (last accessed 12 April 2019).

Ferguson, William. *Scotland's Relations with England: A Survey to 1707* (Edinburgh: John Donald, 1977).

Ferns, Chris. *Narrating Utopia: Ideology, Gender, Form in Utopian Literature* (Liverpool: Liverpool University Press, 1999).

Findlay, Bill. 'Performances and Plays', in Thomas Owen Clancy and Murray Pittock (eds), *The Edinburgh History of Scottish Literature, Vol. One: From Columba to the Union (until 1707)* (Edinburgh: Edinburgh University Press, 2007), pp. 253–62.

Fitzmaurice, Andrew. *Humanism and America: An Intellectual History of English Colonisation, 1500–1625* (Cambridge: Cambridge University Press, 2003).

Florida Center for Instructional Technology. 'Middle Colonies 1620–1702' (University of South Florida 2009). Florida Center for Instructional Technology, College of Education, University of South Florida <https://etc.usf.edu/maps/pages/3800/3864/3864.htm> (last accessed 11 November 2019).

Fraser, Alexander. *Nova Scotia: The Royal Charter of 1621 to Sir William Alexander* (Toronto: University of Toronto Press, 1922). Project Gutenberg Canada Ebook <https://gutenberg.ca/ebooks/frasera-novascotiaroyalcharter/frasera-novascotiaroyalcharter-00-h-dir/frasera-novascotiaroyalcharter-00-h.html> (last accessed 9 April 2019).

Frohock, Richard. *Heroes of Empire: The British Imperial Protagonist in America, 1596–1764* (Newark: University of Delaware Press, 2004).

Fry, Michael. *The Scottish Empire* (East Lothian: Tuckwell Press, 2001).

Frye, Northrop. *Anatomy of Criticism: Four Essays* (Princeton: Princeton University Press, 1957).

—. 'Varieties of Literary Utopias', in Frank E. Manuel (ed.), *Utopias and Utopian Thought* (Boston: Houghton Mifflin, 1966), pp. 25–49.

Galbraith, Douglas. *The Rising Sun* (London: Pan Macmillan, 2000).

Gallup-Diaz, Ignacio. *The Door of the Seas and Key to the Universe: Indian Politics and Imperial Rivalry in the Darién, 1640–1750* (New York: Columbia University Press, 2002). Gutenberg-e <http://www.gutenberg-e.org/gdi01/> (last accessed 14 September 2019).

Gardiner, Michael. 'Interdisciplinarity After Davie: Postcolonial Theory and Crises of Terminology in Scottish Cultural Studies'. *Scottish Studies Review* 2.1 (Spring 2001): 24–38.

—, Graeme Macdonald, and Niall O'Gallagher (eds). *Scottish Literature and Postcolonial Literature: Comparative Texts and Critical Perspectives* (Edinburgh: Edinburgh University Press, 2011).

Geographicus Rare Antique Maps. '1625 Alexander Map of New England and Nova Scotia (first map to name Cape Cod)'. <https://www.geographicus.com/P/AntiqueMap/NewEnglandNovaScotia-alexander-1625> (last accessed 3 June 2019).

Gerbner, Katharine. 'Antislavery in Print: The Germantown Protest, the "Exhortation", and the Seventeenth-Century Quaker Debate on Slavery'. *Early American Studies* 9.1 (2011): 552–75.

Gilroy, Paul. *Darker Than Blue: On the Moral Economies of Black Atlantic Culture* (Cambridge, MA: Harvard University Press, 2010).

—. *The Black Atlantic: Modernity and Double Consciousness* (Cambridge, MA: Harvard University Press, 1993).

Glass, Bryan S. *The Scottish Nation at Empire's End* (London: Palgrave Macmillan, 2014).

Gordon, Robert. *Encouragements, For Such as Shall Have Intention to Bee Vnder-takers in the New Plantation of Cape Briton, now New Galloway in America, By Mee Lochinvar* (Edinburgh: Iohn Wreittoun, 1625). Early English Books Online <https://quod.lib.umich.edu/e/eebogroup/> (last accessed 28 May 2019).

Gould, Rebecca Ruth. 'The Aesthetic Terrain of Settler Colonialism: Katherine Mansfield and Anton Chekhov's Natives'. *Journal of Postcolonial Writing* 55.1 (2019): 48–65.

Graham, Ian Charles Cargill. *Colonists from Scotland: Emigration to North America, 1707–1783* (Ithaca: Cornell University Press, 1956).

Greenblatt, Stephen. *Marvelous Possessions: The Wonder of the New World* (Oxford: Clarendon Press, 1991).

—. *Renaissance Self-Fashioning: From More to Shakespeare* (Chicago: University of Chicago Press, 1980).

—. *The Swerve: How the World Became Modern* (New York: Norton, 2011).

Greene, Roland. *Unrequited Conquests: Love and Empire in the Colonial Americas* (Chicago: Chicago University Press, 1999).

Griffiths, N. E. S., and John G. Reid. 'New Evidence on New Scotland, 1629'. *William and Mary Quarterly* 49.3 (July 1992): 492–508.

Grove, Richard H. *Green Imperialism: Colonial Expansion, Tropical Island Edens and the Origins of Environmentalism, 1600–1860* (Cambridge: Cambridge University Press, 1995).

Guthry, Richard. 'A Relation of the Voyage and Plantation of the Scotts Colony in New Scotland under the Conduct of Sir William Alexander Younger 1629', in N. E. S. Griffiths and John G. Reid, 'New Evidence on New Scotland, 1629'. *William and Mary Quarterly* 49.3 (July 1992): 492–508 [500–8].

Hadfield, Andrew. 'Afterword', in Chloë Houston (ed.), *New Worlds Reflected: Travel and Utopia in the Early Modern Period* (Farnham: Ashgate, 2010), pp. 219–22.

—. *Shakespeare, Spenser and the Matter of Britain* (Basingstoke: Palgrave Macmillan, 2004).

Hale, Matthew. *The Primitive Origination of Mankind Considered and Examined According to the Light of Nature* (London: Godbid, 1677). Early English Books Online <https://quod.lib.umich.edu/e/eebogroup/> (last accessed 4 September 2019).

Hariot, Thomas. *A Briefe and True Report of the New Found Land of Virginia* [1588] (New York: Dodd, Mead, 1903).

Harrington, James. *The Commonwealth of Oceana and A System of Politics*, ed. J. G. A. Pocock (Cambridge: Cambridge University Press, 1992).

Harris, Walter. *A Defence of the Scots Abdicating Darien: Including an Answer to the Defence of the Scots Settlement there* [1700]. The Making of the Modern World <https://www.gale.com/intl/primary-sources/the-making-of-the-modern-world> (last accessed 30 March 2016).

Hart, Francis Russell. *The Disaster of Darien: The Story of the Scots Settlement and the Causes of its Failure 1699–1701* (London: Constable, c. 1930).

Hart, Jonathan. *Empires and Colonies* (Cambridge: Polity, 2008).

Harper, Marjory, and Michael E. Vance (eds). *Myth, Migration, and the Making of Memory* (Halifax: Fernwood, 1999).

Hayman, Robert. 'To the Right Honorable Knight, Sir William Alexander, Principall, and Prime Planter in New-Scotland: To Whom the King Hath Giuen a Royall Gift to Defray his Great Charges in that Worthy Busines', in Charles Rogers (ed.), *Memorials of the Earl of Stirling and of the House of Alexander*, Vol. 1 (Edinburgh: William Paterson, 1877), p. 111.

Hechter, Michael. *Internal Colonialism: The Celtic Fringe in British National Development, 1536–1966* (Berkeley: University of California Press, 1975).

Hiatt, Alfred. 'Mapping the Ends of Empire', in Ananya Jahanara Kabir and Deanne Williams (eds), *Postcolonial Approaches to the European Middle Ages: Translating Cultures* (Cambridge: Cambridge University Press, 2005), pp. 48–76.

Hill, Christopher. 'Introduction', in Gerrard Winstanley, *The Law of Freedom and Other Writings*, ed. Christopher Hill (Cambridge: Cambridge University Press, 1983), pp. 9–68.

Hobsbawm, Eric, and Terence Ranger. 'Introduction: Inventing Traditions', in Eric Hobsbawm and Terence Ranger (eds), *The Invention of Tradition* [1983], 10th edn (Cambridge: University of Cambridge Press, 2009), pp. 1–14.

Hogan, Sarah. 'Of Islands and Bridges: Figures of Uneven Development in Bacon's *New Atlantis*'. *Journal for Early Modern Cultural Studies* 12.3 (2012): 28–59.

—. *Other Englands: Utopia, Capital, and Empire in an Age of Transition* (Stanford: Stanford University Press, 2018).

—. 'Utopia, Ireland, and the Tudor Shock Doctrine: Spenser's Vision of Capitalist Imperialism'. *Journal of Medieval and Early Modern Studies* 42.2 (2012): 461–86.

Houston, Chloë. *The Renaissance Utopia: Dialogue, Travel and the Ideal Society* (Farnham: Ashgate, 2014).

Hume, David. 'Of the Populousness of Ancient Nations', in Thomas Hill Green and Thomas Hodge Grose (eds), *The Philosophical Works*. 4 vols. Vol. 3 (Aalen: Scientia, 1964), pp. 381–443.

Hunt, Margaret. 'Women and the Fiscal-imperial State in the Late Seventeenth and Early Eighteenth Centuries', in Kathleen Wilson (ed.), *A New Imperial History: Culture, Identity and Modernity in Britain and the Empire, 1660–1840* (Cambridge: Cambridge University Press, 2004), pp. 29–47.

Insh, George Pratt. *Scottish Colonial Schemes: 1620–1686* (Glasgow: MacLehose, 1922).

—. *The Darien Scheme* (London: Staples Press, 1947).

Iser, Wolfgang. *The Act of Reading: A Theory of Aesthetic Response* (Baltimore: Johns Hopkins University Press, 1980).

Jackson, Clare. *Restoration Scotland, 1660–1690: Royalist Politics, Religion and Ideas* (Woodbridge: Boydell Press, 2003).

Jajdelska, Elspeth. 'Unknown Unknowns: Ignorance of the Indies among late Seventeenth-century Scots', in Siegfried Huigen, Jan L. de Jong and Elmer Kolfin (eds), *The Dutch Trading Companies as Knowledge Networks* (Leiden: Brill, 2010), pp. 393–414.

James VI and I. 'Ane Schort Treatise, Conteining Some Revlis and cautelis to be obseruit and eschewit in Scottis Poesie'. *The Essayes of a Prentise, in the Diuine Art of Poesie* (Edinburgh, 1585), pp. 41–3. Early English Books Online <https://quod.lib.umich.edu/e/eebogroup/> (last accessed 30 September 2019).

—. *Nova Scotia: The Royal Charter of 1621* (Toronto: University of Toronto Press, 1922), repr. from the Transactions of the Royal Canadian Institute, Vol. 14, Part 1, pp. 25–51.

—. *The Basilicon Doron of King James VI*. Vol. 1, ed. James Craigie (Edinburgh: William Blackwood, 1944).

Jowitt, Claire. 'The Uses of "Piracy": Discourses of Mercantilism and Empire in Hakluyt's *The Famous Voyage of Sir Francis Drake*', in Chloë Houston (ed.), *New Worlds Reflected: Travel and Utopia in the Early Modern Period* (Farnham: Ashgate, 2010), pp. 115–35.

Joyce, L. E. Elliott. 'Introduction, Notes and Appendices', in Lionel Wafer, *A New Voyage & Description of the Isthmus of America*, ed. L. E. Elliott Joyce (Oxford: Hakluyt Society, 1934), pp. xi–lxxi and 133–201.

Kantorowicz, Ernst H. *The King's Two Bodies: A Study in Medieval Political Theology* (Princeton: Princeton University Press, 1957).

Kastner, L. E., and H. B. Charlton. 'Introduction', in Sir William Alexander, *The Poetical Works of Sir William Alexander, Earl of Stirling: The Dramatic Works*, ed. L. E. Kastner and H. B. Charlton. 2 vols. Vol. I (Manchester: Manchester University Press, 1921), pp. xvii–ccxvii.

Keats, John. 'On First Looking into Chapman's Homer', in Duncan Wu (ed.), *Romanticism: An Anthology*, 4th edn (Malden, MA: Blackwell, 2012), pp. 1396–7.

Keith, George. *An Account of the Great Divisions, Amongst the Quakers, in Pensilvania, &c. As appears by Their Own Book, Here Following, Printed 1692. And Lately came from thence, Intituled, viz. The Plea of the Innocent, against the False Judgment of the Guilty* (London: John Gwillim and Richard Baldwin, 1692). Early English Books Online <https://quod.lib.umich.edu/e/eebogroup/> (last accessed 28 June 2019).
—. *Help in Time of Need from the God of Help* [1664]. Early English Books Online <https://quod.lib.umich.edu/e/eebogroup/> (last accessed 28 June 2019).
—. *The Christian Faith of the People of God, Called in Scorn, Quakers in Rhode-Island (Who Are in Unity with all Faithfull Brethren of the Same Profession in all Parts of the World) Vindicated from the Calumnies of Christian Lodowick, that Formerly Was of that Profession, but Is Lately Fallen There-from: As also from the Base Forgeries, and Wicked Slanders of Cotton Mather, Called a Minister, at Boston, who hath Greatly Commended the Said Christian Lodowick, and Approved His False Charges Against Us, and Hath Added Thereunto Many Gross, Impudent and Vile Calumnies Against Us and Our Brethren, in His Late Address, so called, to Some in New-England, the Which in Due Time May Receive a More Full Answer, to Discover his Ignorance, Prejudice and Perversion Against our Friends in General, and G.K. in particular, Whom He Hath Most Unworthily Abused* [1692]. Early English Books Online <https://quod.lib.umich.edu/e/eebogroup/> (last accessed 28 June 2019).
—. *An Exhortation & Caution to Friends Concerning Buying or Keeping of Negroes* (William Bradford, 1693). Early English Books Online <https://quod.lib.umich.edu/e/eebogroup/> (last accessed 29 June 2019).
Kenny, Kevin. 'Ireland and the British Empire: An Introduction', in Kevin Kenny (ed.), *Ireland and the British Empire* (Oxford: Oxford University Press, 2004), pp. 1–25.
Kewes, Paulina. 'Julius Caesar in Jacobean England'. *The Seventeenth Century* 17 (2002): 155–86.
Kidd, Colin. *British Identities before Nationalism: Ethnicity and Nationhood in the Atlantic World, 1600–1800* (Cambridge: Cambridge University Press, 1999).
—. *Subverting Scotland's Past: Scottish Whig Historians and the Creation of an Anglo-British Identity, 1689–c. 1830* (Cambridge: Cambridge University Press, 1993).
—. *The Forging of Races: Race and Scripture in the Protestant Atlantic World, 1600–2000* (Cambridge: Cambridge University Press, 2006).
Knapp, Jeffrey. *An Empire Nowhere: England, America, and Literature from Utopia to The Tempest* (Berkeley: University of California Press, 1992).
Kumar, Krishan. *Utopianism* (Milton Keynes: Open University Press, 1991).
Laing, David (ed.). *Royal Letters, Charters, and Tracts, Relating to the Colonization of New Scotland, and the Institution of The Order of Knight Baronets of Nova Scotia. 1621–1638* (Edinburgh: The Bannatyne

Club, 1867). Internet Archive <https://archive.org/details/royalletter-sc11400lainuoft> (last accessed 1 June 2019).

Landsman, Ned C. *Crossroads of Empire: The Middle Colonies in British North America*. Regional Perspectives on Early America (Baltimore: Johns Hopkins University Press, 2010).

—. 'Introduction: The Context and Functions of Scottish Involvement with the Americas', in Ned C. Landsman (ed.), *Nation and Province in the First British Empire: Scotland and the Americas, 1600–1800* (Lewisburg, PA: Bucknell University Press, 2001), pp. 15–35.

—. *Scotland and Its First American Colony, 1683–1765* (Princeton: Princeton University Press, 1985).

Leaming, Aaron, and Jacob Spicer (eds), *The Grants, Concessions, and Original Constitutions of the Province of New-Jersey. The Acts Passed During the Proprietary Governments, and Other Material Transactions Before the Surrender Thereof to Queen Anne. The Instrument of Surrender, and Her Formal Acceptance Thereof. Lord Cornbury's Commission and Instructions Consequent Thereon: Collected by Some Gentlemen Employed by the General Assembly. And Afterwards Published by Virtue of an Act of the Legislature of the Said Province with Proper Tables Alphabetically Digested, Containing the Principal Matters in the Book.* (Philadelphia: W. Bradford, 1758). Eighteenth Century Collections Online <https://www.gale.com/intl/primary-sources/eighteenth-century-collections-online> (last accessed 6 September 2019).

Levitas, Ruth. *The Concept of Utopia* (Hemel Hempstead: Philip Allan, 1990).

Lindsay, Maurice. *History of Scottish Literature* [1977], rev. edn (London: Robert Hale, 1992).

Linebaugh, Peter, and Marcus Rediker. *The Many-Headed Hydra: Sailors, Slaves, Commoners, and the Hidden History of the Revolutionary Atlantic* (Boston: Beacon Press, 2000).

Locke, John. *Essays on the Law of Nature: The Latin Text with a Translation, Introduction and Notes, Together with Transcripts of Locke's Shorthand in His Journal for 1676*, ed. Wolfgang von Leyden (Oxford: Clarendon Press, 2002).

—. *Second Treatise of Government* [1690]. Project Gutenberg EBook <https://www.gutenberg.org/files/7370/7370-h/7370-h.htm> (last accessed 16 October 2019).

Lockhart, George. *A Further Account of East-New-Jarsey by a Letter Write [sic] to One of the Proprietors Thereof, by a Countrey-man, who has a great Plantation there: Together with the Discription of the said Province, as it is in Ogilbies Atlas, Printed in the year, 1671* (Edinburgh: John Reid, 1683). Early English Books Online <https://quod.lib.umich.edu/e/eebogroup/> (last accessed 10 August 2019).

Loomba, Ania. *Colonialism/Postcolonialism*. New Critical Idiom (London: Routledge, 1998).

Lythe, S. G. E. *The Economy of Scotland in its European Setting, 1550–1625* (Edinburgh: Oliver and Boyd, 1960).

McDiarmid, Matthew P. 'Some Versions of Poems by Sir Robert Aytoun and Sir William Alexander'. *Notes and Queries* 4 (1957): 32–5.

Macinnes, Allan I. *Union and Empire: The Making of the United Kingdom in 1707* (Cambridge: Cambridge University Press, 2007).

Mack, Douglas. *Scottish Fiction and the British Empire* (Edinburgh: Edinburgh University Press, 2006).

McKay, Ian, and Robin Bates. *In the Province of History: The Making of the Public Past in Twentieth-Century Nova Scotia* (Montreal: McGill-Queen's University Press, 2010).

MacKenzie, John M., and T. M. Devine (eds). 'Introduction', in John M. MacKenzie and T. M. Devine (eds), *Scotland and the British Empire*. Oxford History of the British Empire Companion Series (Oxford: Oxford University Press, 2011), pp. 1–29.

—. *Scotland and the British Empire*. Oxford History of the British Empire Companion Series (Oxford: Oxford University Press, 2011).

Mackenzie, Roderick. *An Exact List of all the Men, Women, and Boys that Died on Board the Indian and African Company's Fleet, during their Voyage from Scotland to America, and since their Landing in Caledonia, Together with a Particular Account of their Qualities, the Several Days of their Deaths, and the Respective Distempers or Accidents of which they Died* (Edinburgh: George Mosman, 1699). Early English Books Online <https://quod.lib.umich.edu/e/eebogroup/> (last accessed 1 June 2019).

McNeill, John R. *Mosquito Empires: Ecology and War in the Greater Caribbean, 1620–1914* (Cambridge: Cambridge University Press, 2010).

McPhail, Bridget. 'Through a Glass, Darkly: Scots and Indians Converge at Darien'. *Eighteenth-Century Life* 18 (November 1994): 129–47.

MacQueen, John (ed.). *The Phanaticks*, by Archibald Pitcairne (Woodbridge: Boydell and Brewer, 2012).

Mannheim, Karl. *Ideology and Utopia: An Introduction to the Sociology of Knowledge*, trans. Louis Wirth and Edward Shils (New York: Harcourt, Brace, 1953).

Manuel, Frank E., and Fritzie P. Manuel. *Utopian Thought in the Western World* (Cambridge, MA: Belknap, 1979).

Marx, Karl, and Friedrich Engels. *Manifesto of the Communist Party* [1848], trans. Samuel Moore in cooperation with Friedrich Engels [1888], ed. Friedrich Engels. *Projekt Gutenberg* <http://www.gutenberg.org/cache/epub/61/pg61-images.html> (last accessed 14 November 2019).

Mason, John. *A Briefe Discourse of the New-Found-Land with the Situation, Temperature, and Commodities therof, Inciting our Nation to Goe Forward in that Hope-full Plantation Begunne* (Edinburgh: Andro Hart, 1620). Early English Books Online <https://quod.lib.umich.edu/e/eebogroup/> (last accessed 22 March 2019).

Mignolo, Walter D. *Local Histories/Global Designs: Coloniality, Subaltern Knowledges, and Border Thinking* (Princeton: Princeton University Press, 2000).

Milton, John. *Areopagitica and Other Political Writings of John Milton*, ed. John Alvis (Indianapolis: Liberty Fund, 1999).

Montaigne, Michel de. 'Of the Caniballes'. *Montaigne's Essays*. Vol. 1, trans. John Florio, 1603 (University of Oregon, Renascence Editions, 1999) <http://www.luminarium.org/renascence-editions/montaigne/> (last accessed 23 November 2019).

Montaño, John Patrick. *The Roots of English Colonialism in Ireland* (Cambridge: Cambridge University Press, 2011).

Moran, Michael G. *Inventing Virginia: Sir Walter Raleigh and the Rhetoric of Colonization, 1584–1590* (New York: Peter Lang, 2007).

More, Thomas. *The Complete Works of St. Thomas More*. Vol. 4, ed. Edward Surtz and J. H. Hexter (New Haven: Yale University Press, 1965).

—. *Utopia*, trans. Ralph Robinson, in Susan Bruce (ed.), *Three Early Modern Utopias*: Utopia, New Atlantis *and* The Isle of Pines (Oxford: Oxford University Press, 2008), pp. 1–148.

Morris, Michael. *Scotland and the Caribbean, c. 1740–1833: Atlantic Archipelagos* (New York: Routledge, 2015).

Moylan, Tom. *Demand the Impossible: Science Fiction and the Utopian Imagination* (New York: Methuen, 1986).

Nairn, Tom. *After Britain: New Labour and the Return of Scotland* (London: Granta, 2000).

National Humanities Center. '6. Failed Colonies' (Research Triangle Park, NC: National Humanities Center, 2006) <http://nationalhumanitiescenter.org/pds/amerbegin/exploration/text6/text6read.htm> (last accessed 3 November 2019).

Neville, Henry. *The Isle of Pines*, in Susan Bruce (ed.), *Three Early Modern Utopias*: Utopia, New Atlantis *and* the Isle of Pines (Oxford: Oxford University Press, 2008), pp. 187–212.

Nicholls, Andrew D. *A Fleeting Empire: Early Stuart Britain and the Merchant Adventurers to Canada* (Montreal: McGill-Queen's University Press, 2010).

Nicol, David. *The Fundamentals of New Caledonia* (Edinburgh: Luath Press, 2003).

Nussbaum, Felicity A. 'The Theatre of Empire: Racial Counterfeit, Racial Realism', in Kathleen Wilson (ed.), *A New Imperial History: Culture, Identity and Modernity in Britain and the Empire 1660–1840* (Cambridge: Cambridge University Press, 2004), pp. 71–90.

Ó Ciardha, Éamonn, and Micheál Ó Siochrú. 'Introduction: The Plantation of Ulster: Ideas and Ideologies', in Éamonn Ó Ciardha and Micheál Ó Siochrú (eds), *The Plantation of Ulster: Ideology and Practice* (Manchester: Manchester University Press, 2012), pp. 1–17.

Orr, Julie. *Scotland, Darien, and the Atlantic World, 1698–1700* (Edinburgh: Edinburgh University Press, 2018).

Østergaard Nielsen, Jimmi, and Stuart Ward. 'Three Referenda and a By-election: The Shadow of Empire in Devolutionary Politics', in Bryan S. Glass and John M. MacKenzie (eds), *Scotland, Empire and Decolonisation in the Twentieth Century* (Manchester: Manchester University Press, 2015), pp. 200–22.

Ovid. *Ovid's Metamorphoses. Books I–V*, ed. William S. Anderson (Norman: University of Oklahoma Press, 1997).

Parkinson, David. 'Arcadia, Emulation and Regret in Sir William Alexander's *Encouragement to Colonies*', in Kevin J. McGinley and Nicola Royan (eds), *The Apparelling of Truth: Literature and Literary Culture in the Reign of James VI. A Festschrift for Roderick J. Lyall* (Newcastle upon Tyne: Cambridge Scholars, 2010), pp. 252–65.

Paterson, William. 'A Proposal to Plant a Colony in Darien; To Protect the Indians Against Spain; And to Open the Trade of South America to All Nations' [1701]. *The Writings of William Paterson, Founder of the Bank of England.* 3 vols. Vol. 1, ed. Saxe Bannister [1859], 2nd edn (New York: Augustus M. Kelley, 1968), pp. 115–60.

—. 'Proposals and Reasons for Constituting a Council of Trade' [1701]. *The Writings of William Paterson, Founder of the Bank of England.* 3 vols. Vol. 1, ed. Saxe Bannister [1859], 2nd edn (New York: Augustus M. Kelley, 1968), pp. 7–105.

Perceval-Maxwell, M. 'Sir William Alexander of Menstrie (1567–1640): Earl of Stirling, Viscount Canada and Lord Alexander of Tullibody'. *Scottish Tradition* xi/xii (1981–2): 14–25.

Pitcairne, Archibald. *The Assembly; Or, Scotch Reformation. A Comedy* [1692] (Edinburgh, 1766), Eighteenth Century Collections Online <https://www.gale.com/intl/primary-sources/eighteenth-century-collections-online> (last accessed 26 May 2019).

Pittock, Murray G. H. *Poetry and Jacobite Politics in Eighteenth-Century Britain and Ireland* (Cambridge: Cambridge University Press, 1994).

—. *Scottish Nationality* (London: Palgrave Macmillan, 2001).

—. *The Invention of Scotland: The Stuart Myth and the Scottish Identity, 1638 to the Present* (London: Routledge, 1991).

Plattes, Gabriel. *A Description of the Famous Kingdome of Macaria: Shewing its Excellent Government* (London, 1641). Early English Books Online <https://quod.lib.umich.edu/e/eebogroup/> (last accessed 18 March 2019).

Pomfret, John E. *The Province of West New Jersey, 1609–1702* (Princeton: Princeton University Press, 1956).

Pratt, Mary Louise. *Imperial Eyes: Travel Writing and Transculturation* (London: Routledge, 1992).

Prebble, John. *The Darien Disaster* (London: Secker & Warburg, 1968).

Ramsey, Peter Herbert (ed.). *The Price Revolution in Sixteenth-Century England* (London: Methuen, 1971).

Raleigh, Walter. *The Discoverie of the Large, Rich, and Bewtiful Empyre of Guiana*, ed. Neil L. Whitehead (Manchester: Manchester University Press, 1997).

Reid, John G. *Acadia, Maine, and New Scotland: Marginal Colonies in the Seventeenth Century* (Toronto: University of Toronto Press, 1981).

—. 'The Conquest of "Nova Scotia": Cartographic Imperialism and the Echoes of a Scottish Past', in Ned C. Landsman (ed.), *Nation and Province in the First British Empire: Scotland and the Americas, 1600–1800* (Lewisburg, PA: Bucknell University Press, 2001), pp. 39–59.

Riach, Alan. *Representing Scotland in Literature, Popular Culture and Iconography: The Masks of the Modern Nation* (London: Palgrave Macmillan, 2005).

Ricœur, Paul. *Lectures on Ideology and Utopia* (New York: Columbia University Press, 1986). Internet Archive <https://archive.org/stream/pdfy-oRPzWEh3nXrYxehT/Lectures+on+Ideology+and+Utopia+-+Paul+Ricoeur_djvu.txt> (last accessed 30 May 2019).

Ridpath, George. *Scotland's Grievances Relating to Darien &c. Humbly Represented to the Parliament* [1700]. The Making of the Modern World <https://www.gale.com/intl/primary-sources/the-making-of-the-modern-world> (last accessed 3 September 2019).

Romaniello, Matthew P. 'Through the Filter of Tobacco: The Limits of Global Trade in the Early Modern World'. *Comparative Studies in Society and History* 49.4 (2007): 914–37.

Roper, L. H., and B. van Ruymbeke (eds). *Constructing Early Modern Empires: Proprietary Ventures in the Atlantic World, 1500–1700* (Leiden: Brill, 2007).

Rosenberg, Philippe. 'Thomas Tryon and the Seventeenth-Century Dimensions of Antislavery'. *William and Mary Quarterly* 61.4 (2004): 609–42.

Royan, Nicola, with Dauvit Broun. 'Versions of Scottish Nationhood, c. 850–1707', in Thomas Owen Clancy and Murray Pittock (eds), *The Edinburgh History of Scottish Literature. Vol. One: From Columba to the Union (until 1707)* (Edinburgh: Edinburgh University Press, 2007), pp. 168–83.

Sandrock, Kirsten. 'Ancient Empires and Early Modern Colonialism: William Alexander's *Monarchicke Tragedies*'. *Renaissance Studies* 31.3 (2017): 346–64.

—. 'Postcolonial Perspectives on the Scottish Independence Debate', in Klaus Peter Müller (ed.), *Scotland 2014 and Beyond – Coming of Age and Loss of Innocence?* (Frankfurt: Peter Lang, 2015), pp. 337–52.

Sassi, Carla, and Theo van Heijnsbergen (eds). *Within and Without Empire: Scotland Across the (Post)colonial Borderline* (Newcastle upon Tyne: Cambridge Scholars, 2013).

Scot, George. *A Brief Advertisement Concerning East-New-Jersey, in America* [1685]. Early English Books Online <https://quod.lib.umich.edu/e/eebogroup/> (last accessed 6 August 2019).

—. *The Model of the Government of the Province of East-New-Jersey in America: And Encouragements for such as Designs to be Concerned there. Published for Information of such as Are Desirous to Be Interested in that Place* (Edinburgh: John Reid, 1685). Early English Books Online <https://quod.lib.umich.edu/e/eebogroup/> (last accessed 6 August 2019).

Scott, Walter. *Tales of a Grandfather: Being Stories from Scottish History* (London: Routledge, 1870).

Shaw, Karl. *The Mammoth Book of Losers* (London: Constable & Robinson, 2014).

Sidney, Philip. *The Countesse of Pembrokes Arcadia* [1590], ed. Carl Dennis (Kent, OH: State University Press, 1970).

Spivak, Gayatri Chakravorty. 'Subaltern Studies: Deconstructing Historiography', in Ranajit Guha and Gayatri Chakravorty Spivak (eds), *Selected Subaltern Studies* (Oxford: Oxford University Press, 1988), pp. 3–32.

Spurr, David. *The Rhetoric of Empire: Colonial Discourse in Journalism, Travel Writing, and Imperial Administration* (Durham, NC: Duke University Press, 1993).

Stevenson, David. *Union, Revolution and Religion in 17th-Century Scotland* (Aldershot: Varorium, 1997).

Stewart, Laura A. M. 'Introduction: Publics and Participation in Early Modern Britain'. *Journal of British Studies* 56 (2017): 709–30.

Stroh, Silke. *Gaelic Scotland in the Colonial Imagination: Anglophone Writing from 1600 to 1900* (Evanston, IL: Northwestern University Press, 2017).

—. *(Post)Colonial Scotland? Literature, Gaelicness and the Nation* (Frankfurt: Johann Wolfgang Goethe-Universitaet zu Frankfurt am Main, 2009).

Sydserf, Thomas. *Tarugo's Wiles: Or, the Coffee-House. A Comedy* (London: Printed for Henry Herringman, 1668). Early English Books Online <https://quod.lib.umich.edu/e/eebogroup/> (last accessed 22 March 2019).

The Articles of the Union as They Passed with Amendments in the Parliament of Scotland, and Ratified by the Touch of the Royal Scepter at Edinburgh, January 16, 1707, by James Duke of Queensbury, Her Majesty's High Commissioner for that Kingdom. London: Parliamentary Archives, Houses of Parliament, 1707. Eighteenth Century Collections Online <https://www.gale.com/intl/primary-sources/eighteenth-century-collections-online> (last accessed 21 May 2020).

'The Virginia Company of London'. Jamestown-Yorktown Foundation <https://www.historyisfun.org/pdf/Laws-at-Jamestown/VA_Company.pdf> (last accessed 21 May 2020).

Thomas, Gabriel. *An Historical and Geographical Account of the Province and Country of Pensilvania and of West-New-Jersey in America. The Richness of the Soil the Sweetness of the Situation, the Wholesomeness of the Air, the Navigable Rivers, and others, the prodigious Encrease of Corn, the flourishing Condition of the City of Philadelphia, with the stately Buildings, and other Improvements there. The strange Creatures, as Birds, Beasts, Fishes, and Fowls, with the several sorts of Minerals, Purging Waters, and Stones, lately discovered. The Natives, Aborogmes, their Language, Religion, Laws, and Customs; The first Planters, the Dutch, Sweeds, and English, with the number of its Inhabitants; As also a Touch upon George Keith's New Religion, in his second Change since he left the Quakers. With a Map of Both Countries. By Gabriel Thomas, who resided there about Fifteen Years.* (London: A. Baldwin, 1698). Early English Books Online <https://quod.lib.umich.edu/e/eebogroup/> (last accessed 12 September 2019).

Urquhart, Thomas. *The Jewel* [1652], ed. R. D. S. Jack and R. J. Lyall (Edinburgh: Scottish Academic Press, 1983).

Vaughan, William. *The Golden Fleece: Diuided into Three Parts, Vnder Which Are Discouered the Errours of Religion, the Vices and Decayes of the Kingdome, and Lastly the Wayes to Get Wealth, and to Restore Trading so much Complayned of. Transported from Cambrioll Colchos, out of the southernmost part of the iland, commonly called the New-foundland, by Orpheus Iunio, for the general and perpetuall good of Great Britaine* (London: William Stansby, 1626). Early English Books Online <https://quod.lib.umich.edu/e/eebogroup/> (last accessed 3 May 2019).

Veracini, Lorenzo. *Settler Colonialism: A Theoretical Overview* (London: Palgrave Macmillan, 2010).

Virgil. *The Eclogues by Virgil*, trans. John Jefferys (Edinburgh: Mundell & Son, 1799).

Wafer, Lionel. *A New Voyage & Description of the Isthmus of America*, ed. L. E. Elliott Joyce (Oxford: Hakluyt Society, 1934).

Warburton, Eliot. *Darien; Or, The Merchant Prince. A Historical Romance.* 3 vols. (London: Colburn, 1852).

Watt, Douglas. *The Price of Scotland: Darien, Union and the Wealth of Nations* (Edinburgh: Luath Press, 2007).

Wells, Heather. '"A New Toot out of an Old Horn": Re-evaluating the Relevance of Seventeenth-Century Scottish Drama'. *eSharp* 25:2 (2017): 57–69 <https://www.gla.ac.uk/media/Media_551164_smxx.pdf> (last accessed 2 November 2019).

Whyte, Ian. *Scotland and the Abolition of Black Slavery, 1756–1838* (Edinburgh: Edinburgh University Press, 2006).

—. *Send Back the Money! The Free Church of Scotland and American Slavery* (Cambridge: James Clarke, 2012).

Williamson, Arthur H. 'Britain and the Beast: The Apocalypse and the Seventeenth-Century Debate about the Creation of the British State', in J. E. Force and R. H. Popkin (eds), *Millenarianism and Messianism in Early Modern European Culture. Vol. III: The Millenarian Turn: Millenarian Contexts of Science, Politics, and Everyday Anglo-American Life in the Seventeenth and Eighteenth Centuries* (Dordrecht: Kluwer, 2001), pp. 15–27.

Wilson, Kathleen. 'Introduction: Histories, Empires, Modernities', in *A New Imperial History: Culture, Identity and Modernity in Britain and the Empire 1660–1840* (Cambridge: Cambridge University Press, 2004), pp. 1–26.

Winstanley, Gerrard. *The Law of Freedom in a Platform: Or, True Magistracy Restored. Humbly presented to Oliver Cromwel, General of the Common-wealths Army in England. And to all English-men my brethren whether in Church-fellowship, or not in Church-fellowship, both sorts walking as they conceive according to the Order of the Gospel: and from them to all the Nations in the World. Wherein is Declared, What is Kingly Government, and what is Commonwealths Government. By Jerrard Winstanley* (London: Giles Calvers, 1652). Early English Books Online <https://quod.lib.umich.edu/e/eebogroup/> (last accessed 1 June 2019).

—. *The True Levellers Standard Advanced: Or, The State of Community Opened, and Presented to the Sons of Men* [1649]. Early English Books Online <https://quod.lib.umich.edu/e/eebogroup/> (last accessed 1 June 2019).

Winthrop, John. 'A Model of Christian Charity' [1630]. Boston: Massachusetts Historical Society 7 (1838): 31–48 <http://history.hanover.edu/texts/winthmod.html> (last accessed 13 May 2019).

Withers, Charles W. J. 'Emergent Nation: Scotland's Geography, 1314–1707', in Thomas Owen Clancy and Murray Pittock (eds), *The Edinburgh History of Scottish Literature. Vol. One: From Columba to the Union (until 1707)* (Edinburgh: Edinburgh University Press, 2007), pp. 144–52.

Wolfe, Brenda. 'Virginia Company of London'. *Encyclopedia Virginia*. Virginia Humanities in partnership with Library of Virginia <https://www.encyclopediavirginia.org/virginia_company_of_london> (last accessed 25 September 2019).

Wolfe, Patrick. *Settler Colonialism and the Transformation of Anthropology: The Politics and Poetics of an Ethnographic Event* (New York: Cassell, 1999).

Wormald, Jenny. 'Confidence and Perplexity: The Seventeenth Century', in Jenny Wormald (ed.), *Scotland: A History* (Oxford: Oxford University Press, 2005), pp. 123–49.

—. 'The "British" Crown, the Earls and the Plantation of Ulster', in Éamonn Ó Ciardha and Micheál Ó Siochrú (eds), *The Plantation of Ulster: Ideology and Practice* (Manchester: Manchester University Press, 2012), pp. 18–32.

Worthington, David. 'Introduction', in David Worthington (ed.), *British and Irish Emigrants and Exiles in Europe, 1603–1688* (Leiden: Brill, 2010), pp. 1–27.

—. *Scots in the Habsburg Service, 1618–1648* (Leiden: Brill, 2004).

Index

References to images are in *italics*; references to notes are indicated by n.